The Globalization of
Supermax Prisons

CRITICAL ISSUES IN CRIME AND SOCIETY
Raymond J. Michalowski, Series Editor

Critical Issues in Crime and Society is oriented toward critical analysis of contemporary problems in crime and justice. The series is open to a broad range of topics including specific types of crime, wrongful behavior by economically or politically powerful actors, controversies over justice system practices, and issues related to the intersection of identity, crime, and justice. It is committed to offering thoughtful works that will be accessible to scholars and professional criminologists, general readers, and students.

For a list of titles in the series, see the last page of the book.

The Globalization of Supermax Prisons

EDITED BY JEFFREY IAN ROSS
FOREWORD BY LOÏC WACQUANT

RUTGERS UNIVERSITY PRESS
New Brunswick, New Jersey, and London

Library of Congress Cataloging-in-Publication Data

The globalization of supermax prisons / edited by Jeffrey Ian Ross.
    p. cm. — (Critical issues in crime and society)
    Includes bibliographical references.
    ISBN 978-0-8135-5741-0 (hardcover : alk. paper) — ISBN 978-0-8135-5740-3
(pbk. : alk. paper) — ISBN 978-0-8135-5742-7 (e-book)
    1. Prisons.   2. Prison administration.   3. Prisons—United States.   4. Prison
administration—United States.   I. Ross, Jeffrey Ian.
    HV8665.G53   2013
    365'.33—dc23
                                                                    2012012091

A British Cataloging-in-Publication record for this book is available
from the British Library.

Visit our website: http://rutgerspress.rutgers.edu

Manufactured in the United States of America

To Jeffrey P. Wyndowe, MD

CONTENTS

FOREWORD: PROBING THE META-PRISON

IT IS OFTEN FORGOTTEN that, during the 1960s and into the mid-1970s, the United States was a global leader in progressive penality, much as it had been about a century earlier when Gustave de Beaumont and Alexis de Tocqueville crossed the Atlantic to learn about American innovations in humane punishment for the benefit of European rulers.[1] Through practical experience and in-depth policy analysis, federal authorities had arrived at the view that the prison is an institution that feeds, rather than fights, crime; that the building of custodial facilities should be stopped and juvenile confinement phased out; and that only a vastly enlarged effort at rehabilitating inmates, whose constitutional rights were just beginning to be recognized and enforced by the courts, would improve the output of criminal justice. Local authorities were experimenting in correctional reform on multiple fronts, from jail processing to community mental health to prisoner unionization, with the aim of limiting the scope and injurious effects of captivity. The inmate count was going down slowly but steadily; decarceration was on the agenda; and mainstream penologists, historical analysts, and radical critics were nearly unanimous in holding that the penitentiary had entered into irremediable if not terminal decline. With some 380,000 behind bars circa 1973, the United States seemed poised to hoist the banner of liberty aloft again and to lead other nations onto the path to "a world without prisons."[2]

Then came the *triple backlash* to the socioracial turmoil of the 1960s and the stagflation of the 1970s that turned penal trends around on a dime and sent the country into a carceral frenzy on a scale, span, and duration unknown in human history. The first was a racial reaction against the advances of the civil rights movement and the partial closing of the social gap between blacks and whites; the second a class reaction against the broad gains of labor at the bloom of the Fordist-Keynesian regime; and the third a political reaction against a welfare state perceived to cosset and coddle undeserving categories, *primus inter pares* the welfare recipients and street criminals newly "painted black" in the wake of the ghetto riots of 1964–1968.[3] These three strands coincided and converged into a sweeping reengineering of the state and propelled the deployment of a disciplinary poverty policy mating restrictive "workfare" and expansive "prisonfare" that has turned the United States into the undisputed world champion in incarceration, with 2.4 million behind bars (representing fully one-quarter of the planet's population under lock) and nearly 8 million under justice supervision, even as criminal victimization first stagnated and then receded during that same period. The United States also became a major exporter of punitive penal categories, discourses, and policies: with the help of a transnational network of promarket think tanks, it spread its aggressive gospel of "zero-tolerance" policing, judicial blackmail through plea bargaining, the routine incarceration of low-level drug offenders, mandatory minimum sentences for recidivists, and boot camps for juveniles around the world as part of a neoliberal policy package, fueling a global firestorm in law and order.[4]

One of the most startling products of this unforeseen surge and unprecedented expansion of the penal state has been the invention of yet another American "peculiar institution": the so-called supermaximum-security facility, aka the *supermax prison*. It arose from within the entrails of the correctional administration, in the early 1980s, just as carceral hyperinflation was accelerating, ostensibly in a technical effort to seclude the "worst of the worst inmates," those deemed too disruptive or dangerous to mix with the general population or even to be handled by conventional high-security wards.[5] As a flood of convicts seemingly impervious to penal discipline and splintered by gang-fueled racial violence met a new generation of prison wardens committed to neutralization as the primary, if not the sole, mission of their overcrowded establishments, this "no-nonsense" contraption officially designed to tame recalcitrant and predatory prisoners through intensified isolation solidified. Bureaucratic mimetism, lavish federal funding, and the wish to signal penal severity to lawbreakers, politicians, and the media then fostered its proliferation across the nation. By the year 2000, as the United States passed the red mark of 2 million inmates, such facilities were present in three dozen states and held 2 percent of the country's prisoners, amounting to some 25,000 convicts—twice the *entire* carceral population of the Scandinavian countries. Despite their dubious constitutionality and apparent violation of the International Covenant on Civil and Political Rights (of which the United States is a signatory country), extreme physical austerity, constant social sequestration, the extinction of programming, and enduring sensory deprivation became the normal parameters of long-term detention for these inmates.

In sum, instead of rehabilitating convicts, the United States *rehabilitated the prison* and turned it into a device for the punitive containment of marginality and the reassertion of state sovereignty on the outside. Then it fashioned a new *neutralizing "prison within the prison" to discharge the same function inside* the bloated penal system, granting the supermax a pivotal place in the panoply of "unthinkable punishment policies"[6] that have propelled the drive to hyperincarceration in the age of revanchism. Just as the penitentiary is massively overused as a *vacuum cleaner for the social detritus* of a society ravaged by economic deregulation, welfare retrenchment, and ethnoracial anxiety, supermax facilities are grotesquely overused inside to subdue and store *the refuse and the refuseniks of carceral rule.* The supermax prison thus stands as the hyperbolic product and iconic expression of the ravenous remaking of the American penal state,[7] for which incapacitation has supplanted rehabilitation and the invisibilizing of problem categories has become a prime technique of government. So much to say that its study has much to contribute to our understanding of the internal and external politics of punishment in contemporary society, as demonstrated by the collection of inquiries assembled here by Jeffrey Ian Ross.

The first merit of this volume is to take a broad *cross-national approach* to its topic and to situate the booming rise of the supermax prison in the United States within the spectrum of nations that have expanded their use of high-security units, wards, or establishments over the past quarter century. One of the most severe limitations of the American scholarly and policy debate over the causes, modalities, and consequences of the gargantuan expansion of the country's carceral apparatus has been its studied parochialism: the vast majority of contributors focus narrowly on the national scene, in utter disregard for or blissful ignorance of germane developments, countertendencies, or contrasting trends in neighboring or comparable societies. Yet many central tenets and claims of that debate instantly vaporize when they are held up to international scrutiny. Thus the commonly held notion that high (or rising) crime rates beget high (rising) incarceration rates is directly refuted by crossing America's border to the north: the incidence of criminal victimization (outside of homicidal violence) in Canada is similar to that in the United States, yet Canadian incarceration has stagnated around 110 inmates per 100,000 population over against 740 per 100,000 in the United States.[8] Similarly, it is impossible to spot the stunning disconnection of custodial standards from human rights norms in the United States, where these standards have been elaborated internally by justice practitioners led by the American Correctional Association, unless one realizes that in every other postindustrial nation the enforcement of human rights statutes sharply limits the use of solitary confinement and thus virtually forbids the large-scale deployment of supermax-like arrangements.[9]

Breaking with the doxically US-centric perspective of mainstream criminology, Ross and his collaborators take us on a whirlwind tour of eleven countries on four continents and even include in their purview two infamous American prisons of contested legal and ambiguous territorial status, Guantánamo on Cuban soil and Abu Ghraib in freshly invaded Iraq. The complement of cases brought together in this panorama allows the contributors to raise a series of provocative questions: Is the expanded use of security-focused facilities and regimens of penal confinement the result of changes internal to criminal justice or a response to external demands made by political and other operators? Does it emerge when it does in the different nations through concurrent adaptation and convergent innovation, or is it the spawn of imitation and diffusion? Is emulation or counteremulation (as when the United States serves as foil rather than model) an effect of "globalization," construed as a general and generic process of transnational circulation and unification, or a product of "refracted Americanization" whereby the United States imposes its practices as beacons of modernity and efficiency, effectively legitimating its own practices by turning them into universal yardsticks?[10] Ross portrays intergovernmental organizations and corporations as the main agencies of cross-national dissemination, but what of the action of think tanks and the influence of academic and mercenary intellectuals in the sending and in the receiving countries? The transnational travels and travails of mass solitary confinement as technique of carceral management adds an instructive chapter to the ongoing saga of penal policy transfer, translation, and mutation across borders.[11] The international diversity of the cases gathered in this book is moreover amplified by the diversity of perspectives brought by a team of investigators that mixes academic criminologists, correctional professionals, justice activists, and consultants and even includes former prisoners—in line with the inspiration of the "convict criminology" of which Ross is one of the cofounders.[12]

The second, correlative, virtue of the present volume is to raise in a pointed manner the question of what constitutes a "supermax." As soon as they cross the American border, readers will wonder and ponder (as some of their authors candidly do), are the different chapters chasing after the same animal? What are the shared traits and the distinguishing features of an American-style *supermax prison*, a Canadian Security Handling Unit, a Dutch *Extra Beveiligde Inrichtingen* or a French *quartier de haute sécurité*—let alone a (Mexican) *centre de seguridad máxima* in a penal system where the social conditions of rationalization and professionalization are not granted? Internationalizing the inquiry irrevocably problematizes the very notion at its epicenter, which is all for the good. For the boundaries of the "supermax" are wooly, its genealogy disputed, and its demography imprecise in the very country where it was invented for a simple reason:[13] it is an *administrative notion*, designed by and for correctional professionals, that has been smuggled into the social science of the prison without sufficient scrutiny. And, as Robert Merton reminds us, before we rush to explain any social phenomenon, we must imperatively take pains to establish it and specify its defining properties.[14] So what, then, constitutes a "supermax" facility? Is it the physical layout, the regimen to which inmates are subjected, the types of convicts simultaneously brought together and apart in it, the reasons behind their segregation, or the effects that this type of confinement has on them, or some combination of these? More precisely, does it take a dedicated establishment and a distinctive design permitting direct and permanent close supervision? How many daily hours of solitude and how little human contact must inmates endure for the facility that holds them to qualify? What about the frequency of lockdowns and the routine use of leg restraints and waist chains; are they defining or derivative features, essential or accidental? These questions apply *ad libitum* to every characteristic used to depict this or that presumed instance of a "supermax" or deviation from it.

This book does not resolve these quandaries, but it offers valuable materials to move us from a vague and shifting *folk construct* of the "supermax prison" to a rigorous *analytic concept* of the same, shorn of its contingent ties to a short segment of the arbitrary history of punishment in one country. In the spirit of pushing this collective reflection forward, let me essay the following specification: "supermax" designates a species of *meta-prison*, a prison for the prison, a facility dedicated in all or most of its aspects (architecture, technology, activities, schedules, social relations, etc.) to *redoubling* the treatment that the penitentiary inflicts on those most recalcitrant to it, and therefore geared to dissolving—or, rather, "disappearing"—the gaps, failings, and contradictions of that treatment. In the current era, the meta-prison transposes the philosophies of neutralization and retribution from the outside to the inside of the carceral institution,[15] applying them, as it were, to the "meta-criminals" who repeatedly violate the laws of the administration of penal sanction. It is the materialization of *reflexive punitive penality*, that is, punishment turned back onto itself and not just redoubled but squared. Rather than "a routine and cynical perversion of penological principles," as argued by Roy King, the neutralizing prison-inside-the-prison is a straightforward extension of current punishment policy to the carceral institution itself that brings the simmering "crisis of penal modernism" to a boil by simultaneously singling out and entombing those inmates who embody it.[16]

This analytic specification allows us to displace the United States from its purported Archimedean position, which stems from historical usurpation and not analytic necessity. It enables us to distinguish and explore two dimensions along which countries may vary and journey: the degree to which they differentiate and autonomize the meta-prison within the penal apparatus it serves and the extent to which this meta-prison prioritizes the practical imperative of safety and security as the foundation of carceral order over and against other possible penal purposes (deterrence, neutralization, retribution, rehabilitation).[17] This conceptualization also suggests that we can fruitfully employ the supermax and germane contraptions as a magnifying glass for comparative justice inquiry, insofar as it acts as *practical revelator* of the characteristic traits, structural evolution, and enduring contradictions of a given national carceral system.

Indeed, a third contribution of the present tome is to sound an urgent clarion call for further international research into the social determinants of regimes of criminal confinement so as to connect the phenomenology of imprisonment as everyday lived reality at ground level and the revamping of punishment as a core state activity at the macro-institutional level. For this we need precise empirical descriptions and analytic dissections of (1) the ordinary routines and practical workings of procedures inside custodial facilities of the kind offered for France by Anne-Marie Marchetti in *Perpétuités* and for England by Ben Crewe in *The Prisoner Society*; (2) the inner architecture and administrative functioning of criminal justice, and of the battles roiling the carceral sector within it, as supplied in the case of California by Joshua Page in *The Toughest Beat*; and (3) the shifting position of criminal justice inside the structure of the local and national state, including how incarceration has become the ground, stake, and product of struggles waged across the fields of government, politics, and the media, as sketched by Lisa Miller in *The Perils of Federalism* and Vanessa Barker in *The Politics of Imprisonment*.[18] Pierre Bourdieu's notion of "bureaucratic field" as the set of agencies that successfully monopolizes the definition and distribution of public goods, among them the "negative" government benefit of punishment, supplies a powerful tool for seamlessly integrating these analytic levels. By tying the fleshly experience of hyperconfinement in a supermax-style prison to the broader revamping of the state in the neoliberal era,[19] it can help us discover under what conditions the theater of sovereignty can come to take the perplexing form of a solitary soul in a twelve-by-seven-foot box of barren concrete.

Loïc Wacquant
Paris, February 2012

ACKNOWLEDGMENTS

THE PROCESS OF DEVELOPING and editing this book has been interesting. Each new book I write or edit presents a series of challenges, some of which I have encountered before, others of which I have forgotten, and some of which are completely new. All in all, the process of helping to create a publication keeps me engaged with my discipline, my colleagues, and my students.

In any given project, there are numerous people to thank, and this one is no different. I would like to extend my appreciation initially to Ray Michalowski (University of Northern Arizona), the series editor, for seeing merit in this idea, and to Peter Mickulas (Rutgers University Press), acquisitions editor, for signing this book. Thanks to Joseph A. Dahm for copyediting the entire manuscript. My gratitude also extends to the University of Baltimore, which provided me with a sabbatical during which I formulated the bulk of the ideas for this project, assembled the contributors, and was able to travel to conduct some of the research contained in this book. I also need to thank Margarita (Magui) Cardona and Marc Lennon, of the University of Baltimore's Sponsored Research Division, who helped me craft the research grant proposal from which some of this book derives.

As always, I would like to thank my contributors for their scholarship and patience. I am also grateful to my colleagues both inside and outside the academy. This includes, but is not limited to, James Binnal, K. C. Carceral, Todd Clear, Francis Cullen, Ikponwosa (Silver) Ekunwe, Preston Elrod, Karen Evans, Jeff Ferrell, Rosemary Gido, Marianne Fisher-Giorlando, Mark Hamm, Keith Hayward, Allen Hornblum, Michael (Lee) Johnson, Robert Johnson, Richard S. Jones, Michael Lenza, Shadd Maruna, Gary Marx, Greg Newbold, Stephen C. Richards, Dawn L. Rothe, Frank Shanty, Michael Stohl, Charlie Sullivan, Jon Marc Taylor, Richard Tewksbury, Austin T. Turk, Ron Weitzer, Aaron Winter, Barbara Zaitzow, and Miguel Zaldivar.

Whether they are scholars, practitioners, convicts (or ex-cons), in subtle but important ways they have helped shape my thinking about this book. I also extend my gratitude to my students—many of whom are former or current convicts, police, probation or parole officers and administrators, and other criminal justice practitioners—for enduring portions of this work through lectures and/or required readings. Furthermore, I wish to thank the many invaluable sources who gave freely of their time to respond to my numerous questions and to help me contextualize this material.

I am also indebted to Dawn L. Rothe, who volunteered (or, more appropriately, was pressed into service) to look at selected chapters. Thanks to Rachel Hildebrant for copyediting my chapters. I also extend my gratitude to the anonymous reviewers of the proposal and the final manuscript for their helpful comments; these individuals encouraged me to rethink many of the ideas I initially presented.

Thanks to Loïc Wacquant for writing an excellent foreword.

I would be remiss to not also thank the production people at Rutgers University Press.

Last but certainly not least, I extend my never-ending gratitude to my wonderful family. I thank Natasha J. Cabrera, my wife and fellow scholar, for providing encouragement and feedback at several critical times, for serving as a sounding board for my ideas, and for trying her best to keep me focused. I also recognize Keanu and Dakota Ross-Cabrera, our children, who are a constant source of inspiration and joy and who frequently tolerate their father's divided attention more times than necessary.

The Globalization of
Supermax Prisons

CHAPTER 1

The Globalization
of Supermax Prisons

AN INTRODUCTION

Jeffrey Ian Ross

OVER THE CENTURIES, the way that societies sanction and punish deviants and criminals has significantly changed. From an almost exclusive focus on corporal punishments, governments, through their criminal justice apparatuses, especially the correctional system, now seem to focus on actual and alleged lawbreakers' souls (Foucault 1977/1995). As part of this process, punishment is increasingly meted out beyond the public view, hidden inside large, bureaucratic, state-run structures called jails and prisons. Supermax prisons (also known as administrative control units, special or security handling units, and control handling units) seem to epitomize this kind of punishment and can be considered the next step in the trajectory whereby the individual is removed from the public view, as well as from other inmates.

Supermax prisons are an American invention in penal practice. They are typically reserved for inmates who are considered a serious ongoing threat to the security of correctional institutions, in particular the safety of other convicts and correctional personnel. Supermax prisoners have usually engaged in high levels of violence behind bars and attempted or successfully completed an escape. They are often gang leaders or convicted political criminals, such as terrorists and spies. Collectively, supermax inmates are pejoratively referred to and considered to be the "worst of the worst." Because of this, supermax prisoners are usually locked in their cells for up to twenty-three hours a day and typically have minimal contact with other inmates and with correctional staff. Moreover, supermax inmates appear to be prisoners who are the most detached from the outside world. Rarely are they able to see out of the prison or have contact with the outside world. Short of a death sentence, time in a supermax prison is the most intense type of punishment the state has at its disposal.[1] Not only does the Federal Bureau of Prisons (FBOP) operate a separate supermax prison (i.e., ADX Florence), but almost every state in the United States has either a stand-alone supermax facility or a prison with a supermax tier or wing (Ross 2007b).

The situation is much different outside of the United States. Throughout history, most countries have had dedicated high-security, long-term segregation units (aka solitary confinement) for "incorrigibles." Although these tiers and wings (which share many similarities with supermax prisons) exist within standard correctional facilities, the adoption of the stand-alone supermax model is less common.[2] This trend, however, seems to be expanding. Although only nine countries have gone on record to confirm that they operate supermax prisons per se,[3] others run supermax-type facilities under different labels and names. Why has this occurred? There are no simple answers.

This book examines why nine prominent advanced industrialized countries have adopted the supermax model or a variant thereof. In particular, the supermax phenomenon seems to be a product of democracies because in this type of political arrangement citizens expect human and civil rights to be protected regardless of the crimes individuals commit. In authoritarian and totalitarian regimes, we expect physical brutality. Particular attention has been given to the economic, social, and political processes that have affected each case. Attempts have been made to answer the following broad questions: (1) What kind of support or opposition to the building of such a facility occurred, and if the opposition failed, why did it not succeed? (2) To what extent was the decision to build a supermax influenced by developments in the United States? (3) Has any controversy surrounding the building of a supermax continued after its construction?

Why is this topic important? Understanding the individuals, constituencies, and contexts behind the decision-making processes related to resorting to supermax facilities is necessary given the diverse and critical reactions from both the domestic general public and international organizations (Human Rights Watch 1997). In recent years, supermax prisons have become one of the most debated correctional initiatives among activists, scholars, correctional planners, policy makers, and politicians. Because of supermaxes' controversial nature, however, countries that operate them often deny their existence or dissociate their facilities from American-style supermaxes by calling them by other names. Much of this negative response has been caused by the repeated allegations of human rights abuses within supermax facilities.

The establishment of supermax prisons cannot be simply attributed to either the official crime rate or the incarceration rate in a country or jurisdiction. If this were the case, then all countries with higher rates would have supermax prisons and in proportion to these rates.[4] Clearly there are both macro/global-level and micro/country-level factors at work that affect the decisions of countries and their respective departments/ministries of corrections to propose and/or build supermax prisons.

At the micro or individual country level, supermax prisons are often proposed by legislators, correctional officials, and practitioners to fix and/or improve a number of problems (e.g., boost the local economy, demonstrate that departments of corrections are keeping up with the times, and placate correctional officers and their unions that complain about lax safety policies and practices).

At the macro level, the culture of fear, the growing awareness of risk management, and the control of surplus populations originating in neoliberal governance are also behind the resort to supermax prisons. Some scholars (e.g., Garland 2001) have argued that the growth of supermax prisons could be interpreted as part of a "punitive turn" that has occurred in Western societies over the past three decades. In the United States at least, these measures include harsher sanctions such as boot camps and the reintroduction of the death penalty, chain gangs, and so on. Alternatively, supermax prisons can be seen as part of the introduction of neoliberal policies and practices that emphasize efficiency and effectiveness (e.g., O'Malley 1999; Pratt 2002). This risk-management approach has been emphasized by numerous criminologists over the past two decades (e.g., Feeley and Simon 1992). Although some penologists see these two positions as opposites, they are more complementary than different. More important, however, is the need for understanding the supermax facilities in terms of the relationship among criminal justice (and specifically punishment), neoliberalism, and globalization processes.

Globalization, through the twin processes of communication and transportation, has facilitated the worldwide dissemination of things, people, and ideas. This is as true for cars and information technology as it is for "best practices" in particular fields. Although a growing body of research seeks to address how selected aspects of American culture—including food, fashion, values, and even criminal justice policies (e.g., Jones and Newburn 2002, 2007)—have become globalized, less attention has been paid to how American ideas about correctional practices, specifically supermax prisons, have been adopted and adapted by other countries. Undoubtedly, due to a confluence of factors, the United States has been at the forefront of innovative correctional practices, and the supermax model has proliferated in slightly differing forms and degrees in places such as the United Kingdom, New Zealand, and Australia. This trend has been linked to attitudes concerning retributivism and penal populism (i.e., a perception that dangerous and high-risk individuals are beyond reform and redemption).[5]

Examining the international dissemination of the American supermax correctional facility model fills a gap in the literature (Miller 2007). The globalization of the supermax is an important area of research because, given current political and social debates over the detention of terrorists and other dangerous criminals, there is a possibility that supermax prisons will become the option of choice for countries seeking maximum protection for their citizens (in terms of national and homeland security). Understanding the decision-making processes that have led to the adoption of these types of facilities is crucial given the frequently negative reactions they receive from the general public and from human rights organizations.

SITUATING THE STUDY

The Globalization of Supermax Prisons sits at the crossroads of scholarly and practical developments in the fields of policy convergence, diffusion, and transfer of innovations; comparative corrections; globalization and criminal justice; and supermax prisons. The following section briefly reviews these areas of study as they relate to the globalization of the supermax prisons.

Policy Convergence, Diffusion, and Transfer of Innovations

Building upon the work of Everett Rogers (1962/2003) on the diffusion of innovations, scholars from different disciplines have applied and analyzed the degree to which certain policies and practices are a result of policy convergence, diffusion, and/or the transfer of innovations (e.g., Jones and Newburn 2002). A handful of pieces in the field of criminal justice have acknowledged this intellectual foundation both in the United States and elsewhere. The analysis of diffusion has been applied to general criminal justice policies (Jones and Newburn 2002; Bergin 2010; Newburn 2010) and specific practices such as crime mapping (Weisburd and Lum 2005). This approach has primarily been restricted to processes, and with the exception of boot camps and private prisons, has avoided other kinds of correctional programs and institutions (e.g., the supermax prison).

Comparative Corrections

Comparative research on corrections can be traced back to the work of John Howard (1777) and Gustave de Beaumont and Alexis de Tocqueville (1833/1964). By the end of the nineteenth century, widespread agreement existed among both correctional administrators and reformers that comparing prisons was essential in order to design and improve (i.e., make more humane) countries' penal systems. "Comparative analysis also has been furthered through international congresses on imprisonment, which have convened in Germany since 1846 and which are now organized by the United Nations" (Kaiser 1982, 2).

In the past thirty years, there has been increased scholarly interest in corrections from a comparative perspective. Some researchers have tried to analyze and compare processes across various prison systems (Kaiser 1982;

Lynch 1987, 1988; Carlie and Minor 1992; Vagg 1994; van Zyl Smit and Dünkel 2001; Walmsley 2003; Cavadino and Digman 2006b; Othmani 2008). Alternatively, a small number of single-authored and coedited books contain chapters that review the prison systems in different countries. Both kinds of books have introductions and conclusions that make cross-national comparisons (e.g., Wicks and Cooper 1979; Downes 1988; Ruggiero, Sim, and Ryan 1995; Weiss and South 1998; Russell 2006; Dikötter and Brown 2007). Finally, several scholarly articles focus comparatively on subtypes or processes within the corrections systems (e.g., Morgan 2000; Sparks 2001, 2003). With the exception of King (1999), who compared the need for ADX Florence (the FBOP's supermax prison) to Britain's declaration that it did not and would not operate American-style supermax prisons, none of the above research has specifically addressed the issues surrounding the dissemination of the supermax prison concept from an international comparative perspective.

Globalization, Criminal Justice, and Corrections

In more recent years, a number of scholars have studied the impact of globalization on crime and on criminal justice, including the transfer of policies and practices (Wacquant 1999, 2009; Jones and Newburn 2002, 2007; Whitman 2003). A subset of this work has concentrated on the effects of globalization on corrections (Gilmore 1999; Worrall 2000; Baker and Roberts 2005; Morrison 2006). These studies focus on the following topics: foreign disdain for US prison policy and practices (Stern 2002; Mallory 2007), changes in the way governments criminalize populations (Sudbury 2002; Mallory 2006), the growth in correctional facility construction, the expansion of the prison-industrial complex (Beyens and Snacken 1996; Goldberg and Evans 1998; Mallory 2007; Wood 2007), the rise of the prison abolition movement (Stern 2002), the increasing numbers of individuals who are incarcerated (Sudbury 2002), and the incarceration rates and patterns of women (Sudbury 2002).

Some of the most insightful research on the globalization of corrections has been produced by Michael Cavadino and James Dignan (2006a, 2006b). They present a thoughtful view of America's place in the international realm of global influences:

> the progress of all these "globalizations" has been uneven, and in particular non-American cultures have remained in many ways stubbornly, even sometimes defiantly, non-American. In some countries, national pride can provide an incentive to *differentiate* oneself from the USA sometimes rather than slavishly imitating it in all things. For although globalization enables people to gain a greater awareness of others, how people choose to use such information will be influenced by their own local cultures. (Cavadino and Dignan 2006a, 437)

These authors explain that "[t]here has certainly been an enormous increase in the international traffic of information about punishment, and much greater readiness to import ideas and practices from elsewhere" (Cavadino and Dignan 2006a, 438). Moreover, Cavadino and Dignan state that "while we may see an acceleration of *penal convergence* in many ways, we are still a long way from global *homogenization of punishment*, which may never occur. To the extent that 'penal globalization' does exist, its process and effects are uneven, but the influence of the USA undoubtedly retains predominance" (Cavadino and Dignan 2006a, 438). Cavadino and Dignan ascribe the impact of the US model not only to policy makers but also to corporations and intergovernmental organizations. Finally, it must be understood that American influences are often interpreted as products or forces of hegemony and globalization (cultural, economic, military, etc.), and thus the distinction of and relationship among American influences, hegemony, and globalization are important.

Research on Supermax Prisons in the United States

Most studies pertaining to prisons explore the processes that take place within the facilities. With respect to high-security control prisons, a disproportionate emphasis has been placed on studying the effect these institutions have on inmates (e.g., Jackson 1983; Haney and Lynch, 1997; Haney 2003; Rhodes 2004).

Although numerous books on corrections, jails, and prisons have been published for trade, classroom, and professional audiences, only a limited number of studies offer in-depth perspectives on the supermax prisons. One such research effort is a book published by the American Correctional Association titled *Supermax Prisons: Beyond the Rock* (Neal 2002). Consisting of seven chapters written by prison officials, this compilation functions as a technical guide for the prison administrators who supervise these types of facilities. Besides its technical nature, *Supermax Prisons* is of limited use to general and scholarly readers because of the biases of its sponsor and a relatively small target audience. Written in a different tone, *The Big House: Life Inside a Supermax Security Prison* (2004) is a memoir authored by Jim Bruton, the former warden of the Minnesota Correctional Facility–Oak Park Heights. Although this book was pitched as a memoir of a supermax administrator, Oak Park is primarily a maximum-security facility; only one of the nine complexes at this site is used as an Administrative Control Unit (or supermax). Most recently, Sharon Shalev wrote *Supermax: Controlling Risk through Solitary Confinement* (2009). This book is an excellent review of the main practical concerns surrounding supermax prisons. It examines not only the history of the supermax concept but also the experience of living and working within one. Although these works are of varying degrees of interest and utility, none of the books described above examines the international proliferation of the supermax idea on a comparative basis or discusses the role of globalization as a driving force for countries to adopt this kind of institution.

Research on Supermax / High-Security Control Institutions in Other Countries

In recent years, research into foreign-based high-security control institutions has disproportionately focused on Guantánamo (e.g., Ratner and Ray 2004; Margulies 2006; Council of Europe 2007; Human Rights Watch 2009). Although numerous case studies of Alcatraz, Marion, and ADX Florence exist (e.g., Churchill and Vanderwall 1992; Haney and Lynch 1997; Ward and Werlich 2003; Richards 2008), very few English-language scholarly treatments of high-security correctional institutions and/or supermaxes in other countries have been written. Exceptions include Bree Carlton's (2007; 2009) contributions on supermax prisons in Australia and a handful of studies on the supermax prison in Vught, the Netherlands (e.g., Boin 2001; Resodihardjo 2009).

Carlton's (2007) research documents the dynamics of disciplinary power and prisoner resistance within the Pentridge Jika Jika High-Security Unit, one of Australia's first supermax institutions. In particular, she reviews prisoner intransigence and official responses to these campaigns which culminated in a fatal protest fire in 1987 and the deaths of five prisoners. Her follow-up piece (2009) extends the analysis to the Katingal Special Security Unit in New South Wales. In this article, Carlton examines the official reasons why the prison system chose to construct these two high-security facilities. Carlton's analysis does not discuss the reasons why Goulburn High Risk Management Unit (HRMU), Australia's current supermax prison was built, as this facility was opened only in 2001, after her two pieces were published.

Both Arjen Boin (2001) and Sandra Resodihardjo (2009) describe the Dutch use of the supermax model. These studies were prompted not only by widespread discussions about the advisability of the Dutch Prison Service's construction of a supermax prison but also by the crisis the Dutch Prison Service faced during this period. Cell shortages and escapes (often accompanied by violence) indicated that the Dutch Prison Service's administrative framework was malfunctioning. In fact, the large number of problems and incidents led Dutch policy makers to feel that they had no policy option but to opt for the supermax solution. Starting with a description of the special security units (SSUs) (Extra Beveiligde Inrichtingen)—the predecessors of the supermax prisons—Boin and Resodijardjo both present the crisis in the Dutch Prison Service as the motivation behind the adoption of the supermax concept.

On a related note, an article by Roy King and Sandra Resodihardjo (2010) reviews the reasons why the Netherlands, England, and Wales have pursued different policy responses toward supermax-type prisons. Although King's thesis in regard to England and Wales is well formulated, his definition of supermax prisons is overly narrow and would eliminate many facilities (especially in the United States) that corrections professionals and scholars unquestionably identify as supermax prisons. His definition also excludes Belmarsh Prison and the units that house suspected and convicted terrorists. These institutions, however, share many of the features of American-style supermax prisons.

Filling in the Gaps

Although some of the previously mentioned studies address the debates concerning the adoption of American-style supermax prisons, no empirical/scholarly studies of the supermaxes in Canada (i.e., the Special Handling Unit, Sainte-Anne-des-Plaines, Québec, and the former Special Handling Unit in Prince Albert, Saskatchewan), the United Kingdom, South Africa, Colombia, and Brazil exist to date. Also absent from this body of work is a larger comparative study of supermax prisons and an analysis of the reasons behind various countries' decisions to adopt the American model. Consequentially, the chapters contained in this volume provide a new focus and analytical perspective to the existing body of literature.

The research presented in this book seeks to answer the following questions:

1. Why were supermax prisons deemed necessary in the various countries examined?
2. What particular circumstances led to the creation of supermax prisons in these countries? For example, what constituencies were involved?
3. To what extent was the construction of supermax institutions prompted by a perception or evidence that prisoners were becoming more incorrigible and increasingly dangerous? What role did public pressure for get-tough policies play in the decision-making process?
4. What role has international terrorism played in each country's desire to construct a supermax facility?
5. What is the profile of the typical supermax inmate?
6. What are the similarities and differences between American supermaxes and those elsewhere?
7. What level of public scrutiny have supermax prisons in other countries engendered?
8. Why did the countries that built American-style supermax facilities pursue this policy and practice?
9. Why have some countries officially rejected the introduction of supermax prisons?

This book consists of chapters written by an international team of experts who have conducted both primary/field and secondary data collection research into this area. The writers range in profession from scholars to prison activists; one author was formerly incarcerated at one of the supermax prisons. The research process included reviews of newspaper and magazine articles, scholarly materials, and documents available on the World Wide Web as well as examinations of debates in legislatures and among administrative authorities about the construction of supermax prisons in the countries under investigation. Many of the contributors have conducted face-to-face interviews with the political, administrative, and executive personnel who made the key decisions about the construction of the selected supermax facilities. Many of the researchers have also spoken with local community activists and confidential informants who were involved in the deliberations surrounding the construction of the institutions in question. Finally, some of the contributors have toured the facilities under investigation and spoken with inmates, correctional workers, and administrators associated with them.[6]

The book contains thirteen chapters. The first ten examine specific countries' attempts to develop supermax prisons (i.e., the United States, Canada, Mexico, Great Britain, the Netherlands, South Africa, Australia, New Zealand, and Brazil).[7] The last two chapters explore the US experience in the implementation of the high-security prisons in Abu Ghraib, Iraq, and at Guantánamo, Cuba. The conclusion integrates the diverse threads of scholarship presented in this book and makes suggestions for future research and policy in this area.

CONCLUSION

No current book addresses the subject of the globalization of the American supermax concept or utilizes a comparative approach to generate new and unique perspectives. This publication seeks to examine the impact of the overarching themes of globalization, power, politics, and economics on the decisions to construct and operate supermax prisons in democratic societies and the implications of US policies and practices on two correctional facilities US personnel have run outside of the United States. Although scholars, policy makers, and correctional administrators will be interested in this book, it should also appeal to instructors and students at the university level. This includes readers in the fields of criminology/criminal justice, political science, sociology, and law.

CHAPTER 2

The Invention of the American
Supermax Prison

Jeffrey Ian Ross

OVER THE PAST THREE DECADES, a phenomenal number of
individuals in the United States have been sentenced to jails and to state or
federal prisons. However, not all correctional facilities are the same. Prisoners
are sent to a wide array of institutions. These jails and prisons typically vary
based on the level of security, ranging from minimum to maximum. Since the
mid-1980s, however, a dramatic change has influenced corrections in the
United States. Specifically, correctional systems at both the state and federal
levels have introduced or expanded the use of supermax prisons. Supermax
prisons, also known as special (or security) handling units (SHUs), control
units, or control handling units (CHUs), incarcerate almost 2 percent of all
prisoners (men only) doing time in the United States.[1] For some inmates,
being housed in a supermax is like a badge of honor, a source of pride. For
others, including prison activists, it constitutes cruel and unusual punishment.[2]

This chapter presents an overview of the American experiment with
supermaximum security prisons. It describes the historical development of
"supermax" facilities from their roots in the early prisons in America through
the present day and explains various shifts in practice, the growth of correctional support for these institutions, and the emergence of resistance to these
forms of confinement. The chapter also reviews various relevant legal challenges and rulings, as well as the international responses to these institutions.

Historically, most jails and prisons temporarily housed "problem"
inmates in a tier that was colloquially called solitary confinement but over
time officially dubbed administrative segregation (also known as "ad seg") or
administrative/disciplinary segregation (both known as "the hole").[3] Prisoners transferred to these units typically violated one or more facility rules (e.g.,
fighting, possessing contraband, etc.). If they are suspected of such an infraction, inmates are formally issued a ticket or incident report (also known as a

shot) by a correctional officer; they may then receive some sort of superficial administrative hearing, and if "officially" convicted, they are then sentenced to ad seg. Although conditions vary from one correctional facility to another, ad seg/administrative detention/disciplinary segregation (A.D./DS) inmates are typically required to stay in their cell twenty-three out of twenty-four hours a day and have only minimal contact with other prisoners and correctional workers. The inmates may eat the same meals as the general population, eat sack lunches, or be placed on a restricted diet, including a prison loaf (e.g., nutraloaf), which consists of food that is typically served to other inmates that day but is ground up, poured it into a baking pan, and reheated for the ad seg/A.D./DS inmates.

Unlike the ad seg/A.D./DS tiers, supermaxes are usually stand-alone facilities where prisoners have minimal contact with other inmates and in many cases correctional officers too. In the United States, supermax prisons are characterized by their physical layout, the regime to which prisoners are subjected, the types of inmates who are incarcerated, and the effects of this type of incarceration on prisoners.

THE HISTORICAL ORIGINS
OF THE SUPERMAX IDEA

Supermax prisons in the United States can be traced back to a reliance on solitary confinement and the use of administrative segregation. This kind of sanction is not solely exclusive to jails and prisons since a considerable number of mental hospitals use this kind of practice as well. In terms of chronology, there are four major periods in the growth of supermaxes and supermax-like facilities: the early period (e.g., Walnut Street Jail, Eastern Correctional Facility), the turn of the century (i.e., Alcatraz Prison), the 1950s–1980s (e.g., conversion of Marion Prison), and the past two decades (the failure of USP Marion and the building of ADX Florence, Colorado).

Since the inception of prisons, segregation and solitary confinement have been staples of the incarceration experience. These methods originated in the punitive penal practices of the nineteenth century, which included various kinds of torture (e.g., flogging, shackling prisoners to the cell wall, sweat boxes, etc.). The history of corrections in the United States can be traced back to colonial times. During this period, deviance and law breaking were typically dealt with through the process of shaming.

> The Puritans in New England used correctional punishment as a means to enforce their strict Puritan codes. They viewed the deviant as wilful, a sinner, and a captive of the devil. Informal community pressures, such as gossip, ridicule, and ostracism, were found to be effective in keeping most citizens in line. Mutilations, hangings, burnings, and brandings were used to punish serious crimes. Fines, confinement in the stocks and the public

cage, banishment, and whippings were other frequently used methods of control, and any citizen who was not a respected property owner was rejected from the town. The jail, which was brought to the colonies soon after the settlers arrived from England, was used to detain individuals awaiting trial and those awaiting punishment. (Bartollas 2002, 46)

Over the history of correctional policy and practice, the pendulum has swung back and forth between a concentration and a dispersal model for the incarceration of dangerous and problem convicts. The practice of placing inmates in solitary confinement began with the Walnut Street Jail, which was constructed in 1790 by the Quakers (the Society of Friends) in Philadelphia. Some of the prisoners were required to spend the majority of their days in the newly constructed and separate penitentiary block, isolated in their cells, and the only diversion they were given was a copy of King James Bible, which they were asked to read. With the rest of their time, the inmates were asked to reflect on the sins they had committed. This approach to treatment was called the "silent but separate" system. After several reforms were proposed, larger and more comprehensive structures were built as part of the Pennsylvania correctional system; these included Western Penitentiary (built in 1818 in Pittsburgh) and Eastern State Penitentiary (built in 1829 in Philadelphia). It was not until 1913, however, that "the Pennsylvania legislature dropped 'solitary' from sentencing statutes, and housing arrangements at Eastern State became congregate. From that point forward, specialized housing units were developed for management and control of troubling inmates" (Schmalleger and Smykla 2008, 320). Later, as the region grew in population, a competing corrections philosophy developed in a neighboring state, at the prison in Auburn, New York. The organizers of this prison believed that a military regime under which convicts lived and worked together (but remained silent) would have a more rehabilitative effect. This alternative was called the "silent but congregate" system.

During the late 1800s, many states began building "big house" prisons (e.g., Sing Sing, San Quentin, Joliet), also known as penitentiaries. These large structures were usually located in rural or remote parts of their respective states. The institutions were typically constructed out of local stone, were constructed by convicts, and loosely resembled castles. Physically, penitentiaries had high walls, large tiers, a yard, shops, and industries.

During the 1940s and 1950s, more jails and prisons were built, and corrections became recognized as a profession. The penitentiaries became increasingly obsolete, and the architecture of prisons started changing, as did their locations. A number of correctional experiments took place during this period. One noticeable change was the introduction of prisoner classification into different levels of security. Another experiment related to the implementation of rehabilitative programs, which were based on medical models (e.g., Rothman 1980). Crime was now perceived as a disease, and convicts afflicted with this malady were to be cured. In this context, a variety of psychological, drug, and alcohol treatment programs were introduced. This period also witnessed the beginning of the professionalization of corrections as a field. Correctional officers were now required to take tests before being allowed to work in the prison system and before being promoted to more senior positions in the institutions or with the state department of corrections (DOC) and Federal Bureau of Prisons (FBOP).

The 1960s were characterized by a desire to experiment with various community corrections programs. These initiatives went beyond simply probation and parole and included innovations such as diversion, work and educational release, and house arrest. This change in practice was designed to keep those individuals who could best be treated or rehabilitated in their communities out of jail and prison. During the 1980s, however, as a response to the public's fear of crime and to simplistic, negative interpretations linked to rehabilitation studies (e.g., Martinson 1974) and crime-reducing experiments (Austin and Irwin 2001, xiii–xiv; Austin 2003), a conservative agenda took hold of the criminal justice field. Many of the gains that had been made during the so-called community corrections era were scaled back. Congress and numerous state legislatures passed a variety of criminal laws that reversed such time-honored practices as indeterminate sentencing. The result was an array of laws that extended prisoners' sentences in custodial facilities. Politicians also passed legislation that enabled states to build more correctional facilities. The prison-building boom increased with towns and cities lobbying their state legislatures and the federal government for new correctional institutions. Jails and prisons were now seen as a way to make up for the job loss and population displacement that had happened because of business closure and relocation (Hallinan 2003).

American supermax prisons can trace their origins to a well-documented turning point in the nation's history of corrections. In October 1983, after the brutal stabbing deaths of two correctional officers by inmates at the federal maximum-security prison in Marion, Illinois, the facility implemented a twenty-three-hour-a-day lockdown of all convicts. The institution slowly changed its policies and practices and was retrofitted to become what is now considered a supermax prison. After considerable debate and difficulties with Marion, in 1994 the federal government opened its first specially designed supermax prison in Florence, Colorado.

Originally intended to house the most violent, hardened, and escape-prone criminals, supermaxes are increasingly used for persistent rule breakers, convicted leaders of criminal organizations (e.g., the mafia, street gangs), serial killers, and political criminals (e.g., spies and terrorists) (Suedfeld et al. 1982;

Barak-Glantz 1983; Riveland 1998; National Institute of Corrections 1997; Lovell et al. 2000). In some states, the criteria for admission into a supermax facility and the review of prisoners' time inside are very loose or even non-existent. These facilities are known for their strict lockdown policies, lack of amenities, and prisoner isolation techniques. Escapes from supermaxes are so rare that they are statistically inconsequential.

In the United States alone, 7.2 million people are under the control of the criminal justice system. Approximately 2.3 million are behind bars in jails or prisons, while the balance are in some form of community corrections (e.g., probation or parole) (Glaze 2009). The supermax in Florence (i.e., referred to as Administrative Detention Maximum, or ADMAX or ADX for short), which is maintained by the FBOP (or BOP for short), has a rated capacity for 490 inmates and currently houses such notable political criminals as "Unabomber" Ted Kaczynski and Oklahoma City bombing (1995) coconspirator Terry Nichols. Only a fraction of those incarcerated in state and federal prisons are ever sent to a supermax facility.[4] Although official statistics on the total number of inmates in supermax facilities do not exist, it has been argued that approximately twenty-five thousand individuals are currently imprisoned in these kinds of facilities (Briggs, Sundt, and Castellano 2003; Mears 2008). Most of the supermaxes in the United States were constructed as completely new units or involved the retrofitting of existing institutions at some point in the past two decades. In recent years, the number of convicts being sent to the supermax prisons has been growing.[5]

WHY THE FBOP DEVELOPED THE SUPERMAX PRISON CONCEPT

Although the elements of solitary confinement and administrative segregation have been present in all FBOP prisons, only three institutions were specifically designed or modified by the FBOP for high-security prisoners.

Alcatraz (California)

In 1933, the US Department of Justice acquired Alcatraz, a former military prison. The FBOP decided to use Alcatraz for intractable prisoners from other FBOP facilities, such as escape-prone inmates like Robert Stroud, dubbed the Birdman of Alcatraz, gangsters like Al Capone and Machine Gun Kelly, and spies like Morton Sobel. The FBOP believed that solitary confinement would be an appropriate management tool for these individuals. One hundred of the most dangerous criminals and troublemakers in the federal system were transferred there (Ward 1994). In 1963, because of the prison's deteriorating conditions, then attorney general Robert Kennedy closed Alcatraz. It was deemed a failure. The remaining prisoners were dispersed to other maximum-security facilities in the FBOP.

Marion (Illinois)

In 1963, the FBOP built USP Marion to house some of the Alcatraz prisoners and other difficult-to-manage convicts in the system. The facility had a rated capacity for five hundred inmates, who were allowed controlled movement throughout the facility. Despite this extra freedom, there were problems with Marion: "Open cell-fronts were a major limitation in Marion's design to control the toughest prisoners. Through their cell bars, inmates threw trash, urine, and faeces at corrections officers; passed contraband; set fires; and verbally harassed and lunged at staff and other prisoners as they walked by. Tension, hostility, violence, and murder were all too common" (Schmalleger and Smykla 2008, 320).

In October 1983, correctional officers Kluts and Hoffman were stabbed to death by a member of the Aryan Brotherhood. Almost immediately, a state of emergency was declared by the warden, and the facility implemented a twenty-three-hour-a-day lockdown of all convicts within its walls. Marion effectively became a "control unit" (Richards 2008). Due to numerous safety and design issues, the FBOP made plans to construct "a supermax facility that would implement construction features for controlling difficult inmates" (Schmalleger and Smykla 2008, 20).

ADX Florence (Colorado)

In 1994, the federal government opened its first uniquely designed supermax prison in Florence, Colorado. The facility was pejoratively dubbed the "Alcatraz of the Rockies" or the "Hellhole of the Rockies." ADX Florence includes four prisons: a minimum-level camp, a medium-security correctional institution, a maximum-security penitentiary, and an administrative maximum-detention facility. This correctional institution enforces strict discipline with few privileges; prisoners are not allowed the normal "controlled movement" from cells to the dining hall, work assignments, and recreational opportunities. The facility has a rated capacity of 490 inmates, and as of this writing 424 individuals are incarcerated there.[6] Empty cells are reserved for intake prisoners who may be transferred in from rebellious or rioting institutions. The prisoners are locked in their cells for twenty-three hours of every day, and they are normally allowed one hour of exercise in recreational pens. All meals are consumed in their individual cells. When necessary, the prison staff uses four-point spread-eagle restraints, forced feedings, cell extractions, mind-control medications, and chemical weapons to incapacitate prisoners (Levasseur 1998a, 1998b).

ADX Florence was built not only to eliminate escapes but also to provide defense against outside attack. To this end, an "outrider" (a guard patrol outside the fence or wall) patrols the perimeter of the facility in a white armored personnel carrier (similar to a tank without a cannon). At any given time, the outrider is occupied by three guards carrying automatic weapons (Austin et al. 2001).

Problems at ADX Florence are caused not only by the inmates. In 1999, allegations surfaced that a group of correctional officers, dubbed the "cowboys," was brutalizing inmates. In 2000, five officers were charged with this offense. The lawsuit included fifty-two indictments involving twenty inmates. Among other allegations, the correctional officers were charged with an array of offenses ranging from choking the inmates to placing excrement in the inmates' food. Other correctional officers who witnessed the acts against the inmates were threatened by their commanding officers, who claimed that aid would not be forthcoming if the witnesses revealed the identity of the officers involved in the torturing and harassment of the inmates.

CONDITIONS OF CONFINEMENT

Supermax prisons share common characteristics in terms of their physical layout, the regime to which prisoners are subjected, and the effects of incarceration on the prisoners. The following pages provide a brief review of these features.

Physical Layout

Supermax facilities have a higher degree of security and more rings of security than normal maximum-security prisons. Although cells vary in size and construction, on average they are twelve by seven feet in dimension. A cell light usually remains on twenty-four hours a day, and cell furnishings consist of a bed, a desk, and a stool, all made out of poured concrete, and a stainless steel sink and toilet. Supermax prisons are more expensive to build and run than less secure correctional facilities. Two reasons account for this. Supermax institutions depend on an expanded degree of technology to observe and control inmates in order to minimize human contact and the threat of attack to correctional workers by the inmates. The correctional officer to inmate ratio is also higher, thus leading to higher salary costs.

Regime

One of the more notable features of supermax prisons is the fact that prisoners are usually locked down twenty-three out of twenty-four hours every day. The hour outside of the cell is typically used for recreation or bathing/showering. Technically the law provides that all prisoners in SHUs, control units, or supermax prisons must be released from their cells once a day for one hour. Nonetheless, no legal authority actually enforces this rule. Without official oversight, many prisoners spend the whole day in their cells without the one-hour reprieve. Whenever inmates are actually removed from their cell, they are typically obliged to kneel down with their back to the door. Then they are required to place their hands through the food slot in the door to be handcuffed. While inmates are outside of their cells, the correctional officers typically search the rooms. Excepting the supermax facilities that allow double bunking (e.g., Pelican Bay State Prison), prisoners have virtually no contact with other people (including fellow convicts or visitors) besides the correctional officers. Supermax prisoners have very limited access to privileges such as watching television or listening to the radio. Access to phones and mail is strictly supervised and restricted. Reading materials are often prohibited.

Supermax prisons generally do not allow inmates to either work or congregate during the day. In addition, there is no personal privacy; everything the convicts do is monitored, usually through a video camera that is on all day and night. Communication with the correctional officers typically takes place through a narrow window in the steel door of the cell and/or via an intercom or microphone system. In the supermaxes, inmates rarely have access to educational or religious materials or to religious services. Almost all toiletries (e.g., toothpaste, shaving cream, and razors) are strictly controlled (Hallinan 2003). Given these sparse conditions, rehabilitation programs are almost impossible to implement.

The Effects of the Supermax Experience on Inmates

Not only do many supermax inmates enter the prisons with psychological problems, but because of the austere conditions and lack of or minimal human contact, supermax prisoners can develop these kinds of symptoms. "At one Supermax in California, more than two hundred inmates, or about one in every nineteen, were diagnosed as psychotic. Doctors who visited the prison reported finding 'bug-eyed' inmates who were incoherent, heard voices, or hallucinated. One wrote a suicide note in his own blood" (Hallinan 2003, xiv–xv). During their incarcerations, supermax prisoners often develop severe psychological disorders, including delusions and hallucinations, which may have long-term negative effects (Grassian 1983; Grassian and Friedman 1986; Haney 1993; Haney and Lynch 1997; Zinger, Wichmann, and Andrews 2001; Briggs, Sundt, and Castellano 2003; Gibbons and Katzenbach 2006). The potentially harmful conditions inside the supermax prisons have led several corrections and human rights experts and organizations (including Human Rights Watch and the American Civil Liberties Union) to question whether these facilities are a violation of the Eighth Amendment of the US Constitution, which prohibits the state from engaging in cruel and unusual punishment. The groups have also argued that the supermaxes are in conflict with the European Convention on Human Rights and the UN Universal Declaration of Human Rights, which were drafted to protect the rights of not only people living in the free world but also those behind bars. Although short-term stays in solitary confinement may have negligible effects on prisoners (Gendreau and Bonta 1984), the isolation, lack of meaningful activity, and shortage of human contact during long-term solitary confinement are much more debilitating in their impact.

Supermax prisons have plenty of downsides, and these affect not just the inmates (Lippke 2004). Some scholars have suggested that the supermax prisons are part of the correctional industrial complex (Christie 1993/2003). Most of the American supermaxes were constructed relatively recently. Others are retrofitted facilities that now fit the supermax paradigm. As one could expect, the economic requirements for these facilities are huge. According to a recent study by the Urban Institute, the annual per-cell cost of a supermax is about US$75,000, a large amount when compared to an average per-cell cost of US$25,000 for cells in an ordinary state prison.[7]

CRITICISMS AGAINST AMERICAN SUPERMAX PRISONS

As to be expected, several cases involving the constitutionality of the supermaxes have gone to court in recent years. One of the most famous legal cases that has come out of the SHU experience is *Madrid v. Gomez* (1995 W.I. 17092, N.D. Cal 1995). In 1993, prisoners in the Pelican Bay Supermax Prison in California initiated this class-action suit in federal court. The judge in the case concluded that the inmates had been subjected to cruel and unusual punishment, excessive violence, and substandard medical care.

According to Roy King (2001, 164), the treatment of inmates in the supermaxes is in clear violation of both national and international legal standards:

> Although the effective reach of international human rights standards governing the treatment of prisoners remains uncertain, there seems little doubt that what goes on in a number of Supermax facilities would breach the protections enshrined in these instruments. . . . The International Covenant on Civil and Political Rights, which the United States has ratified, for example, has a more extensive ban on "torture, cruel, inhuman or degrading treatment or punishment" than the Eight Amendment prohibition of "cruel and unusual" punishment, and requires no demonstration of intent or indifference to the risk of harm, on the par of officials.

WHAT LANDS PRISONERS IN SUPERMAX PRISONS?

In some states, the criteria for sentencing a convict to a supermax facility and the review of prisoners' time inside are quite vague or even nonexistent. Although placement in a supermax can be caused by a range of reasons, the most influential factors are the recommendations outlined in a presentence investigation, the sentence a judge passes, classification processes at reception centers, and the behavior of inmates during incarceration.

For some convicts, the decision about which correctional facility they are sent to is a product of sentencing guidelines (which take into account the inmate's criminal history), judge's discretion, and the result of a presentence investigation (i.e., an evaluation during an assessment process conducted by the respective DOC or FBOP). In some cases, the decision is made long before the inmates begin their sentences, specified by the judges in their cases. For example, Ramzi Yousef, one of the convicted bombers in the 1993 terrorist attack of the World Trade Center, was sent directly to ADX Florence.

Alternatively, most prisoners who are new to the system are initially transferred to a receiving and departure tier, wing, or facility where they are classified into the appropriate receiving facilities. Officially, prison systems utilize classification systems as a means to designate prisoners to different security levels. Typically, the hard-core, violent convicts serving long sentences are assigned to maximum-security facilities, the incorrigible prisoners serving medium-length sentences are sentenced to medium-security prisons, and those serving short sentences for relatively light infractions are sentenced to minimum-security camps, farms, or community facilities (Ross and Richards 2002).

Although much has been written on the subject of jails, prisons, and corrections, the mass media and the academic community have justifiably been relatively silent with respect to supermax prisons. It is difficult for journalists and scholars to gain access to prisoners, correctional officers, and administrators in these kinds of facilities. Only a very limited number of publicly available government reports have been published (e.g., National Institute of Corrections 1997; Riveland 1998). These have primarily consisted of statistical compilations related to the supermax facilities throughout the United States and the composition of the inmates housed within their walls. The academic treatments (journal articles or chapters in scholarly books) fall into three groups. The first category consists of overviews of the topic (Suedfeld 1974; Rogers 1993; King 1999; Kurki and Morris 2001; Toch 2001). The second group centers on the individuals who are sent to solitary confinement or assigned to supermax prisons (Suedfeld et al. 1982; Barak-Glantz 1983; Lovell et al. 2000). And the last category concentrates on the effects of supermax prisons on inmates and others (Grassian 1983; Grassian and Friedman 1986; Haney 1993; Haney and Lynch 1997; Zinger, Wichmann, and Andrews 2001; Briggs, Sundt, and Castellano 2003). To date, the research has focused disproportionately on supermax prisons in the United States, ignoring their introduction in other countries. Rigorous comparative examinations of foreign-based supermax prisons have yet to be performed.

THE STATE SUPERMAXES AND
WHY THEY HAVE PROLIFERATED

The state supermaxes outnumber the federal facilities; thus, it stands to reason that considerable variability exists among these types of prisons. The states' control units differ in terms of conditions of confinement and procedures. According to the National Institute of Corrections, "Supermax facilities of one stripe or another exist or are rapidly being built in three dozen states, and in 1996 such facilities housed from 8 to 10 percent of those behind bars, or roughly one hundred thousand individuals—about twice as many as a decade ago" (Hallinan 2003, 129). Most states are ostensibly proud of their supermaxes, "which were almost invariably referred to as 'state of the art' institutions. DOC administrators highlight their supermaxes' technological sophistication, pride in their sheer enormity and expense, but pride most of all in the notion that they had figured it out . . . finally found a way to beat the inmate. In this sense, the supermaxes had become symbols, flags flown in victory" (Hallinan 2003, 130). Some of the more well-known or infamous state-level supermaxes include the North Branch Correctional Institution (Cumberland, Maryland), Colorado State Penitentiary (Canon City), Pelican Bay State Prison (California), Wallens Ridge in Big Stone Gap (Virginia), Walpole (Massachusetts), and Tamms (Illinois).

Since the mid-1980s, many state DOCs have built their own supermax prisons (Dowker and Good 1993). The exact number of existing supermax prisons is difficult to determine. For example, in 1997 a study by the National Institute of Corrections determined that fifty-seven separate units were in operation. However, in 1999, this official number dropped to thirty-four.

TABLE 2.1
Some of the more notable supermax prisons in the United States

Federal supermax prisons

United States Penitentiary Administrative Maximum Facility (ADX), Florence, Colorado, opened in 1994

State supermaxes

Minnesota Correctional Facility–Oak Park Heights (MCF-OPH), Stillwater, Minnesota, opened in 1983

Maryland Correctional Adjustment Center (MCAC), Baltimore, Maryland, opened in 1988

Tamms Correctional Center, Tamms, Illinois, opened in March 1998

Wallens Ridge State Prison, Big Stone Gap, Virginia, opened in April 1999

Varner Supermax, Grady, Arkansas, opened in 2000

Although some states do not have supermax prisons, others, like Texas, have sixteen units (Abramsky 2002, 26).

Several reasons account for the proliferation of the supermax prisons. First, many states have had tragic experiences similar to that which took place at Marion. In Minnesota, for example, after the escape of a prisoner, correctional officers were held hostage and a warden was stabbed to death. These events set off a series of prison disturbances during the early 1970s. Thus, the situation was ripe for the construction of a new facility that would house the worst of the prison population (Bruton 2004, 27–28).

Second, anecdotal evidence suggests that the public is, in general, supportive of supermax prisons.

> These prisons, though, have proven widely popular. Thirty years ago, Americans watched as their prisons spun out of control. They saw guards killed at Attica and inmates rioting at San Quentin, and what they wanted from their prisons, more than anything, was control. This is what the Supermax provided. In Tamms, Illinois, I found people who so loved their new Supermax that the local sandwich shop renamed its specialty in honor of the prison: the Supermax burger. Like the prison, I was told, it came with "the works." The super-prisons set the tone for the rest of the system. Across the country, politicians began calling for harsher conditions of confinement. (Hallinan 2003, xv)

Third, the construction and administration of supermax prisons are part of the correctional industrial complex, a loose network of people and corporations that keep the jails and prison system growing. Nils Christie (1993/2003) outlines how recent trends indicate that the modern world has an ever-increasing supply of individuals for the criminal justice system to monitor; furthermore, a vast network of public and private enterprises financially benefit from this phenomenon. Though Christie's argument was directed at the criminal justice systems in all advanced industrialized countries, he mainly focused on the United States, particularly its correctional system. He examined the rationales that led to an increase in the number of jails and prisons being built and operated, the rising numbers of inmates, and the political, economic, and cultural mechanisms that support the prison system. Arguing that the United States leads the world in incarcerated individuals, Christie reviewed how other countries have dealt with the problem of criminality and the sanctioning of offenders. As a source of this phenomenon, Christie primarily blamed the American obsession with controlling lawbreakers through organizations such as the American Correctional Association and the impact of privatization on the system at large. Other scholars have built upon Christie's notion and fleshed it out to include the idea of a prison industrial complex (PIC). According to journalist Eric Schlosser (1998, 54), who first popularized the concept, a PIC is composed of "a set of bureaucratic, political, and economic interests that encourage increased spending on imprisonment, regardless of the actual need. The prison-industrial complex is not a conspiracy, guiding the nation's criminal-justice policy behind closed doors. It is a confluence of special interests that has given prison construction in the United States a seemly unstoppable momentum." If Schlosser is correct, a whole panoply of nonprofit organizations and for-profit businesses capitalizes on a seemingly insatiable need to incarcerate individuals and build prisons, ultimately making money from the pain and suffering of others behind bars. Since the publication of Schlosser's article, other authors have provided additional evidence of the profits made by businesses and corporations tied to the PIC (e.g., Sheldon and Brown 2000; Sheldon 2005). Articles challenging the legitimacy of the PIC have also been published in recent years (e.g., Mahmood 2004; Platt 2004).[8]

Fourth, another explanation for the growth of the supermax prisons lies in the existence of a conservative ideology linked to criminal justice in general and offenders in particular. This trend started in the 1970s and continued during the 1980s. Often labeled the "new penology" (Feeley and Simon 1992), this trend represents a reaction to an increase in the public's fear of crime and to the demise of the "rehabilitative ideal." In the aftermath of this shift, a punitive agenda took hold of the criminal justice field, and it led to an increased number of people being incarcerated (Kramer and Michalowski 1995). This approach to criminal justice was carried forward by Ronald Reagan's Republican successor, George H. W. Bush (1989–1993). During this time, the number of people entering jails and prisons increased dramatically. This was facilitated by the following factors: the construction of new correctional facilities; new, more stringent sentencing guidelines (particularly "truth in sentencing" legislation, mandatory minimums, and determinate sentencing); the passage of "three strikes, you're out" legislation; and the "war" on drugs. Thus, many of the gains that had been part of the so-called community corrections era of the 1960s were scaled back. Congress and state legislatures passed various laws that reversed time-honored practices, such as indeterminate sentencing, and invoked an array of new laws that increased the sentences of those convicted of crimes.

Fifth, the careerism of correctional administrators has contributed to the proliferation of supermax prisons. Without the leadership of particular wardens, government "rainmakers," commissioners, and DOC secretaries, the supermax facilities would not have been built. In order to advance their careers, these professionals developed new kinds of policies and practices, emulating other facilities being built at both the federal and state levels. After all, no self-respecting director of corrections would want to be singled out in the history of corrections or accused by his or her state legislators as lagging behind current correctional practice.

Sixth, the federal government's National Institute of Corrections (NIC) (a branch of the FBOP) helps to disseminate policies and practices and train senior correctional administrators at the state level. The NIC acts as a clearinghouse for information on the latest developments in the field of corrections. Some of this work has involved the training of supermax wardens and employees in the state DOCs. During the training sessions, psychologists lecture on classification and mental health, and lawyers speak about the major legal cases affecting the supermaxes. Encouraging a peer learning model, the NIC helps states to direct correctional policy through collaborative technical assistance, training programs for managers, and academic course work.[9]

Finally, in many respects, supermaxes are a symbol of the failure of rehabilitation endeavors to think and act creatively with respect to incarceration. Supermaxes also serve a symbolic function by demonstrating to both lawbreakers and those in other countries that the American correctional system is prepared to severely punish those who engage in the most violent or heinous of crimes.

FUTURE PROSPECTS

The United States has plenty of superexpensive supermax facilities, but they were designed when street crime was considered a growing problem.[10] Today, the country has a lower violent-crime rate that shows no sign of changing in the foreseeable future.

Few, if any, state directors of corrections or correctional planners will admit that the supermax concept was a mistake. It is clear these prisons cannot be replaced by equivalent facilities that are significantly less expensive. Nonetheless, prison experts are beginning to realize that, just like a city with a shrinking population that finds itself with too many schools or fire departments, the supermax model must be made more flexible in order to justify its size and budget (*Corrections Digest* 2002).

One solution involves converting these facilities to house different types of prisoners. In May 2006, for example, Wisconsin DOC officials announced that over the previous sixteen years the state's supermax facility in Boscobel—which cost US$47.5 million to build (in 1990) and which has a capacity of five hundred inmates—had an average occupation of one hundred cells fewer than its capacity. Boscobel now houses supermax inmates and maximum-security prisoners, serious offenders who do not qualify for incarceration with the state's most violent offenders. Similarly, the Maryland Correctional Adjustment Center opened in 1989 at a cost of US$21 million and provided space for 288 inmates. The prison operation relocated in 2011, and the existing facility was then taken over by the FBOP.

Converting cells is one approach, but it is not the only one. Other ideas include building more regional supermaxes and filling them by shifting populations from other states. This would result in emptying some of the larger supermaxes and then closing them or converting them to other uses.

Another possibility would involve combining some elements of the supermax model with the approaches linked to traditional prisons. This would result in the creation of a hybrid facility that could serve a wider population. However, the differing types of inmates would need to be kept separate from each other—a logistical problem of no small concern.

The invention and adoption of the supermax prison model is perhaps the most significant indictment of the way prisons are operated and the broader culture of correctional facilities. The United States incarcerates more people per capita then any other advanced industrialized country, and yet the average American rarely questions this fact. Furthermore, most Americans believe that individuals doing time are guilty of the crimes of which they are accused. The question remains, what does the creation and reliance on supermaxes say about the field of corrections and about American society at large? The supermax phenomenon has deep cultural and political implications, a reality that this book attempts to address.

This chapter reviewed the success and failures in responding to the supermax prison model. It explored the development of new policies, legislation, and practices. In conclusion, the future of supermax prisons in light of the events of 9/11, allegations and investigations of human rights violations, and greater government intrusiveness into citizens' private affairs were considered. At this time, three possible future scenarios exist: keeping things the way they are (the do-nothing approach), improving the supermaxes (the reform option), and the abolishment of the supermaxes. Only time will tell which course will dominate the future of the supermaxes.

CHAPTER 3

How Canada Built Its Supermax Prison

Jeffrey Ian Ross

As one of the world's leading advanced industrialized democracies, Canada has not missed its opportunity to build and run its own supermax facility.[1] However, unlike its neighbor to the south, a country in which almost every state has a supermax facility either as a stand-alone structure or as separate wing or annex of an existing correctional facility (Ross 2007b), only one supermax facility currently exists in Canada. At the present time, Canada operates a Special Handling Unit (SHU), which is located in Sainte-Anne-des-Plaines, Québec (just outside of Montréal). The fact that Canada only has one supermax prison while its neighbor to the south, with which it shares many cultural, economic, and legal similarities, has a federal supermax and a supermax facility in almost each state is somewhat unusual. The sequence of events surrounding and leading to this current state of affairs is long and complicated. This chapter reviews the process by which Canadian correctional practitioners experimented with different supermax-like facilities and recounts the events that led to the construction of the current facility in Sainte-Anne-des-Plaines.

In order to accomplish this goal, this study primarily relies upon a review of secondary data. The research focuses on scholarly materials, publicly available government documents, newspaper and magazine articles, and materials available on the World Wide Web concerning the construction and management of SHUs in Canada.[2]

The Development of the Canadian Special Handling Unit

Similar to the United States, Canada has both provincial and federal prisons. Individuals convicted of crimes warranting sentences of two years less a day are sent to provincial prisons, operated by the provincial governments'

Ministry of Corrections, and those who commit crimes with sentences of two years or longer are sent to federal prisons operated by the Correctional Services of Canada (CSC). In 2008 and 2009 (the most recent statistics available), 22,240 inmates were supervised by CSC; 13,531 convicts were behind bars, and 8,709 fell under various kinds of community corrections supervision. The prison system costs Canadian taxpayers about Can$3.85 billion, or roughly US$3.94 billion (http://www.publicsafety.gc.ca/res/cor/rep/2010-ccrso-eng.aspx#b1). Out of the fifty-seven federal correctional facilities (seventeen minimum security, nineteen medium, eight maximum, and sixteen multilevel), only one is designated a supermax penitentiary (Calverley 2010). The CSC is governed by two federal statutes: the Correctional and Conditional Release Act (CCRA) and the Correctional and Conditional Release Regulations. Neither of these documents outlines the role of supermax facilities. Needless to say, the CSC considers the supermax as a type of maximum-security facility. Canada's history with supermax facilities can be described as constantly evolving. The development of corrections and, by extension, control units in Canada can be broken up into a number of periods. Although others (e.g., Ekstedt and Griffiths 1988) have divided the history of Canadian penal philosophy into separate eras, for simplicity's sake the discussion below is organized according to decades starting with the 1960s.

One final caveat is in order. The reader must keep in mind that the composition of prisoners in Canada is not the same as it is in the United States. According to John Lowman and Brian MacLean (1991, 134), "Gang affiliations in U.S. prisons are not, for the most part, nearly as important in Canada in shaping prison social structure. The proportion of African American, Hispanic, and Native prisoners far outweighs their proportion in the general population; in Canada, it is primarily First Nations (i.e., Native people) who are vastly overrepresented. Yet the differences between the two systems are far more dramatic than this."

1960s

The origins of the ideas behind the first SHU in Canada can be traced back to a handful of federal government reports (e.g., "The Fauteux Report" 1956), senior-level discussions between the federal minister of justice and the attorney generals of the provinces (i.e., Dominion Provincial Conference 1958), the creation of a Correctional Planning Committee in the Department of Justice (1960), and the writing and release of a "10 Year Plan of Institutional Development" (Joseph 1983, 1–2).[3] The original plan called for the construction of four "Special Correctional Units" specifically designed to house disruptive prisoners; the units were to be geographically distributed among four designated regions (Atlantic, Québec, Ontario, and Western). The first of these institutions was built in Laval, Québec (a suburb located south of Montréal), and it opened in 1968. The planners originally intended that this facility would hold 160 inmates. The Special Correctional Unit in Laval was subsequently evaluated, and the construction of the remaining three institutions was dependent on the success of the first one (Joseph 1983, 3–4). Initially, the Laval facility was to be populated with prisoners transferred from the other regions who were to be placed in a specially designed, four-phase program of treatment. However, it was soon determined that "there were not enough 'dangerous offenders' to fill the institution. Many of the inmates in the Special Correctional Unit were in fact protective custody inmates, not dangerous offenders" (Joseph 1983, 7).

1970s

In the 1970s, well-publicized riots rocked Canadian penal institutions (Culhane 1985). One of the most famous altercations occurred at Kingston Penitentiary (Ontario). It started on April 14, 1971, and lasted ninety-six hours. In the end, "two prisoners were murdered; sixteen sex offenders were stalked, bound, and beaten; several correctional officers were taken hostage; and major sections of the institution were destroyed" (Welch 2004, 260). The riot was finally quelled with the assistance of the Canadian army. The riots were investigated by a royal commission of inquiry that was headed by Justice J. W. Swackhamer (1972). Both Swackhamer and other observers attributed the causes of the riot to harsh conditions, punitive treatment, and prisoner resistance to the construction and implementation of the maximum-security prisons. Within four days of the riot's termination, four hundred prisoners were transferred to Millhaven Prison, a maximum-security prison in Bath, Ontario (outside of Kingston), which was in the final stages of construction. To punish the inmates who had participated in the Kingston uprising, correctional officers repeatedly beat the newly arrived inmates. One shocking example of the brutality involved prisoners who were forced to run a gauntlet (i.e., a situation where correctional officers would line a hallway and officers would beat prisoners as they walked or ran through). Over the next six years, there were numerous disturbances and outbreaks of prison violence, not only at Millhaven but in other prisons across Canada as well (MacGuigan 1977).

In 1972, a CSC report evaluating the Special Correctional Unit in Laval was completed. The document concluded that although the facility should continue to house the same types of inmates as it had in the past, the prisoners should henceforth be required to undergo a "therapeutic community orientation" program. In order to carry out this change in rehabilitation, the institution was slated for renovation. In June 1973, however, five inmates escaped, forcing the CSC to put the construction plans on hold. All of the convicts were removed from the Special Correctional Unit and placed in other facilities across Canada, and the institution was mothballed until 1975. In 1976, 110 inmates who had participated in a riot at the nearby Laval Penitentiary were transferred to the Special Correctional Unit, which was subsequently called the Correctional Development Centre (CDC) (Jackson 2002a, 8). Michael Jackson (2002a, 8) states that "[a]lthough conceived as an alternative to long-term administrative segregation, places where prisoners could participate in specially designed, phased programs to earn increasing privileges, the new units proved to be a cruel parody of reform." Jackson, who visited the CDC, lamented that the phased program existed only in theory: "The phase program, designed to distinguish between Special Handling Units and the old-style segregation units, was the focal point for most of the criticism directed at the new units by prisoners I interviewed in 1980" (Jackson 2002b, sec. 02.1, 1).

In 1977, the CSC established an Offenders Program Branch, and one of its tasks was to develop "programs aimed at controlling the new 25-years-to-life population" (Lowman and MacLean 1991, 146). The branch later appointed a task force to develop a revised security classification system. The task force developed a seven-tiered framework "with the 'S7' designation—the highest level of security—being the SHU. The system was adopted in fiscal year 1981–1982 and became operational in 1983" (Lowman and MacLean 1991, 146).

During the 1970s, a series of reports (e.g., "Annual Report of the Correctional Investigator," "The Study Group on Dissociation," "The Sub-Committee on the Penitentiary System in Canada," "The Response of the Solicitor General to the Parliamentary Sub-Committee Report on the Penitentiary System") addressed the need for a special institution to house uncooperative, violent, and dangerous inmates. The study's authors differed on exactly where these inmates should be placed. Ultimately, the studies resulted in the creation of SHUs to deal with the problem (Joseph 1983, 10–11). Since March 1978, an SHU with a capacity for eighty inmates has been operating within the walls of the CSC (Joseph 1983, 8).

1980s

During the 1980s, the SHU facilities were focused around four institutions: Millhaven, the CDC, Prince Albert (Saskatchewan), and Sainte-Anne-des-Plaines (Québec).

I. MILLHAVEN AND CDC. By the early 1980s, two temporary SHUs were operational: one at Millhaven Penitentiary in Bath, Ontario, and another at the CDC in Laval, Québec. These prisons were primarily used to house violent inmates (Malarek 1980). In Millhaven, the cells were equipped with steel desks, sinks, toilets, and beds that were bolted to the walls. In terms of supervision, three levels of custody, or "phases," were in place. In phase 1, inmates were allowed out of their cells for only one hour a day. Phase 2 convicts were permitted out of their cells for six hours a day. Inmates in phase 3 were allowed out of their cells for eight hours a day. In both phase 2 and phase 3, inmates were provided with television sets in their cells. In the communal space of the facility, a couple of cells were converted into recreational rooms equipped with instruments, musical accessories, and punching bags (Malarek 1980). Unlike inmates of most American-style supermaxes, Canadian inmates are allowed visits from family members. These visits were typically done through barriers of cages, windows, and screens.

Transfer to the SHU occurred when an inmate assaulted or murdered a correctional officer or another convict or if he or she had been involved in an incident that resulted in a hostage situation. "Confinement in the units is relatively free of bureaucratic red tape. A warden holds an in-penitentiary review of the cases and makes a recommendation that goes to regional headquarters and then to the special handling unit board in Ottawa" (Malarek 1980).

In December 1980, the commissioner of the CSC issued a directive regarding prisoners in the SHUs. The categories of "particularly dangerous inmates" who could be transferred to such facilities now included inmates "whose documented actions or demonstrated intentions while in custody or under sentence constitute a persistent and serious threat to staff, inmates or other persons" (Jackson 2002b, 02.1, 2). Furthermore, the directive stipulated the creation of a national SHU review committee, consisting of "senior officials of the CSC under the chairmanship of the Deputy Commissioner Security" who were responsible for reviewing "applications from wardens to transfer prisoners to a SHU" (Jackson 2002b, 02.1, 2). To expedite transfers in and out of the SHU, potential cases are assessed by the "National Review Committee, made up of heads of Canada's maximum security institutions and other correctional officials. Each case is reviewed at least every four months" (Harris 2001a).

In terms of the duration of incarcerations, "[p]risoners in SHUs spend three years moving in stages from complete isolation to an eventual reintegration with the prison population" (Strauss 1982). Although official counts of SHU inmates are hard to find, in 1982, 135 inmates were in SHUs and 60 others were on probation from these units in the general population.

Besides these two SHUs, alternative solutions for violence-prone inmates included the building of an SHU in Renous, New Brunswick, to house eighty inmates (intended completion date of 1985). However, a considerable backlash to this proposal came from prison activists, who argued that the CSC could not build its way out of its problems. Some CSC officials also spoke out against the new facility, citing the remote nature of the location and its distance from the majority of the prisoners' families (Makin 1984). Shortly after the construction company broke ground, the government shut down the project. In 1986, then auditor general of Canada Kenneth Dye was quoted as stating that this decision led to a waste of Can$10 million in taxpayer money (McIntosh 1986).

2. SHU IN PRINCE ALBERT, SASKATCHEWAN. In 1984, the CSC closed down the SHU units at Millhaven and CDC and opened an SHU inside the Saskatchewan Penitentiary (SaskPen) in Prince Albert as well as another one in Sainte-Anne-des-Plaines (Québec). During its history, the SHU in Prince Albert held such infamous Canadian criminals as Charles Ng, Clifford Olson, and Carney Nerland. The ratio of correctional officers to inmates was approximately one-to-one, and the facility had a holding capacity of eighty inmates. In terms of physical spaces, the cells measured eight by twelve feet. "The Prince Albert SHU had five cell blocks radiating off a central dome-controlled area. In each block, there were 16 cells. . . . [T]he prisoners' cells . . . were much bigger than those in the old SHUs at Millhaven and the CDC and indeed in any segregation unit. . . . The distinguishing feature of the new SHUs . . . was that of separation of staff from prisoners and the pervasive influence of security and surveillance" (Jackson 2002b, 02.1, 1). In 1997, the Prince Albert unit was closed and the inmates were transferred to the maximum-security facility at Sainte-Anne-des-Plaines.[4]

3. SAINTE-ANNE-DES-PLAINES, QUÉBEC. In 1989, the CSC opened an SHU at Sainte-Anne-des-Plaines. By the late 1980s, this location already had three detention facilities in the same complex, with a total of 204 beds and 169 inmates (Gazette 1995). The SHU was the fourth prison to be built at this site. The new facility was originally designed to have thirty separate cells, but today it can accommodate ninety inmates thanks to the construction of additional cells. The expansion phase was completed in 1996 by the Canvar Group, a Montréal-based construction company, at a cost of Can$4.8 million.

Kathleen Harris (2001b) provides a detailed description of the facility:

> Set in a desolate, barren, faceless location, the buildings are secured by heavy gates and 12-foot fences topped by double coils of razor wire. The perimeter is laced with sensor monitors, and watchtowers survey the sprawling site. Inside, every detail is designed to confine and maximize security. . . . Eight guards walk the main floor, while another three patrol a darkened catwalk above. Lights are kept dim so prisoners below can't see shadows to determine the guards' whereabouts. . . . A central area reaches out to five "ranges" each with its own classification of inmate privileges. Here, guards control every movement within the institution and communicate with staff on the floor and prisoners in their cells. . . . Some prisoners are completely segregated; a camera fixed in the corner of the cell monitors

every turn and motion. Few privileges are granted, including just one hour out each day. On a less restrictive wing, inmates are permitted three hours out each day; they are able to leave cells and are paid to carry out simple tasks like cleaning floors or delivering meals to inmates. Some are allowed time in a common room, where they are closely monitored to ensure they don't attack or kill one another. (Harris 2001b)

Michael Jackson (2002a, 8) states, "[T]he architects of the new SHUs had taken to heart the panoptical vision of English political reformer Jeremy Bentham in laying out the observation galleries; these permitted total surveillance of prisoner activity. Separation of prisoners from staff by glass and steel barriers was a central theme of these units, allowing total control over prisoner movement and intensifying the repressive nature of imprisonment." In the late 1980s, for reasons unknown, these institutions were renamed "High Maximum Security Institutions," but the name was changed back at a later date to "Special Handling Units."

At the time of Harris's writing, and according to Correctional Service of Canada, the typical SHU inmate was "single white, 35 years old, who [had] been convicted of a violent crime. He [had] been sentenced to more than 10 years in prison and [was] more than two years away from his possible release" (Harris 2001b). With respect to officers, they were disproportionately "young, averaging seven or eight years' experience in the field. Only two guards [were] women" (Harris 2001b).

1990s

In 1990, a new policy was introduced to help manage the incarceration of dangerous inmates: "This policy embodied the philosophy and objectives of the Mission [of the SHU] and changed the SHUs to more program-oriented facilities. The policy provided for a new definition of 'dangerous inmates' and emphasized that inmates were to be admitted to a SHU only when their needs could not be addressed in a less secure facility" (O'Brien 1992). According to Lowman and McLean (1991, 146), although the decisions to transfer inmates to an SHU were originally made by an SHU Review Committee in Ottawa, "more recently, the practice has been for prisoners to be transferred into this classification without the committee reviewing the case. . . . [Now] SHUs have been used proactively. Prisoners who are deemed to present a threat to life and security can be sent to SHU without having committed an act so interpreted."

During the 1990s, approximately seventy inmates were held in the Sainte-Anne-des-Plaines SHU. According to Linda Mariotti, a spokesperson for the facility, the SHU "does not offer many programs, but inmates can choose from courses offering advice on dealing with anger or substance abuse.

In addition, they are given exercise time in small groups and have access to a communal television" (Campbell 1999, R2). She further explained how decisions regarding inmate movements were made: "The only inmates who are locked in their cells almost 24 hours a day are those who refuse to get involved in programs or limited work opportunities." The same article quotes Mariotti on the topic of American penal practices. She stated that "there are no plans by Correctional Services [Canada] to adopt the U.S. practice of dealing with hard-core disruptive inmates by isolating them virtually around-the-clock. The goal in Canada remains rehabilitation" (Campbell 1999, R2).

The Sainte-Anne-des-Plaines facility has had a rocky history. In 1998, it was discovered that the officers had encouraged gladiator-style fights among the prisoners, similar to what occurred in the Corcoran corrections facility in California (1989–1993). The fights achieved national attention when inmate Mark Gamble launched a Can$50,000 lawsuit against the facility (Cairns 1998). In 2001, *Toronto Sun* reporter Kathleen Harris wrote a two-part article focusing on the facility and the lives of five inmates: Clifford Olson, one of Canada's most infamous serial killers, accused of murdering eleven children; Cory Cameron, whose sentence was increased for crimes committed behind bars; Tommy Ross Jr., convicted of murder; Bernie Ruelland, convicted of a variety of violent crimes and escaping custody; Allan Legere, convicted of multiple murders and escape; and Maurice (Mom) Boucher, a well-known former leader of the Montréal chapter of the Hells Angels biker gang.

2000

In 2005, CSC officers (members of the Union of Canadian Correctional Officers/Syndicat des agents correctionnels du Canada) started lobbying for the construction of a supermax facility for female inmates. The federal government opposed the proposal, and the idea was eventually abandoned (Harris 2005). During the early 2000s, the SHU concept did not develop substantially. Periodic news media reports profiled the stories of infamous criminals who were incarcerated in the facility, but little other media coverage appeared. Although the typical inmate transferred into an SHU has been convicted of assault, armed robbery, or murder, the recent increase in terrorist acts (or the fear thereof) has led to the incarceration of a small number of inmates who have been issued and held under Security Certificates (Larsen and Piché 2009).

Shortly after the 9/11 attacks in 2001, the Canadian government arrested various individuals on suspicion of participating in terrorism. Most of these inmates were placed in provincial jails. Because of public and legal concerns over housing these people in provincial jails, an agreement was signed in 2006 between the Canadian Border Services Agency and CSC; the contract pertained to housing individuals on Security Certificates in the Kingston

Immigration Holding Center (KIHC), also pejoratively called "Guantánamo North." Located inside Millhaven Penitentiary, this facility has only six cells and has held as many as four detainees and as few as one. According to Mike Larsen, Sophie Harkat, and Mohamed Harkat (2008, 37), "This is a prison within a prison, with its own perimeter and security gate, its own specially cross-trained workforce of 'multi-function detention officers' with its own set of rules, guidelines, President's Directives and Standing Orders."

CONCLUSION

Over the past five decades, the Canadian government, in particular CSC, has pursued a varied but measured course in the building and use of supermax prisons. In most instances, the construction of such facilities was implemented as a response to some sort of persistent and headline-grabbing crisis (such as the riots of the 1970s). In the aftermath of the event or events, a formal investigation was initiated, which resulted in the production of a report. The study usually recommended the transfer of inmates to other federal penitentiaries, the closure of a facility, or the construction of a new one. According to Robert Joseph (1983, 26),

> A major reason for the implementation of Special Handling Units within the Correctional Services of Canada was that such facilities were needed to reduce the level of violence in Federal penitentiaries. By identifying and removing the violent inmate from the general inmate population, it was believed that the number of incidences of violence would decrease. . . . Such has not been the case. . . . The Special Handling Unit program has not had an identifiable deterrent effect on perpetrators of violence in penitentiaries. Neither is it a humanitarian treatment-oriented program. The only objective it appears to have achieved is the successful containment of violent inmates.

In recent decades, some scholars have argued that Canada's move to more punitive correctional facilities was based on the ascendance of a right-wing agenda that various theorists trace back to Thatcherism, Reaganism, and Mulroneyism (Lowman and MacLean 1991). Others, such as Dawn Moore and Kelly Hannah-Moffat (2005), take issue with the punitive turn thesis (e.g., Garland 2001) as applied to Canada and contend that the rehabilitative model that seems to dominate Canadian penal practice is in fact grounded in coerciveness. Both of these arguments are possible explanations behind the creation of the Canadian SHU system, but they do not necessarily negate the possibility that globalization was an underlying process in the development. Nevertheless, in the case of Canada, many of the decisions about the SHUs predate the existence of the current government (i.e., the political party that is in power at any given time). Thus, the new government inherits a legacy that they must skillfully manage in order to avoid negative public opinion and repercussions. Overall, it appears that in the case of Canada, the construction of the SHUs was mainly motivated by internal dynamics and had nothing to do with external factors (i.e., globalization).

In order to gain a deeper understanding of the SHUs in Canada, follow-up research might include an examination of the debates about the prison system that occurred in the Canadian Parliament (e.g., through an examination of the Hansard). Additional research into the discussions in the provincial legislatures and municipalities where the supermaxes were built would also be warranted, and information might be obtained through requests using the federal Access to Information Act. The scope of this study could be further expanded to include interviews with the political, administrative, and executive personnel who made key decisions about the construction of the various supermax facilities. Interviews could also be conducted with community activists and union personnel (both those in favor of and those against the facilities) who were involved in the deliberations surrounding the construction of the institutions in question. Moreover, this research could extend to interviews with representatives of the construction and architectural firms that were responsible for building the facilities. Further research could examine any instances where the Canadian SHU system was criticized by international human rights organizations. Finally, future studies could incorporate tours of the facilities under investigation and, if possible, conversations with inmates, correctional workers, and administrators. In order to properly understand why other countries have adopted American-style supermax prison models, it is necessary not only to gather, assemble, and analyze secondary source information but also to conduct field research.

CHAPTER 4

Supermaxes South of the Border

Patrick O'Day and Thomas O'Connor

GLOBALIZATION IS AS VAGUE a concept (Scholte 2000) as supermax (Shalev 2009), so it is no wonder that confusion often ensues when examining whether the supermax phenomenon has any global implications. George Ritzer (1997, 2004) uses the term "globalization" to refer to the spread of a number of American-style characteristics throughout the world, and Matthew Robinson (2002) believes it includes the spread of American-style criminal justice in different countries. Jeffrey Ian Ross (2007b) suggests that supermaxes, defined as architecturally distinct stand-alone facilities, wings, or annexes, either new or retrofitted, that house the most persistent rule breakers under a very strict monitoring, surveillance, and control regime, may be proliferating. Given the lack of rigorous comparative examination of supermax prisons, it is important to study whether the American "supermax" model has truly proliferated on a worldwide scale.

This chapter explores whether the supermax model has been adopted by Mexico, America's southern neighbor, which for geographical reasons alone should have been significantly affected by the globalization trend. Nevertheless, it is entirely possible that a reverse trend—Mexicanization instead of Americanization—has happened. For instance, in selected jurisdictions, the overwhelming corruption in Mexican law enforcement has spilled over into American law enforcement (Miller 2009). With Mexico as a case study, sufficient similarities and differences that make for good comparative analysis may be found.

Some of the specific questions this study hopes to answer are the following: (1) Why were supermax prisons deemed necessary in Mexico? (2) What particular circumstances led to the creation of supermax prisons in Mexico? (3) To what extent was the construction of supermax prisons prompted by perceptions that prisoners were becoming more incorrigible and increasingly dangerous, as perceived by either the Mexican public or governmental elites? (4) What role has international terrorism played in Mexico's desire to construct a supermax facility? (5) What is the profile of the typical supermax inmate? (6) What are the similarities and differences between American supermaxes and those in Mexico? and (7) What level of public scrutiny have supermax prisons engendered in Mexico?

MEXICO'S PRISON SYSTEM

For historical background, conventional wisdom has it that the first federal civilian correctional facility was Mexico City's Lecumberri Prison (which opened in 1902), which was designed to hold as many as five thousand inmates. In truth, as Louis Brister (1986) has noted, Lecumberri was just the signature penological expression of the many fin de siècle glitzy excesses of the Porfiriato dictatorship (1876–1910), such as the (unfinished until 1934) Fine Arts Palace, with its famous Tiffany stained-glass curtain As such, Lecumberri can best be seen as little more than a state-of-the-art upgrade of the much older Fortaleza de San Carlos in Perote, Veracruz, which, along with other facilities, housed Mexico's inmate population throughout the nineteenth century and before. Mitchel Roth (2005) has pointed out that Lecumberri was built on the radial Pennsylvania penitentiary style and served as the model for a great many similar state facilities until the outbreak of the 1910 revolution. This important event, which profoundly changed the country's zeitgeist, gave pause to the Mexican penchant for massive, decorative, architectural facilities that would be more at home in Vienna or Rome than in Mexico City or Guadalajara.

The idea of a high-security prison in Mexico is often believed to have been inspired from the first US federal high-security correctional facility on Alcatraz (Pelican) Island in San Francisco's North Bay, first designed to house Confederate prisoners of war. It is noteworthy, however, that Mexico had already begun public discussions some three years earlier on the desirability of establishing another island-based high-security facility to complement its venerable San Juan de Ulloa fortress prison, which was located on an island in the harbor of the city of Veracruz. Although this idea did not bear fruit in Mexico proper until the 1930s, when the Islas Marías prison was finally established, it is nevertheless possible that the idea for the hemisphere's first "supermax" facility originated in Mexico and then migrated to the city of San Francisco, which was part of Mexico until 1848 (Ornelas 2004).

Much like Alcatraz, the Islas Marías prison had some unique architectural and geographic features. Both prisons restricted contact with the outside world, primarily via geography, but also by housing those classified as escape prone. Ross (2007b) identifies those so classified as supermax prisoners, along with gang leaders, serial killers, and political prisoners. The Islas Marías prison had fifty-eight miles of water separating the penal colony from Mexico's west coast. Also, with extensive land at its disposal, Islas Marías provided breathing room to some of Mexico's seriously overcrowded other prisons, such as San

Juan de Ulloa and Lecumberri and even Santiago Tlaltelolco, the nation's military prison, from which the legendary bandit and sometime revolutionary Pancho Villa was to escape. The Islas Marías correctional facility was built to serve a perceived need for escape-proof conditions. It was based on autonomous models and not foreign designs. As Alberto Tinoco (2005) has argued, it was also established by the nation's governing elite for purposes other than merely detaining the most hardened offenders. Yet, at this stage in Mexico's history, some prisoners were also handled by execution and exile.

The revolution of 1910 launched Mexico on a sui generis path of development that, among other things, virtually guaranteed its immunity from global trends in incarceration practices. The revolution coincided with an inward-looking nationalism and a degree of initial harshness. For example, the bloody revolutionary general Álvaro Obregón was eliminated by assassination, and another, the cold, sinister Plutarco Elías Calles, was exiled in the United States. After these harsh steps were taken, Mexico's penultimate military president, the revered general Lázaro Cárdenas (1934–1940), took charge to develop Mexico's own distinct political identity.

MEXICO'S POLITICAL IDENTITY

Cárdenas built a corporatist party (Partido Revolucionario Institucional, or PRI) with bases of support: the military as well as labor, peasant, and business/professional organizations. More important, he developed the doctrine of revolutionary nationalism, which was, in the words of one author, "a vague ideology that extolled the goals of the Mexican Revolution, the official party and a strong, independent state—[which] largely immunized the nation's workers and peasants from Marxism, Maoism, Castroism, and other leftist doctrines" (Grayson 2009, 8).

Cárdenas did his job so well that his successor, General Manuel Ávila Camacho, was able to eliminate the military as a component of the corporatist ruling PRI as well as continue systematically to reinforce and solidify the revolutionary nationalism of Cárdenas. Thus, the stage was set for a unique path for Mexico in both foreign and domestic policy, including its prison system.

A striking example of Mexico's inward-looking politics was the fact that its most secure prison, Islas Marías, was eventually used not just to hold political prisoners and other such undesirables securely but also to subject them to a regimen of forced labor. This routine, which involved going from lockdown to forced labor and then back to lockdown, was so brutal and so harsh that it would not be at all unreasonable to think of it as torture. In 1950, *Islas Marías*, a film starring Pedro Infante, Mexico's most famous entertainer of the time, created such an uproar that the resulting reforms once and for all put an end to the association, at least in the Mexican mind, of maximum security incarceration with inhumane treatment. This period of forced labor represented only a small part of Mexican penal history and turned out to be the exception rather than rule in the history of Mexico's supermax.

The eponymous film exposed in searing detail what it was like being forced to work in the broiling sun on the salt flats of the main island of the Islas from sunrise to sundown, mind-numbing day after mind-numbing day, for years on end. By 1950, the penal colony actually bore more resemblance to Devil's Island, the infamous French penal colony off the coast of French Guiana, than to Alcatraz, especially since its inmates were considered to be either subversives or the country's most dangerous and depraved criminals. As a result of the ongoing public criticism of the brutal conditions of prison life on María Madre (the name of the largest island and the only one on which the correctional facility is now located), resources were expended toward improvement, and the shame of Mexico's prison system gradually changed to the point of becoming the showcase of Mexico's detention facilities.

At this point, a contextual footnote is in order. In the 1970s, as the Islas was becoming a model of rehabilitation and enlightened treatment, storm clouds were gathering throughout the rest of Mexico. It seems like the country has its revolutions every fifty years: 1810, 1858, 1910, and finally 1962, with the revolt of the rural school teachers, Lucio Cabañas and Genaro Vasquez Rojas. Their separate rebellions, which were in the west-central states of Guerrero and parts of Michoacán, respectively, did not fizzle out until the mid-1970s, after the deaths of both leaders in separate incidents.

Mexican authorities were obsessed with putting down all the rebellions. It became risible in military circles, for instance, to even mention the notion of civil rights, and as a result, as most of Mexico's Islas Marías supermaximum detention facility was undergoing a breathtaking liberalization, a darker and more sinister parallel reality was also emerging. Rebels and others suspected of subversion were secretly brought to the islands and allegedly put in cells that would flood up to the roof with every fortnightly high tide, when the moon and the sun were in rough alignment.

As the water rose and the inmates stood on their toes in order to keep breathing as the water approached its biweekly high-water mark, they knew that it was only a matter of time before their cells would be flooded all the way to the ceiling. Once they (presumably) confessed to real or imagined crimes, prisoners were executed to keep the whole operation hidden from the public. Thus, the state, which had supermax facilities constructed in part to fight subversion, revolution, and terrorism, engaged in its own brand of state-sponsored terrorism against rebels who were deemed terrorists. Inmates on other parts of the island were benefiting from more liberal conditions, however, and what was taking place more brutally was kept secret. To this day, there are few left who will talk about it if asked (Hayward 2004; Ornelas 2004).

During the 1970s, the Islas had become, for the most part, such a model of rehabilitation that inmates were (and still are) encouraged to bring their families to live on the island. Their children go to school, and the inmates generally live with their families in modest houses and support themselves through their own labor, which includes the open manufacture and distribution of alcohol. Although convicts are subject to three roll calls during the day, they are otherwise free to move around the island as they please. As a result, inmates rarely ask for a reduction in their sentence once they arrive at the islands. In fact, it is almost routine for those who are released to petition to remain right where they are as "libres," a term the prison administration uses for those who are incarcerated at their own request.

Needless to say, only sections of the Islas Marías prison during certain periods of time, because of the conditions of confinement, qualify it to be considered a supermax facility. The civilian guards were unarmed and in possession of only one rather slow motorboat. The island penal colony, with its "impenetrable walls of water," to use the felicitous phrase of José Revueltas, can no longer be considered to be escape proof (Ornelas 2004). Private, unscheduled boats are not permitted within twelve nautical miles of the island, but such restrictions are meaningful only if corruption does not taint the prison administration.

Unfortunately, corruption taints prison administration in Mexico. For example, the petitions of inmates in the federal system to be interned on the Islas Marías are routinely denied if it is determined that the petitioners are of the socioeconomic class that could rather easily facilitate their early departure from the islands through corruption or if their economic prospects would considerably improve if they were to achieve their freedom early through inappropriate means. In the past twenty-five years, there have been an astonishing seventy escapes, and the facility has been downgraded to medium-security status within the federal system.

By the 1990s, during the reform regime of President Ernesto Zedillo (1994–2000), it had become apparent that Mexico had a negative image problem with the islands. France had closed its Devil's Island prisons in 1946; Chile closed down its Isla María facility well before Pinochet left power in 1990; in the same year, Costa Rica closed its San Lucas island prison; and Brazil closed its Isla Grande prison in 1994. Mexico's response, however, was characteristically Mexican. While taking cues from foreign experiments in corrections, Mexico surprisingly converted the islands into a protected zone of biological diversity!

As a result, a vastly reduced number of prisoners, about eight hundred federal inmates and around two hundred state inmates (down from a total of five thousand), together with their families, share their hilly domain with an abundance of wild horses and burros as well as an endless supply of cats who seem to be going feral. In addition, the islands are host to a vast variety of native vegetation (Stevenson 2005). Once again, Mexico can be seen as putting its own stamp on its correctional facilities. Early on, an impenetrable facility was used for the daily torture and even execution of political and criminal incorrigibles, and later it became an island village for those fortunate few who somehow managed to end up there. Now it is increasingly becoming home to freed prisoners and a variety of wild animals. This pattern, albeit in somewhat altered and muted form, seems to characterize the development of Mexico's next generation of supermax prisons.

MEXICO'S CORRECTIONAL SYSTEM

Corrections in Mexico consists mainly of separate systems for each of the thirty-one states, which hold a combination of inmates accused of *fuero común* crimes (violations of state law) and inmates accused of violations of federal law (*fuero federal*), almost all of which are drug related. As recently as 2004, the last year for which the authors have data, the states, which are required to house the federal prisoners sent to their facilities, were compensated at a rate of a little less than US$2,000 per federal inmate per year. That is low even for Mexico, and such an unfunded federal mandate, as it would be called in the United States, has long been an irritant in federal/state relations in Mexico. Mexican states and regions also have their own subsystem of miniprisons, jails, and detention centers. Roth (2005), reports the 2003 numbers (the most current data available) at 448 prisons and an inmate population of 175,253 prisoners (a rate of 169 per 100,000). At this point in time, it should be interjected that the word "super," as in the term "supermax," is not a term generally understood in Mexico. It is an alien term and not one to soon become adopted in such a country that is only now losing much of its xenophobia in reference to the "Colossus of the North." Thus, the term "maximum security" (*seguridad máxima*) is used with shameless ambiguity to refer to a variety of facilities, which in the United States would be designated as anything from mixed medium/maximum facilities to maximum-security prisons to supermax facilities.

At present, there are five federal penitentiaries plus another one under construction. The federal component also consists of several detention centers, a few small jails, and the military prison or prisons, of which there is only grudging acknowledgment and almost no public awareness. In addition, there are holding cells attached to the small army barracks that are found scattered throughout the countryside. To complete the picture, mammoth Mexico City, which is a federal district but operates much like any one of the thirty-one states, has its own prison system.

Apart from Islas Marías, another strictly federal correctional facility is a "psychosocial" correctional facility in Ayala, Morelos, which is often referred to discreetly by the authorities as Cuautla, for the highway on which it is located. Because of its twenty-three-hour lockdown conditions, it can be considered a supermax prison. However, a more appropriate example is the supermax prison in the heart of Mexico's drug trafficking area in Guasave, Sinaloa, which was built in the autumn 1999. Because it was built in a highly vulnerable location, it did not become operational until ten years later and even then was reserved only for kidnappers. There is also a fortress-like supermax facility across the Rio Grande from Brownsville, Texas, on the outskirts of Matamoros, Tamaulipas, which is very heavily guarded and is almost totally hermetic; and finally, as of 2011, a new classification center for the country's growing prison system is under construction in Papantla, Veracruz (*El Universal* 2010).

It is easy to understand why and how these prisons can be considered supermax facilities. In conversations with Mexicans, it is clear that some of the previously mentioned correctional institutions are subject to such popular labeling. For example, Lecumberri, which houses Mexico's national archives, is commonly mistaken as a supermax by passersby, and Guadalajara's legendary Puente Grande, which is often thought of as a state prison but is actually a federal prison, presumes to function as a supermax facility, and is popularly ridiculed with the nickname Puerta Grande (the Open Door) due to its high-profile escapes.

That leaves one federal prison yet to be mentioned, which for all intents and purposes functions as a supermax prison. In 1991, Mexico began the construction of a whole new type of supermax facility, one that became an island of reinforced concrete, for the express purpose of holding the country's most dangerous felons. It was called el Centro Federal de Readaptación Social Número 1 (Cereso #1). It was known for many years as Almoloya de Juárez, after the municipality where it is located. It has undergone several name changes because of growing dissatisfaction on the part of the citizens of Almoloya with having the name of their town appear regularly on the nightly news in association with what has become one of Mexico's most notorious correctional facilities. The name was first changed to La Palma, and then later to its official name, el Penal del Altiplano, or in popular parlance el Altiplano (meaning High Plains Prison).

The supermax facility el Altiplano has integrated state-of-the-art security features for better monitoring and surveillance. Both internal and external controls are cutting-edge and high-tech. Some of its segregation cells are built deep into the earth. Video cameras are everywhere, metal detectors scan visitors for anything metallic, and an X-ray machine performs the most thorough inspections of incoming goods. For fourteen years, the public was regularly assured by the government that there had never been an escape, murder, or even riot (Walker 2005).

SUPERMAXES OR RESORTS?

Starting around 2001, things changed dramatically when drug lords started being sentenced to the supermax prisons. Benjamín Arellano Félix, the principal leader of the Tijuana Cartel, and Osiel Cárdenas Guillén, the leader of the Gulf Cartel, were the first to be imprisoned. When Benjamín Arellano arrived at La Palma (as Altiplano was still being called), in March 2002, he was able to accomplish single-handedly what the other 530 inmates had supposedly been unable to achieve. Aided by Osiel Cárdenas, who arrived a year later, their public tactics of hunger strikes and noisy protests by family members made the prison administration accede to the demands of these high-profile inmates.

Visiting hours were extended, they could dine from a menu, and they were allowed to socialize with other inmates outside their cells for twelve hours a day. The cartel honchos cleverly used public outrage over their cuisine and the absence of other perks to obscure or finesse the ongoing deterioration of the prison's electronic equipment. Orders were given that female visitors were to be searched in only the most cursory manner, thus allowing firearms to be smuggled in. Finally, as S. Lynne Walker (2005) reports, Noe Hernández, the deputy director of el Altiplano, who had been resisting the growing influence over correctional policy by the capos, was gunned down in nearby Toluca in December 2003.

What united the leaders of two previously rival cartels was their mutual antipathy to the rapidly growing Sinaloa Cartel of Joaquín Guzmán. With the ready availability of guns inside the now corrupted supermax facility, the next step of the new drug axis was to strike at their common enemy. As a result, on October 6, 2004, one of Guzmán's associates was shot and killed inside the facility, and on New Year's Eve 2005, the hapless Arturo Guzmán, the younger brother of El Chapo Guzmán, who was known as El Pollo (the chicken), was murdered with seven bullets fired into him while he was talking with his lawyer in the visitor's section of el Altiplano by a low-ranking member of the Tijuana Cartel (Foreign Prisoner Support Service 2006). Shortly after that, the Preventive Police of Mexico's Secretaría de Seguridad Pública, the equivalent of the US Department of Homeland Security, backed by soldiers, surrounded the prison for five days. They were legitimately worried that Osiel's Zeta commandos, led by about sixty-five deserters from Mexico's Special Forces, might indeed have been able to penetrate the meter-thick walls of the facility (Walker 2005).

PUBLIC OPINION AND THE MEXICAN SUPERMAX

The overwhelming show of force during 2005 at the el Altiplano prison brought about something quite rare in Mexican corrections: public scrutiny. Some Mexican officials are used to withstanding public scrutiny, but many are not, so public outrage, once awakened, can indeed make its influence felt. Consequently, many of the most dangerous inmates in el Altiplano were transferred to another facility, Puente Grande, since they had to go somewhere. The Puente Grande supermax will be discussed later.

Today, Mexico's leaders are striving toward a supermax model that sticks to maximum-security consciousness and defeats the tendency for such prisons to evolve or be usurped for other purposes. The goal is to make the supermaxes completely and totally inaccessible to the public and even to academic researchers, and this includes not only those under construction, but the older prisons that hold drug traffickers such as el Altiplano. However, Mexico's prison system also has a strong reformist impulse, exemplified by the practice of conjugal visitation, which has long been a standard tradition and accepted part of prison life in Mexico.

Yet the main challenge that Mexico faces is how to reconcile this approach to supermax development with the ongoing war against the drug traffickers. In October 2009, for instance, the lead author interviewed Juan Escalante (a pseudonym), who entered Mexico City's Reclusorio Norte, the country's most secure prison before La Palma (el Altiplano) was finished. He is the son of a person who was a regional strongman in the border state of Tamaulipas during the 1980s and an associate of Miguel Ángel Félix Gallardo, Mexico's *capo di tutti capi* (i.e., the godfather of the country's drug traffickers). Don Miguel, the strongman, coordinated Mexico's drug trafficking from the time of his arrest on April 8, 1989, well into the early 1990s. El Reclusorio Norte, a medium-/maximum-security facility, is easy for the uninitiated to confuse with the La Palma/Altiplano supermax institution since they both hold the same kind of highly dangerous inmates and hardened and very influential drug traffickers (among others), and both are situated in the same general area. In fact, el Reclusorio Norte is located on an elevated piece of land called La Loma de la Palma.

The first author's informant, Juan Escalante, was sent to el Reclusorio Norte as a *libre* by his father, who was himself incarcerated in a different facility. His father, Julio, "had the plaza" of a large industrial border town in the state of Tamaulipas, which is right across the Rio Grande from south Texas. The expression "having la plaza" means that Escalante, in this case, had all of the government officials with any authority to intervene in drug trafficking on his private payroll. Unfortunately for himself and his family, Don Julio politically supported the wrong candidate for the presidency, and when his pick, Manuel Camacho Solis, lost out in the nomination process of the ruling party, he soon found himself behind bars and was then held up as an example of how Mexico is resolute in fighting drug trafficking.

At about this same time, intense pressure was being applied on Mexico by the Reagan administration over the February 9, 1985, murders of the DEA agent Enrique Camarena and his pilot, Alfredo Zavala Avelar. Escalante claimed that the DEA agent had to be murdered because he would not take what was considered to be a reasonable bribe so as to keep confidential or at least minimize in his reports the twenty-five thousand acres of marijuana that one of the godfather's subordinates, Rafael Caro Quintero, was growing in Búfalo and two adjacent *municipios* (counties) in the northern state of Chihuahua. Also involved in the pressure to crack down on drug trafficking was the fact Carlos Salinas, once he ascended to the presidency in 1988, was willing to do whatever it took to get his pride and joy, the North American Free Trade Agreement, approved by the US Congress.[1]

Because of the sudden and unexpected incarceration of his father, Escalante was given the mission to cajole the funds from Don Miguel that were needed to secure his father's release. Like most Mexican prisons, el Reclusorio Norte is composed of cell blocks. Miguel Félix had his own cell block populated entirely by his own armed guards and various other retainers, or domestic service providers. According to Escalante, one particular cell was of critical importance as it was filled to the ceiling with nothing but cocaine. External and internal security in this type of institution, then, is achieved by reducing all incentive to escape or in any way injure or even threaten custodial personnel. The X-ray machines, surveillance cameras, and the like that are installed are in place not to reveal to the authorities what is going on inside a supermax prison facility but rather to provide a smoke screen between the interior of the facility and the outside world so as to give the impression of total hierarchical control (from the top to the bottom) and to obscure the actual reality of pervasive control from the bottom to the top.

With Don Miguel's continued incarceration, he could no longer maintain the daily operational control that his empire required, and over time he allowed the organization to fragment into the Tijuana Cartel, the Juárez Cartel, and, with the January 19, 2001, escape of Joaquín ("El Chapo") Guzmán Loera from Puente Grande Prison, the Sinaloa Cartel. Perhaps even worse, the very fact of the imprisonment of the larger-than-life figure of Miguel Felix Gallardo revealed to his subordinates the old man's vulnerability to changing circumstances at the same time that it put a certain distance between the godfather and the government official who had him imprisoned, the president of the country. This is not to say that he could not run his own shipments of drugs.

That is the easy part, and his shipments could proceed smoothly, as if on autopilot. The difficult part consisted of coordinating the activities of the country's various drug cartels and in keeping the peace between them. The extent to which a caged lion like Don Miguel could for a period of time keep things reasonably under control from the vantage point of his prison quarters speaks volumes to his unrivaled image as a clan totem, an individual to whom the various cartel leaders could find it expedient to pay homage since at some level they knew that any infighting would hurt everyone in the long run.[2]

Now there are many more cartels, and the fighting, with its steadily increasing death toll, has become a threat to the continued existence of Mexico as a republic. In this view, it is perhaps unfortunate that a person who previously had been coordinating the trafficking of drugs within an entire nation (and in the process keeping the peace among his subordinates) could no longer run his empire as before once he was in prison regardless of how opulent his conditions of incarceration had generally been.[3]

This is not necessarily a fringe view. Recently someone as notable as Jorge Castañeda Gutman, Mexico's foreign minister during the (reform) presidency of Vicente Fox (2000–2006), gave a speech at the Cato Institute, a libertarian American forum, calling for a return to old ways during the domination of the venerable ruling PRI, of having a quiet understanding that would allow the drug trade to proceed smoothly, with discreet guidelines (and payoffs) in place and respected by all (Castañeda 2010a). This perspective, as shocking as it may be to American sensibilities, is clearly growing in popularity in Mexico. Among other things, it bemoans the fact that in being incarcerated, even in the lap of prison luxury, *il capo di tutti capi* should lose the high-level daily contact with the political, administrative, and military figures that is crucial for the conduct of his business.

The imprisonment of the larger-than-life figure of Miguel Félix Gallardo reveals the problems as well as vulnerabilities of Mexican supermax confinement for drug traffickers. On the one hand, it puts a certain distance between them and the government officials who had them imprisoned, but on the other hand, this is not to say that they cannot still run shipments of drugs. That is the easy part, and shipments can proceed smoothly, as if on autopilot. The difficult part consists of coordinating the activities of the country's various drug cartels and in keeping the peace between them. The extent to which a trafficker like Don Miguel could for a period of time keep things reasonably under control from the vantage point of his prison quarters speaks volumes to his unrivaled image as a clan totem, an individual to whom the carious cartel leaders could find it expedient to pay homage since at some level they knew that any infighting would hurt everyone in the long run (O'Day 2001). Similar insights were made by Escalante, as previously noted.

GUADALAJARA'S PUENTE GRANDE

Guadalajara's Puente Grande prison is a Mexican supermax facility with some unique features. It is the prison from which several notorious escapes took place, including the 1991 and 2001 escapes of Glen Godwin (an American drug trafficker operating in Mexico) and El Chapo Guzmán (leader of the Sinaloa cartel). Puente Grande has many elements of American-style

supermax prisons, and since so many of the country's top mafiosi are imprisoned there, it is particularly important to analyze its functioning for the light
that it can throw on the internal life of the Mexico's future development of
supermax facilities.

From the perspective of most Mexicans, including the general public,
government officials, and drug traffickers, there is a hierarchy of supermaxes,
and Puente Grande is at the apex, although it is questionable if the term
"supermax" really applies in this particular case. That is because Jalisco's
Puente Grande, much like Mexico City's Reclusorio Norte, shares similarities to typical supermax facilities. In terms of external security, it would take
a regiment of soldiers to breach its external defenses. Internal security is
achieved by a large and sometimes corrupt correctional staff. For example,
and according to the *Wall Street Journal,* cartel leader El Chapo Guzmán

> brib[ed] nearly everyone, including the warden, who is now in jail. . . .
> El Chapo, together with his longtime associate Mr. Palma, terrorized the
> jail. . . . Female members of the prison staff, ranging from nurses to
> cooks, were paid to have sex with the drug lords. One woman who
> refused was raped, according to documents from the Jalisco state human
> rights agency. . . . Prison guards too were offered money to cooperate
> with the capo. Those who refused were beaten with baseball bats by a
> group run by Mr. Guzmán known as the "batters."
>
> In January 2000, a prison guard named Felipe Leaños filed a
> complaint . . . about the abuses at the jail with the Jalisco state human
> rights commission. In the following months, he persuaded four other
> guards to step forward. The state agency . . . tried to get federal officials
> to intervene in the jail during the course of the year. Leaños disappeared
> in May 2007 and is presumed to have been murdered by Mr. Guzmán's
> men. (Luhnow and de Córdoba 2009)

These tales are eagerly shared by many mafiosi regardless of which family
they belong to, and on January 11, 2005, together with dozens of other
inmates, Rafael Caro Quintero, whose arrest for maintaining a large twenty-
five-thousand-acre marijuana plantation started the process that led to both
his and Don Miguel's incarceration when the plantation was spotted by US
reconnaissance satellites, finally secured an upgrade from La Palma to Puente
Grande (Foreign Prisoner Support Service 2006). Unfortunately for Don
Miguel, however, something seems to have gone horribly wrong, and after a
mere seventeen days at Puente Grande, he was transferred again, this time to
a Cefereso facility, in Matamoros, across the river from Brownsville, Texas
(Tenorio 2005). At this point, it cannot be said for certain if the absolute
secrecy surrounding the latest generation of supermax facilities (those housed
in Guasave, Matamoros, and Papantla) is necessary to keep the inmates in or

just to keep the news of their (presumably opulent) living conditions from leaving the prison. Given such a history, corruption appears to be the biggest impediment to the future development of Mexico's supermax prisons.

CONCLUSION

Although certain Mexican prisons, such as el Altiplano (La Palma), meet the structural criteria (in terms of both physical and social structure) of a supermax facility, underlying this appearance of security is a completely Mexican institutional culture that is totally different from the generally accepted ethos of supermax facilities, as has been argued here. The country's long history of pervasive corruption means that inmates with adequate funds find little impediment to obtaining whatever they may desire (except for freedom itself, of course) while institutionalized. Consequently, the more secure the facility, as with the Islas Marías, the more lax and even entertaining daily life on the inside. Mexico may pay lip service to international norms of human rights, but the expression most characteristic of the country's public administration going back to its earliest days, "Obedezco pero no cumplo" (I obey, but I do not comply), says it all.

In sum, Mexico has built several supermax correctional institutions, primarily due to increasing organized criminal activity, but also to more easily either handle with velvet gloves or absolutely terrorize selected inmates, depending on whether they are affluent mafiosi or revolutionary subversives. The felt need for the facilities in question arose entirely from the exigencies of Mexico's crime problem, with minimal public input, and the occasional public outcry. Mexico has a long history of developing such institutions. Contrary to other countries, international terrorism has had no role whatsoever in the construction of supermax facilities since inward-looking Mexico has long pursued a policy of neutrality and nonalignment in foreign affairs. The typical supermax inmates are drug traffickers, murderers (often in the service of drug traffickers), or kidnappers. And in a comparative sense, Mexican supermaxes, although they started out with the same general intent as their American counterparts, could not keep out the pervasive and endemic corruption of the larger society, and as a result over time they became little more than spas for wealthy incorrigibles.

Finally, are supermax facilities supported by the public? Mexico, with its unprecedented and seemingly unending wave of drug-related violence and mayhem, is becoming bipolar on the issue. As has been noted, a small but growing segment of the Mexican population is so weary of the violence and the general level of insecurity that it is willing to tacitly admit defeat and reach a quiet accommodation with the drug barons. Consistent with this perspective would be a general pardon for all drug-related offenses and a de-emphasis of incarceration as a remedy for the country's concerns about public security. The other segment of the population, a solid 40 percent, believes in going after the cartels tooth and nail, even to the extent of allowing American military units to operate in conjunction with Mexican military units on Mexican territory (Castañeda 2010a).

The issue still to be decided in Mexico's future is primarily the drug war. Although Mexico is quite successful at controlling the petroleum and electricity industries, retirement and health care programs, the public university system, and the armed forces (Grayson 2009), the country may or may not be able to totally eradicate the drug violence problem. Like its neighbor to the north, with its concern over terrorism, Mexico indeed has an ongoing challenge. It has a drug trafficking problem with all the persistence of an addiction, but that does not mean that it is an insurmountable challenge. And whichever path Mexico chooses, the ensuing solution will most likely be distinctly Mexican.

Chapter 5

The Growth of the Supermax
Option in Britain

Angela West Crews

THE UNITED STATES HAS BECOME so prolific at incarcerating law violators (with the assumption that "practice makes perfect") that our ideas and practices are now being seen as the model for others, including many European countries. It seems as if the exchange of correctional ideas across the Atlantic has come full circle, with the American system taking an idea originally developed in Western Europe, modifying it to make it more extreme, and peddling it back to Europe as "better" or even as the "best." The idea of a level of security *more* secure than "maximum" (i.e., "the greatest amount possible") is uniquely and unmistakably American, although the practice of removing problematic prisoners from regular prison environments for security and control has been used in many Western European countries for several decades with varying degrees of success.

Britain, for example, which encompasses the countries of England and Wales, has policies, procedures, and facilities to deal with prisoners who need extra security and additional control. Does this mean, however, that it has Americanized its systems, or has it resisted the trend toward bigger, harsher, tougher, and supermaximum punishment?

This chapter addresses this question by examining the philosophies, policies, procedures, and facilities used in Britain within Her Majesty's Prison Service in England and Wales (HMPS) to handle prisoners who present management and/or security challenges within the prison environment. Current populations, classification systems, philosophies, environments, and brief histories of the treatment of problematic prisoners are described for HMPS, followed by a conclusion as to whether and to what extent it has been "supermaxed."

A DESCRIPTION OF HER MAJESTY'S PRISON
SERVICE IN ENGLAND AND WALES

The fifty-year history of formalized efforts by HMPS to control prisoners who pose specific types of threats to institutional safety and security, as well as to public safety, is complex and often inscrutable. Although well-intentioned, the government's continual and varied assessments and reviews of correctional policies and procedures, changes in social and political ideology, the 2004 creation of the National Offender Management Service (NOMS), the 2007 creation of the Ministry of Justice, the 2008 relocation of responsibility for oversight of HMPS from NOMS to the Ministry of Justice, and changes in legislation (e.g., Counter-Terrorism Act 2008; Criminal Justice and Immigration Act 2008; Coroners and Justice Act 2009; Crime and Security Act 2010) all have contributed to seemingly unending reversals of or amendments to these policies and procedures, making them extremely difficult to follow, to describe, and to interpret. As in the United States, this probably reflects underlying confusion about the purpose of ultra-high-security confinement as well as about the most humane and effective methods of accomplishing that type of confinement. Exacerbating this confusion for Britain is a rather rapid increase in the prison population.

In 2005, the incarceration rate in Britain was 139 per 100,000 (Christie 2005) but had grown to 153 per 100,000 by the end of 2008 (Walmsley 2009), making it the highest per capita incarceration rate in Western Europe (Ramesh 2010). As of March 1, 2011, HMPS held 85,206 prisoners (80,985 males and 4,221 females), 3,080 below maximum capacity (Ministry of Justice 2011), although the prison population had doubled since 1990 (Verkaik 2010) and increased 3 percent since this same time in 2010 (Ministry of Justice 2011).

Prisoners are distributed among 139 facilities, which includes 35 youthful offender institutions (YOIs) and/or juvenile detention facilities, 11 "contracted" or private prisons, 5 women's prisons, 3 immigration removal centers (IRCs), and 2 foreign nationals prisons (FNPs). The remaining 83 are for male prisoners, with 8 designated as high-security prisons (HSPs), 5 "dispersal" prisons (Frankland, Full Sutton, Long Lartin, Wakefield, Whitemoor), and 3 "core local" prisons (Belmarsh, Manchester, Woodhill) for newly sentenced high-security prisoners or for those awaiting trial (HM Chief Inspector of Prisons 2010b). These are discussed in greater detail below.

The structure of HMPS is complex, and oversight for its management currently resides within the NOMS, an umbrella agency that envelopes the Prison Service and the Probation Service (Spurr 2005) and reports to the Ministry of Justice, housed within the Home Office. Britain is divided into ten geographic areas, and all the prisons in each area are managed, respectively, by ten area managers. Management of the eight HSPs is an exception.

Despite geographic location, these all are managed by the director of high security (Spurr 2005).

The Prisons Act 1952 and Offender Management Act 2007 require that every prison in Britain be monitored by an Independent Monitoring Board (IMB) appointed by the minister of justice and composed of volunteer members from the communities that surround each prison. Each IMB is responsible for inspecting and evaluating its home prison to determine if prisoners are treated humanely and justly and if programs and services are adequate and for reporting annually to the secretary of state the extent to which the prison has or has not met standards and requirements (IMB 2009).

In addition to announced and unannounced inspections by IMBs, programs, services, treatment regimes, staff performance, and prisoner attitudes are monitored and evaluated regularly by several internal and external entities. Each prison is subject to Standard Audits by the HMP Standard Audits Unit, to annual announced and unannounced inspections by Her Majesty's Inspectorate of Prisons, and to review by the Commission for Racial Equality. In addition, each prison has a prison ombudsman who serves as a liaison between prisoners and administrators (Spurr 2005).

Security Categories

Upon receipt into the prison system, prisoners are "categorized" (i.e., classified) based on the severity of the crime committed, the sentence length, the probability of an escape attempt, and the danger they would pose to society if they were to escape and are "allocated" (i.e., placed) in prisons with corresponding security classifications. HMPS has four primary classification categories (A, B, C, D): category A prisoners are "highly dangerous" and for whom escape must be made impossible "no matter how unlikely that escape might be"; for category B prisoners, "escape must be made very difficult"; category C prisoners "cannot be trusted in open conditions," but lack "the resources and will to make a determined escape attempt"; and category D prisoners "can reasonably be trusted in open conditions" (Ministry of Justice 2000). Prisoners are reassessed at regular intervals and can move downward or upward in security categorization, although it is a rather complicated process requiring several levels of review.

Category A prisoners are further categorized as to the *actual* risk of escape they pose (1 = *standard risk,* 2 = *high risk,* and 3 = *exceptional risk*) and are distributed among the eight HSPs where they associate with category B prisoners (Ministry of Justice 2010b). This "dispersal" system avoids putting all of the most dangerous prisoners into "one 'Supermax' jail, because it enables prisoners to be moved around individually, preventing the building up of dangerous liaisons, prevents the conditioning of staff and dilutes the risk" (Spurr 2005, 53).

HMPS officials are not restricted by federal/state or state line boundaries and regulate "the mix" of prisoners by carefully monitoring the types of inmates placed together in any given facility. In the United States, the federal system is able to distribute prisoners in this manner, but any particular state system is able to do this only within its own state lines and to the extent it has available resources.

Within the high-security system is a group of smaller units called "close supervision centers" (CSCs) for enhanced prisoner control, similar to the American "supermax." CSC units are scattered throughout the HSP system to hold a maximum of forty-four prisoners, although only twenty-five to thirty prisoners are confined there at any given time. The CSC system opened in 1998 and developed from various other attempts to secure and control problematic prisoners. This evolution is described below. Isolation in segregation units, recently renamed "separation and care units" or "care and separation units" (Kirby 2010), as a solution to short-term problems within the prison environment also is discussed as it is used with CSC prisoners. To understand the CSC system and whether it approximates the American "supermax" system, it is first necessary to understand the history of high security in Britain.

History of High Security in HMPS

The evolution of classification into high security in HMPS is an interesting study in trial and error. Although many things about high-security confinement in HMPS have changed over time, policy makers and administrators always have been aware of two important things: (1) that long-term confinement under high security, especially segregation and/or isolation, is detrimental and inhumane and (2) that there are differences between disruptive prisoners at serious risk of escape (who represent *control* problems) and long-term prisoners with significant outside criminal associations that could facilitate escape (who represent *security* problems). This awareness is clear from legislative history, public discourse, and changes in the use and management of facilities for high-risk prisoners. It also is clear from examining the historical evolution of major initiatives to deal with troublesome prisoners. These initiatives are briefly described below.

SPECIAL SECURITY UNITS. In the mid-1960s, three "special security units" were developed at Leicester, Parkhurst, and Durham to house high-risk prisoners in Britain (Walmsley 1989). These were developed for those who were such security risks that they could not be safely contained "without additional security precautions even within [the] most secure prisons" (Tuck, cited in Walmsley 1989, iii).

From the beginning, however, the public was concerned about the treatment of these prisoners. It is surprising that even the secretary of state and the minister of state argued "it would be wrong" to confine anyone in these facilities "for a prolonged period" (internal minute, as cited in Walmsley 1989, 9). In 1966, this sentiment was reiterated by Lord Mountbatten, when he advocated the use of these facilities only as short-term, "stop-gap" solutions. Alternatively, Mountbatten proposed a "purpose-built prison" for prisoners "who must in no circumstances be allowed to get out" (Mountbatten, as cited in Walmsley 1989, 10) and described these as spies or individuals so violent that they would threaten lives if they got out. He termed these "category A" (see above).

DISPERSAL FACILITIES. In 1968, Professor Leon Radzinowicz disagreed with Mountbatten and argued that such prisoners be *dispersed,* not concentrated, and that "small segregation units in larger prisons" were to be for *control* purposes, not *security* purposes (Home Office 1968, para. 209). Radzinowicz declared that security should be improved through the strengthening of perimeter security systems in the closed prisons within which these segregated units were housed. Following Radzinowicz's recommendations, the Home Office announced a "dispersal program" for category A prisoners to be sent to one of eight HSPs so that the special security units would "cease to be used" for that purpose (Home Office 1968, chap. 2, para. 8).

Although they disagreed on logistics, Mountbatten and Radzinowicz agreed that prisoners should not endure long-term segregation because the units' regimes were unsatisfactory for long-term prisoners (Home Office 1968). Terence Morris (1968, 313) supported this argument by connecting conditions inside these units with several incidents of unrest that had occurred within them and by actively denouncing as "execrable" the purpose-built prison Mountbatten had proposed.

In comparisons between high-security confinement in HMPS and "supermax" confinement in America, one cannot overstate the relevance of Radzinowicz's argument that categorization should distinguish between prisoners who present *security* problems and those who present *control* problems. Security categorization in HMPS has a long history, but control categorization is still undefined (Price 2000), whereas America has security classifications for prisons (e.g., minimum, medium, maximum) and custody classifications for prisoners (e.g., low, medium, close, high). An American prisoner, for example, is *externally* classified to a prison based on the security level that he or she requires (minimum, medium, maximum), then is *internally* classified to a custody (i.e., *control*) level within that prison (low, medium, high), which determines his or her movement within that prison (with implications for jobs, programs, and services). The determination of which prisoners should be under which type of confinement and how to accurately judge which individuals present control problems, which individuals present security problems, and which individuals present both security and control problems continues to be challenging but is the single most critical element in the humane and effective confinement of these prisoners.

CRC/SPECIAL UNITS, AND THE CONTINUOUS ASSESSMENT SCHEME. Eventually, overwhelming public and political consensus judged the "special security units" undesirable and the government decided to close them and disperse remaining prisoners to category A prisons. The units at Chelmsford and Durham closed by 1972, but Durham continued to hold high-security women until 2005, when an investigation revealed a high level of suicides and emotional distress among the women, who were eventually dispersed to more suitable prisons (*BBC News* 2005).

The mission to close all these units was nearly accomplished when plans were derailed by Irish Republican Army (IRA) bombings of London on March 8, 1973. British officials believed that detained IRA bombers would pose a significant security threat that might not be containable within the dispersal system. This led to a 1978 policy reversal in which officials not only abandoned the idea of closing the remaining units but also were convinced to open a third. Officials decided to house this unit within a new dispersal prison being built at Full Sutton (Walmsley 1989).

During construction of Full Sutton, considerable debate still surrounded the distinction between confinement for security and confinement for control. In response, the government formed the Control Review Committee in 1984 to evaluate the strategies and mechanisms for managing (i.e., *controlling*) long-term disruptive prisoners (Home Office 1984; Clare and Bottomley 2001). The committee formed an "advisory group" to plan, coordinate, and evaluate proposed new small "special units" for *control* problems within facilities, as opposed to "special security units," which were for *security* problems (Home Office 1987). This advisory group, in an effort to improve conditions and minimize control problems within the proposed special units (also called "CRC units"), commissioned a report about "lessons-learned" to help develop more "forward-looking regimes" for the new units (Walmsley 1989, 1).

CRC units were introduced after 1989 for prisoners who were the "severest control problems" (Tuck, cited in Walmsley 1989, iii) but not necessarily significant risks to security (Walmsley 1989). Three units operated to hold a total maximum of thirty-five prisoners, although populations rarely approached this number (Bottomley 1995). Between 1989 and 1996, however, several events, including a major riot, high-profile escapes, and a series of five government investigations and six reports, resulted in the discontinuation of CRC units.

First, a merry-go-round called the "Continuous Assessment Scheme" emerged whereby dispersal prisons exchanged problematic prisoners for four- to six-week periods (Flynn 1998; King 1999; Morris 2006) because "[CRC units] didn't work" (senior manager, as cited in Clare and Bottomley 2001, 133). This informal process was formalized and centralized in 1993 to "select more prisoners suitable for the CRC units" and to make the "'underground' process of frequent transfer, more visible" (Clare and Bottomley 2001, 134). The result, however, was that prisoners with difficulties in the CRC units were segregated on a long-term basis, in extremely restrictive conditions, with few opportunities to improve their behaviors and thus reduce their perceived risk (Morris 2006). While this scheme arguably decreased prisoners' danger to others, it increased their risk of suffering significant mental health issues and their threat to public safety from constant transfers between facilities (HM Chief Inspector of Prisons for England and Wales 2000).

Second, the longest, most damaging, and most costly riot in English history at HMP Strangeways (now HMP Manchester) resulted in the Woolf Enquiry and Report, which emphasized the "need to balance security & control with justice & humanity" (Home Office 1991b, as cited in Waddington 1991). A 1991 white paper from the Home Office broadly accepted Woolf's recommendations and provided a long-range strategy to accomplish them (Home Office 1991a).

Third, escapes from HMP Whitemoor's "impregnable walls" in September 1994 and from HMP Parkhurst four months later resulted in the Woodcock and Learmont reports, respectively (Home Office 1994, 1995). The Woodcock report raised general concerns about the security of high-security units and dispersal prisons and triggered a broader investigation by Learmont that also encompassed an inquiry into the Parkhurst escape. Learmont's one recommendation, a supermax facility as a long-term solution to managing prisoners who were seriously disruptive, was rejected as "not politically and budgetary feasible" (Resodihardjo 2009, 182). The government, however, commissioned a "supermax feasibility study," but this was lost in the shuffle of Prime Minister John Major's last days in office (Resodihardjo 2009).

Finally, a threefold investigation into system-wide security policies, management of prisoners who presented serious control problems, and the feasibility of a "strict regime CRC unit" (Clare and Bottomley 2001, 119) resulted in the 1996 Spurr report. This report concluded that some prisoners were too disruptive even for the CRC units and suggested their management within five CSCs characterized by a "coordinated system" of "graded regimes" (Clare and Bottomley 2001, 120). The CSC system was recommended to replace the expensive prior system because, instead of getting prisoners off of the special custody "merry-go-round" and successfully reintegrated, the primary accomplishment of the former system was to "provide relief for the mainstream long-term prisons" (Home Office 1994, 16).

Challenging, Dangerous, Disruptive, or Disordered?

In 1998, after fewer than ten years, the CRC/special unit system was discontinued and replaced with the CSC system to house up to forty-eight "really dangerous and disruptive prisoners who attack staff, take hostages, attack and murder other prisoners, and refuse to conform to normal prison conditions" (HM Chief Inspector of Prisons [HMCIP] 2000, 1). Guidance for the CSC system comes from Prison Rule 46, the "CSC Referral Manual," and the "Managing Challenging Behaviour Strategy." Prison Rule 46 provides the basis for the operation of the CSC system allowing the secretary of state to remove a prisoner from association, for safety or "good order or discipline," and to confine him or her (in one-month renewable increments) within a CSC, defined as "any cell or other part of a prison designated by the Secretary of State" (Home Office 1999/2010). This strategy "bridge[s] the gap between segregation units and the CSC system" by providing "one coordinated system for managing difficult prisoners" (IMB—Woodhill 2010, 23). It also monitors prisoner movement out of the CSC system to assist in reintegration (HMPS 2009, 11). A local "challenging behaviour manager" coordinates local delivery of the strategy and is the point of contact for the central Case Management Group. This group, based at HMP Woodhill, consists of the CSC operational manager (a governor), a senior forensic mental health nurse, a chartered psychologist, and an administration manager (HMPS 2009).

A referral to the CSC system is "the last resort in the management of prisoners" (Ministry of Justice 2009, 8). HMPS aims to keep troublesome prisoners in their "home" prisons by exhausting all in-house management tactics. Prison governors must attempt "local" strategies, including individual case management in consultation with area managers. They must clearly document both the extent of the prisoner's dangerous behavior and the risk he or she poses to others and himself or herself, ensure that all other control and management options under the strategy (ranging from "positive dialogue" to segregation to transfer) have been exhausted, and use evidence to illustrate that other strategies are inadequate for the protection of everyone involved (Ministry of Justice 2005).

The CSC Process

One of the first steps in the initial referral process is the completion by the prisoner's home prison of a minimum of five reports including a psychology, mental health/psychiatric, and security and intelligence report. The psychiatric report is critical because it provides evidence of whether the prisoner should be referred to a CSC, to a high-security hospital, or to a unit for "dangerous persons with severe personality disorder" (DSPD) (Home Office 1999/2010; Ministry of Justice 2009). These reports are reviewed by the local manager, who sends warranted referrals to the support manager at HMP Woodhill, who sends them to the Case Management Group (EIA 2009). The group reviews the reports from the referring prison and may ask for additional or supporting information.

Prisoners whose referrals are approved by the group are transferred from their home prison and confined for up to four months in either Woodhill or Wakefield during assessment; assessments of their suitability for CSC confinement generally take up to three months, followed by one month for report writing and the case conference to decide whether they should be placed in the CSC system. The CSC assessment process consists of six key stages, beginning with a series of reports to provide multidisciplinary risk assessments, including mental health issues and reports from a forensic psychiatrist and a forensic psychologist. During this twelve-week period, several reports from specialists are completed "to fully identify and assess the risks the prisoner presents" (Ministry of Justice 2009, 11). The CSC Management Committee approves or disapproves the referral, and the decision is ratified by the director of high security (UK Government 2009). Prisoners not selected for CSC confinement will be either managed under the strategy by the group and monitored through local panels at their home prisons or referred for confinement in highly secure hospitals or DSPD units (Ministry of Justice 2009; Home Office 1999/2010).

Once selected into the CSC system, prisoners either continue to be confined at Woodhill or are sent to Wakefield, Whitemoor, or a specially designated cell in one of seven other prisons (see the "CSC Units" section). Although the CSC system originally developed as a containment and control strategy with little consideration of working the prisoner toward reintegration back into the general prison population, since late 2005 it has been reframed as a "violence reduction strategy for disruptive prisoners" (HMCIP 2006, 10). This move came after several years of criticism from IMBs and others concerned specifically about the impact of this type of confinement on the mental health of the prisoners. In fact, since 2005, mental health professionals and others have been working directly with the Prison Service to develop and pilot specific violence reduction strategies and programs and have developed treatment models, particularly for DSPD prisoners (HMCIP 2006).

Within four weeks of acceptance into the CSC system, the CSC multidisciplinary team at the receiving prison develops a multidisciplinary "care and management" plan for the prisoner to manage or reduce disruptive and/or violent behavior. The ultimate aim of this plan, reviewed quarterly, is to *deselect* prisoners out of the CSC system and back to the general prison population (HMCIP 2006). In addition, prisoner behavior is evaluated weekly, and monthly monitoring reports are forwarded to the committee. Each prisoner can review these monthly reports and make written comments, as well as review and comment on the report's feedback from the committee (Ministry of Justice 2009).

The dedicated CSC units at Woodhill, Wakefield, and Whitemoor are designed and staffed for varying levels of control and privilege in a "progressive system" from the most restrictive and least privileged "basic" to the least restrictive and most privileged "standard plus." Segregation, not considered part of the progressive scheme, is reserved for those who require even more restriction and control and complete loss of privileges (see below) (Ministry of Justice 2009).

Entering prisoners are placed in a "standard" environment for induction and assessment period with a basic, structured regime, under the assumption that they will then progress to "standard plus" and eventually out of the CSC system. Standard regime prisoners are expected to work or engage in other constructive activity for a specified number of hours per week and are paid accordingly. Prisoners on this regime also may be allowed open association with other prisoners on a limited basis and open association with visitors (Ministry of Justice 2009).

Standard plus prisoners are the most privileged and least restricted in the CSC system. These prisoners are expected to be productively engaged a specified number of hours per week, are allowed more cell furnishings and personal possessions, access to a communal kitchen and meals, and significantly more and lengthier associations, and can wear and launder their own clothing. Prisoners also can shower and make phone calls at any time when they are "unlocked" (i.e., out of cell). This regime also is marked by educational opportunities.

Prisoners on the "basic" regime are under the most stringent controls and restrictions in the progressive system. Basic prisoners are allowed personal possessions of a limited type and number (e.g., twelve photos), a limited number of books and education materials, limited associations with others, cardboard cell furnishings (if assessment deems this a necessary precaution), exercise within secure outdoor exercise yards that resemble cages, and daily showers. In addition, these prisoners are allowed only two prebooked thirty-minute visits per month and up to three prebooked ten-minute phone calls per week (Ministry of Justice 2009).

The CSC Units

The CSC system is composed of three prisons with twenty-eight cells in dedicated CSC units (HMPs Woodhill, Wakefield, and Whitemoor) and sixteen designated cells within the segregation units of seven other high-security dispersal prisons (HMPs Belmarsh, Full Sutton, Frankland, Long

Lartin, Manchester, Wakefield, and Whitemoor). All together, forty spaces are allocated for CSC prisoners. The facilities within which these CSC cells are located are described below.

Woodhill has a "certified normal accommodation" (CNA) of 661 and a maximum capacity of 819. Currently, the prison confines 813 prisoners (HM Prison Service 2011a). Woodhill's A wing is the main national assessment center for prisoners being referred to the CSC system, including preselection CSC referrals and CSC inductees on a "restricted regime," as well as those progressing toward a less restricted regime. The restricted regime on A wing is "equivalent to segregation" (HMCIP 2006, 23), although three levels of regime (basic, standard, standard plus) theoretically make the wing "progressive." In the most restricted regimes, prisoners are fed through hatches and have minimal, if any, daily direct contact with anyone. Overall, however, Woodhill generally is praised for its treatment of CSC prisoners (IMB—Woodhill 2010), but the CSC unit could benefit from a "more structured evidence-based violence reduction programme" (HMCIP 2010b, 35).

Wakefield has a CNA of 751, a maximum capacity of 749, and a current population of 739 (HM Prison Service 2011a). It is a main "lifer" prison housing both category A and category B prisoners, but focusing on serious sex offenders serving more than five years. Wakefield houses up to eight CSC prisoners "in a unique self-contained unit" within its segregation unit on F wing (HM Prison Service 2011b). All of the cells have electricity, and two are fitted with CCTV for constant observation, when necessary. Each cell has both an inner gate that remains locked and an outer door that can be left open, allowing for more interaction between the prisoners and the staff. Despite this unit being described as "a positive development" (HMCIP 2006, 13), Wakefield has been criticized for not adequately differentiating between CSC prisoners and those in segregation, for lacking mental health treatment, and for providing an environment that seems focused on containment rather than progression (HMCIP 2008b; IMB—Wakefield 2010).

Whitemoor has a CNA of 473, a maximum capacity of 458, and a current population of 444 (HM Prison Service 2011a, 3). This unit, newly opened in 2004, provides "a structured and meaningful regime" for up to ten CSC prisoners, focused on reintegrating them back into the prison mainstream (HMCIP 2006, 28). Most CSC prisoners here come from the more restricted regime at Woodhill because they have proven themselves ready for a more open regime. The primary criticism levied again Whitemoor by CSC prisoners is a lack of activities, leading to boredom (HMCIP 2006).

High-Control Cells

Under Prison Rule 46, "high-control cells" are designated to hold CSC prisoners for open-ended periods within the segregation units at dispersal prisons Wakefield, Whitemoor, Frankland, Full Sutton, Long Lartin, and Manchester, and within the segregation unit of Belmarsh. These cells, while primarily used for control, also may be used for the more positive purposes of accumulated visits ("saving up visits" and accumulating them to allow for visits of longer periods of time) or *deselection* (leaving the CSC system) (HMCIP 2006), although this use is "highly unlikely" (C. Hodson, pers. comm., March 25, 2011). Although the CSC system makes frequent use of these cells, record keeping related to their use is poor (HMCIP 2009c). With the exception of Wakefield and Whitemoor, discussed above, these prisons are all described below.

Frankland was the first purpose-built dispersal prison. It has a CNA of 859, a maximum capacity of 844, and a current population of 822 (HM Prison Service 2011a). It also accommodates 80 DSPD prisoners and has twenty-eight cells in the segregation unit. Two additional cells within the segregation unit are set aside for CSC prisoners. The most recent inspection praised the segregation unit for its treatment of prisoners, for its prisoner/staff relations, and for its regime (HMCIP 2011a). Problems, however, were noted in overrepresentation of black and minority ethnic prisoners and of Muslim prisoners in segregation, as well as in support for foreign national prisoners (IMB—Frankland 2010; HMCIP 2011a).

Full Sutton has a CNA of 604, a maximum capacity of 608, and a current population of 598 (HM Prison Service 2011a). The segregation unit has forty cells, with thirty allocated for "normal" segregation, eight for other types of segregation (e.g., dirty protest), and two for CSC prisoners. Reviews of Full Sutton are fairly positive in terms of progressive treatment of prisoners in segregation. During the most recent IMB review, one CSC prisoner was held in Full Sutton, and his treatment and progress were extolled as an "excellent example of patient, sympathetic development" (IMB—Full Sutton 2010, 28). However, inspections express concerns about the growing threat of gangs, particularly Muslim gangs, whose members tend to become segregated more frequently, resulting in their overrepresentation (HMCIP 2011b).

Long Lartin's "Security Care and Control Unit" (i.e., segregation unit) houses up to thirty-eight prisoners in single-cell accommodation and includes four designated cells for CSC prisoners. Two of these cells are monitored by CCTV. Long Lartin has a CNA of 629, a maximum capacity of 622, and a current population of 616 (HM Prison Service 2011a). It generally is praised for good programs, services, and management but suffers from disproportionate confinement of black and minority ethnic and Muslim prisoners in segregation and in the detainee unit (IMB—Long Lartin 2010). Muslim prisoners also express perceptions of poor treatment by staff (HMCIP 2009a).

Manchester, formerly known as Strangeways, was the site of a series of major disturbances between April 1 and April 25, 1990, during which one prisoner was killed and 147 staff and 47 prisoners were injured. Much of the prison was destroyed and had to be rebuilt. In 2003, Manchester became part of the high-security system, and its segregation unit contains two cells designated for CSC prisoners. Manchester's CNA is 965, its operational capacity is 1,250, and its current population is 1,181 men (HM Prison Service 2011a). In the most recent inspection, the chief inspector reported that one CSC prisoner had spent more than three months on the unit and that, in general, "use of special accommodation was high" (HMCIP 2009b, 77). However, staff in the segregation unit were broadly commended for their professionalism.

Belmarsh primarily serves the Central Criminal Court and Magistrates' Courts in South East London but also holds high-security prisoners awaiting trial and on remand (IMB—Belmarsh 2010). It has a CNA of 800, a maximum capacity of 933, and a current population of 866 (HM Prison Service 2011a). It is a large complex prison with a segregation unit that has fourteen regular segregation cells, four other special cells, and two cells for CSC confinement. Reports commend Belmarsh on its treatment of foreign national prisoners and, in general, for taking positive steps toward violence reduction. However, four deaths in custody between 2007 and 2008 were still awaiting inquests as of year-end 2010 (IMB—Belmarsh 2010). Inspectors also are critical of deteriorating health care, mental health care, and support for prisoners with disabilities, insufficient provision of productive activity, insufficient resources for prisoner resettlement (i.e., release and reentry), poor prisoner/staff relations, and negative perceptions of staff and treatment among the black and minority ethnic and Muslim populations (HMCIP 2009c). Although recently abandoned, Belmarsh used to hold CSC prisoners under a "refusal" regime allowing "only sub-basic privileges with the aim of discouraging prisoners from staying" (HMCIP 2006, 19). In general, current reviews of Belmarsh indicate "a predominant focus on security" at the expense of "some important areas of prisoner care and rehabilitation" (HMCIP 2009c, 6).

CSC and Segregation

Although confinement in a CSC and confinement in segregation differ philosophically and practically, there are overlaps. Most individuals referred to the CSC system have spent significant amounts of time in segregation. Even after prisoners have been selected for CSCs, they will still spend time in designated cells within high-security segregation units for adjudication, punishment, "good order or discipline," their own protection, or "reasonable management" (HMCIP 2006). Moreover, some prisoners actively refuse to "progress" because they do not want to be put in general population or because they hope to be transferred to another CSC or segregation unit at another prison.

Early inspections of the CSC system raised concerns over the use of seg-regation with CSC prisoners, particularly as it affected mental health (HMCIP for England and Wales 1999). CSC prisoners who could not be trusted even within the "basic" regime were provided regimes more restricted than segre-gated regular prisoners (HMCIP for England and Wales 1999), locked down twenty-three hours per day with no direct daily human contact, little indi-rect human contact, few or no visits from family (many of whom have to travel great distances to visit a maximum of thirty minutes twice a month), and two prebooked ten-minute phone calls per week. As a result, "prisoners were isolated from anyone who might encourage them to review their position . . . and unable to demonstrate improved behaviour whilst perma-nently locked away" (HMCIP for England and Wales 1999, 10). Moreover, weekly risk assessments to determine the continued need for segregation became "self-fulfilling paper exercises" because restrictions that "equate[d] with punishment" (HMCIP for England and Wales 1999, 3) made showing change difficult.

Distinctions should be made among segregation as punishment, segrega-tion to control immediate risk of harm, and segregation as part of a struc-tured regime, which should mean differentiation among regimes. Property and privilege loss, for example, should accompany segregation as punishment, but prisoners in segregation to control risk of harm or as part of a structured regime should not lose property and privileges and should have safe access to staff at all times. More important, all prisoners "should have the opportunity to make personal progress in prison, and none should be exposed to regimes which might cause a deterioration in their mental or physical health" (HMCIP for England and Wales 1999, 46–47).

A more recent review of "extreme custody" indicates that the system has implemented more mental health support, added a unit at Wakefield for man-aging extremely dangerous prisoners, developed more ways for prisoners to progress, and abandoned the punishment regime in favor of a "violence reduction model" (HMCIP 2006). Concerns still remain about the lack of clinical involvement in the case management of these prisoners, especially those with severe mental health needs, and although use of segregation for control has declined, when used it is for significantly longer periods of time (HMCIP 2006).

Of additional concern is confusion over "ownership" of these segregated CSC prisoners and lack of clarity about the role of IMB monitoring. The chief inspector noted that "disproportionate use of segregation and unfur-nished cells for black and minority ethnic prisoners was not being picked up in monitoring" (HMCIP 2006, 6). In one unit, for example, the inspection showed that 73 percent of those segregated in unfurnished cells were from black or ethnic minority communities (HMCIP 2006).

Nationality, Race, Religion, and Politics

Legislation targeted at terrorism (e.g., Terrorism Act 2000; Terrorism Act 2006) has resulted in more Muslims in custody, and an increase in gang-related activities has led to an increase in black and minority ethnic prisoners. Moreover, Muslim prisoners and black and minority ethnic prisoners are at increased risk of referral to the "managing challenging behavior strategy" if evidence suggests that they are also involved in any extremist or gang-related activity "that is unsuitable and adversely impacting on the good order of an establishment" (HM Prison Service 2009, 7). Currently, 37 to 55 percent of prisoners in high-security prisons are black or minority ethnic prisoners (HM Prison Service 2009), and Muslims, who compose about 3 percent of the population in the United Kingdom, are about 12 percent of the prison population (HMCIP 2010b), although in some prisons this percentage is much higher. Although the current representation of Muslim prisoners in the CSC system is unclear at this time, the representation of black or minority ethnic prisoners in CSC confinement was 29 percent as of April 2009 (HM Prison Service 2009).

Problems surrounding disproportionate confinement of these populations were illustrated in a review of the "specialist unit" for category A detainees at Long Lartin. Seven Arabic-speaking Muslims were detained, six on suspicion of international terrorism and a seventh on an extradition warrant. These prisoners were held for an indefinite period in an extremely isolated and confined environment without appropriate mental or physical health care. Many of these detainees feared and had perhaps previously experienced mistreatment or torture overseas, and most had diagnosable, often severe, mental health issues. Although funds were set aside for their health care, it was not actually being spent for this purpose, partially because the prisoners did not trust the health care staff (HMCIP 2008a).

These issues recently came to the forefront in HMPS, in judicial review proceedings initiated by the Equality and Human Rights Commission. A High Court of Justice decision ruled that NOMS "failed to comply with disability and race laws in its treatment of foreign national prisoners" in May 2009 when it entered into an agreement with the UK Border Agency for the "effective management and speedy removal of Foreign National Prisoners" (Equality and Human Rights Commission 2010, 1). HMPS implemented this transfer policy without considering the impact it might have on ethnic minority or disabled prisoners despite significant evidence from HM Inspectorate of Prisons and IMBs about widespread discrimination and disadvantage already faced by these populations.

HMPS violated the law by failing to conduct an "equality impact assessment" before changing policy. This assessment uses a two-stage process to determine whether any particular policy or function may have a disproportionate impact on any particular group of people by race/ethnicity, gender, gender identity, disability, religion or belief, sexual orientation, or age (HM Prison Service 2009).

The Prison Service's assessment of relevant policies did not happen until several months after the initiation of judicial review of the transfer policy. The first assessment in November 2009 reviewed the "managing challenging behaviors strategy" (HM Prison Service 2009) and identified three issues by which this strategy could have a disproportionate impact: race/ethnicity, religion, and disability. However, only one disabled prisoner was confined at this time under the strategy, and he had refused to participate in the assessment, so disability was identified as an issue only because the evaluators had no information. Race/ethnicity and religion were both related to the presence of Muslim prisoners in the system who were being disproportionately affected by this strategy.

This assessment prompted a "thematic review" of Muslim prisoners' experiences (HMCIP 2010a). The primary conclusion was threefold. First, staff had difficulties working with small terrorist or radical prisoner groups while also working with larger groups of Muslim prisoners and "often did not distinguish adequately between the two," and "a focus on identifying extremism, promoted questionable assumptions about the presence and prevalence of radicalisation" (HMCIP 2010a, 19). Second, Muslim prisoners distrusted the staff and felt that they stereotyped all Muslims from having to deal with small numbers of extremists charged with or convicted of terrorist activities. Third, the Muslim prisoners felt more at risk than non-Muslims; 46 percent of Muslim prisoners felt unsafe, compared to 36 percent of non-Muslim prisoners. The difference between Muslims and non-Muslims was greatest in the dispersal prisons from which CSC populations primarily are drawn (HMCIP 2010a). On a positive note, a significantly larger proportion of Muslim prisoners reported positive interactions and feelings of safety than in a 2007 report (HMCIP 2010a). As a result of the findings from the assessment and from the thematic review, the chief inspector recommends "a national strategy for Muslim prisoners . . . outlining how the needs of Muslim prisoners will be met" (HMCIP 2010a, 43).

DOES CSS EQUAL SUPERMAX?

In theory, the idea of the American "supermax" has been proffered, evaluated, and rejected outright by Britain. According to Clare and Bottomley (2001, 166), "[C]ontemporary United States does not provide a model that we wish to buy wholesale." In practice, however, the CSC system shares several characteristics with the American supermax, including seemingly disproportionate confinement by race/ethnicity for long periods in ultrasecure facilities with extra control, supervision, and deprivation more significant than any other prisoners. In addition, both the CSC system and American supermax are meant for those prisoners who have demonstrated histories of disruptive behavior in general prison populations.

Although these are shared characteristics, several things distinguish the British system from the supermax system in America. Primary among these is the emphasis on the provision of humane treatment and services for CSC prisoners that is evident in the language of the policies, training, manuals, and guides related to the confinement of these prisoners. Second is the transparency of the system to reviewers from both within and outside of the prison establishment (e.g., HM Chief Inspectorate, Institutional Monitoring Boards). The entire prison system is open to daily review and inspection on both announced and unannounced bases, which makes improper or inhumane practices much less likely, whereas in the United States, few are given access to observe daily life in the supermax and only rarely.

Another difference is that Britain seems committed to keeping populations very low in the CSC units. Currently, forty spaces are reserved for these prisoners, and these rarely have been filled. The criteria for CSC confinement, however, recently were expanded to "enable the system to work with offenders who undermine security and good order by their covert activities" (C. Hodson, pers. comm., March 25, 2011), which includes "prisoners considered to be at the heart of extremist activities on the wings" (IMB—Whitemoor 2010, 24). Although the chief inspector expressed concern over this criteria change (HMCIP 2010b), some IMBs were pleased that the criteria had been widened because bringing in more prisoners to the CSC units provides "better value for the cost" (IMB—Whitemoor 2010, 24). Even with the expansion of the criteria, however, the rate of confinement in ultra-high-security prisons in the United States is four times higher than in Britain; about 2 percent of prisoners in the United States are confined in supermax facilities, compared to less than 0.05 percent in CSC units in Britain. Prisoners, however, accuse the CSC and the "managing challenging behaviors strategy" of "trying to institutionalise a system of repression that violates the basic human rights of prisoners" by broadening the definition of "challenging" and by widening the net of high-security confinement to include prisoners who may not present control and/or security problems at the highest levels (Bowden 2009, 29).

Discouraging signs that Britain may be becoming more harsh and following in US footsteps indicate that an American-style supermax system may not be too distant on the horizon. In response to changes in sentencing laws and increasing prison populations in Britain, a recent report recommended the creation of a Sentencing Commission to develop and enforce sentencing guidelines and the construction of three "Titan" prisons that each would hold 2,500 prisoners (Carter 2007). As a result, the Coroner's and Justice Act 2009 established a Sentencing Council for England and Wales and the adoption of Sentencing Guidelines for judges and magistrates (Coroner's and Justice Act 2009). To address burgeoning prison populations, Britain is expanding capacity to 96,000 by 2014 (UK Government 2009). While the government disregarded the "Titans," construction has commenced on five smaller prisons to accommodate up to 1,500 prisoners each (UK Government 2009). A more determinate sentencing structure coupled with prison construction hints at a hardening of the British system, which might eventually reach the CSC system.

Although money apparently is available for prison construction, HMPS has been asked to severely slash spending due to a 23 percent decrease by 2014 in the Ministry of Justice budget (Blunt 2010). It is unclear how these cuts will affect the CSC system, but a recent announcement by the NOMS may give some indication. CSC, DSPD, and segregation units are being "collapsed" into a new division called "Specialist Units" (HSE) for the "care and supervision of high risk offenders within the custodial environment in dedicated and specialist units . . . provided to the highest possible standard of security" (Ministry of Justice 2010a, 3).

This merging of provisions for the severely mentally ill (DSPD), for those who are segregated for various reasons (not all because of patterns of misbehavior), and for the CSC prisoners may indicate a relaxing commitment on the part of the government to maintain high levels of humane treatment and the differentiation necessary to provide treatment, programs, and services relevant to each population. In fact, with increasing populations, accusations of racial and ethnic bias, significant proportions of mental illness among incarcerated populations, decreasing budgets, sentencing guidelines, and more prison construction, perhaps Britain may be following in the footsteps of the United States after all.

CHAPTER 6

Analyzing the Supermax Prisons in the Netherlands

THE DUTCH SUPERMAX

Sandra L. Resodihardjo

WHEN IT COMES TO Dutch supermax, there is hardly any controversy at the moment. It works and almost everyone is happy that it works—though there are some actors (most notably prisoners and their representatives and some lawyers and criminologists) who are not too keen on the concept of a Dutch supermax. But this does not mean that there has been no controversy whatsoever. On the contrary, the decision to build a supermax unit was quite controversial. So-called special security units (SSUs, known in Dutch as Extra Beveiligde Inrichtingen) turned out to be not as escape-proof as anticipated, resulting in the construction of a completely new SSU, which, though not officially called a supermax prison, does fit King's (1999) definition of a supermax. Moreover, there was initially some controversy about the way the supermax was run. Consequently, this chapter consists of two parts. The birth of the Dutch supermax is described in the first part of this chapter, including a description of the crisis that preceded the decision to build a supermax as well as the discussions that were held on this topic. Following a description of the supermax's structure and regime in the second part, the question of whether or not prisoners are treated inhumanely in this prison is addressed.

THE BIRTH OF THE DUTCH SUPERMAX PRISON

In 1992–1993, the Dutch Prison Service faced a crisis. Lack of cells meant that suspects and convicts were sent home to wait until a cell became available for them, while prisoners were released early in order to make room for the next inmates. At the same time, a number of prisoners managed to escape. They managed to escape not only from low-level security complexes but also from SSUs—prisons that were supposed to be escape-proof. In addition, inmates often used violence while escaping—an uncommon phenomenon in the Dutch Prison Service (King and Resodihardjo 2010). Combined, these incidents resulted in the perception that the Dutch Prison Service was failing (Resodihardjo 2009, 53). Faced with such a crisis, policy makers (most notably the minister, the junior minister, and the director of the prison service) had no choice but to reform the prison service. Regime changes were announced, security was increased, additional cells were built, and a supermax prison was created (Resodihardjo 2009). In order to understand why policy makers opted for a supermax prison, one needs to understand the crisis and its background. This section therefore first addresses cell shortage policies and SSUs, before focusing on the crisis itself.

Cell Shortage Policy

Until the end of World War II, Dutch prisons had been modeled along the lines of the Pennsylvania model. In this kind of regime, prisoners are locked up for twenty-four hours a day without being able to talk to anyone (Rothman 1998, 106), thus allowing inmates to reflect on what they had done. Political prisoners and members of the resistance experienced solitary confinement during World War II and were not too happy with the regime (Fick Inquiry 1947, 6). As a result, the Fick Inquiry was established to determine whether it was possible to institute a more humane and effective way to imprison people. The report of the inquiry, published in 1947, suggested a communal system with solitary confinement during the night so that prisoners could still reflect on what they had done (Fick Inquiry 1947). The resulting system of communal confinement during the day and solitary confinement during the night was still in effect in 1992.[1]

One of the effects of this system was that double bunking was never seriously considered in the Netherlands. Instead, one person to one cell was the norm. Every time the prison service could not keep up with the increase in prisoners, there was a cell shortage—which was dealt with either by not admitting new prisoners or by releasing convicts early in order to make room for the next prisoners. Now and again when the number of prisoners sent home was relatively high, a debate would ensue on whether or not to allow double bunking. But each time it was clear that a majority (consisting of academics, the Union of Prison Governors, the Union of Prison Officers, and most political parties) was against double bunking (Franke 1996, 312–316; Resodihardjo 2009, 36). This majority would slowly start to crumble during the crisis, thereby creating the opportunity to allow double bunking in rare cases (Resodihardjo 2009). A few years later the prison service faced another crisis when there were not enough cells to deal with the many drug runners caught at Schiphol airport. As a result, double bunking became possible for other types of offenders as well (Dekker, Jongejan, and Spek 2003; cf. Kelk 2008, 244).

The Need for SSUs

While cell shortages and the discussion of double bunking were recurrent phenomena, the use of violence during escapes was not. Especially the taking of hostages during escapes was a rare phenomenon—one that was dealt with by introducing SSUs.

In the 1980s, prisoners took staff members hostage on a number of occasions while trying to escape. This resulted in prison staff feeling "unsafe while doing their job and there was a feeling of anxiety in Dutch society" (Ministry of Justice 1987, 1). The junior minister of justice assembled a team to establish the best method of dealing with this relatively small number of prisoners who escaped. The group looked at three types of prisoners: those who were escape-prone, those dangerous prisoners who were difficult to control, and those who were both escape-prone and dangerous at the same time (Ministry of Justice 1987; Hoekstra 1992, 31).

From the outset, the team made it clear that these prisoners should be separated from the rest of the prison population. Dispersion (or what the Dutch Prison Service calls dilution) would only burden other inmates because of the higher security measures and stricter regimes needed to deal with these prisoners. Separation of the inmates could be achieved through concentrating them in a single prison or placing them in several units. The team was in favor of the use of several units since that would make it possible to transfer prisoners every six months so that they could not plot their escape (Ministry of Justice 1987).

Coincidentally, the project team's recommendation corresponded with the junior minister of justice's wish to use the entry units of prisons that were being built at the time as SSUs (Ministry of Justice 1987, annex 1). While the project team declared that they came to their conclusion independently, they did stress that the refurbished entry units would have to have better security than the parent prison (Ministry of Justice 1987).

Soon after the SSUs (three remand and four prison units)[2] became operational in 1990, it became clear that the three types of prisoners (i.e., escape-prone, dangerous, and both escape-prone and dangerous) could not be mixed, and each type required a different regime. Consequently, the decision was made to house only those who were either escape-prone or escape-prone with a tendency to use violence during their escape (Hoekstra 1992, 31). As it turned out, the SSUs were not as escape-proof as planned.

A Malfunctioning Prison Service

Cell shortages and escapes alternately dominated the agenda in the early 1990s. In 1992, these issues became linked in the eyes of the media and members of Parliament (MPs) as indicators of a completely malfunctioning prison service. The attention paid to the Dutch Prison Service by media and MPs not only increased but also was negative in nature as questions were raised about the functioning of the policy sector. Especially MPs were very critical of what was happening, while the media gave MPs a forum to express their opinion (Resodihardjo 2009).

By spring 1992, seven of fifty-five SSU prisoners had escaped (Hoekstra 1992, 18). In time-honored fashion, Junior Minister of Justice Aad Kosto installed an inquiry to investigate the SSUs chaired by Secretary-General Rein Jan Hoekstra (Ministry of General Affairs), which started on April 2, 1992. While the inquiry was on its way, the problems surrounding cell shortage became worse (see figure 6.1 for an overview of the number of adults sent away in these years). Incidents such as the sending home of suspects in a million-guilder public transport ticket fraud fueled media and MP attention. Again, double bunking was the focus of heated debate, but the minister and junior minister of justice continued to oppose double bunking. Instead, they announced the building of more prisons (Resodihardjo 2009, 54–58).

While the debate on double bunking was raging and the inquiry was under way, escapes continued to occur (see table 6.1 for an overview of the number of escapes with and without taking people hostage). Some of these escapes were quite spectacular. One prisoner, for instance, escaped from a remand center by helicopter, while four other inmates escaped from an SSU while armed with knives (Resodihardjo 2009, 59).

The Hoekstra report was published in September 1992. It concluded that though the use of SSUs was a good idea, their implementation had been lacking. Instead of residing within independent prison units, SSU prisoners still had to go to the parent prison for certain facilities such as those for sports and

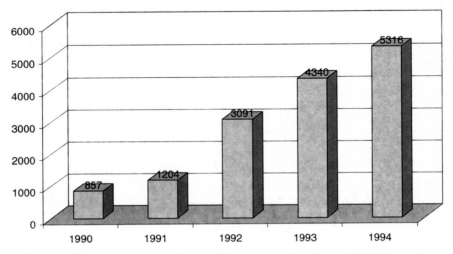

6.1. The number of adults sent away, 1990–1994. Source: DJI (1999, 17). This graph was previously published in Boin and Resodihardjo (2000, 66) and Resodihardjo (2009, 69).

TABLE 6.1

The number of successful escapes from closed prisons with and without taking people hostage, 1991–1995

	1991	1992	1993	1994	1995
Without taking people hostage	50	31	33	18	22
With taking people hostage	0	13	26	3	0
Total	50	44	59	21	22

SOURCE: CBS (1997, 27). This table was previously published in Resodihardjo (2009, 58).

recreation. It was during their stay at the less secure parent prison or during their trip to or from the parent prison that escapes took place (Hoekstra 1992, 9, 31; cf. De Borst 1991). The inquiry recommended building two completely new SSUs that would truly adhere to the SSU philosophy. The SSUs would be self-sufficient prisons with extremely high levels of security systems and policies in place. The high levels of security and the consequent separation of prisoners and staff basically meant that the Hoekstra inquiry was recommending a supermax prison (King and Resodihardjo 2010, 68). Moreover, the inquiry introduced new selection criteria for the SSUs. Prisoners were to be remanded to SSUs if they were likely to escape (with or without outside help) and if their escape would be "socially unacceptable" (Hoekstra 1992, 9).

The recommendation to build two supermax-style prisons was supported by a number of people but was not immediately accepted. Junior Minister of Justice Kosto was hesitant to accept the recommendation and said that he needed to think about it. While doing so, media coverage showed that many supported the recommendation. A populist newspaper, for example, declared that following the recommendation would mean that the prisoners would almost be literally caged in during their stay in prison, "but the Hoekstra inquiry has correctly realized that this is the price that needs to be paid if one wants to be sure that law-abiding citizens' trust in the legal system continues to survive. The number of escapes in the last years has been bad enough as it is" (*De Telegraaf* 1992).

Though there was overall support for the inquiry's proposals, there was some critique as well. One newspaper said that the "Hoekstra inquiry introduced recommendations that were aimed at a draconic reduction of the number of escape attempts" (*De Volkskrant* 1992a). Even though the recommendation was understandable, it was clear that the inquiry allowed the need to avoid any future escapes (since that would make a mockery out of the rule of law) outweigh the fact that prisoners were humans too and needed to be treated as such (*De Volkskrant* 1992b). Another newspaper wrote that one could understand why the inquiry had made these suggestions. "Every escape from a prison is one too many, especially when it is about prisoners who can escape much easier than the poor devil who does not have a powerful [gang] to support him. It is, after all, important to catch these big fishes and keep them as well. . . . [The strict measures in the supermax] are allowed and, to some extent, even desirable. But the [inquiry] should acknowledge that the position of convicted criminals is being restricted" (*Trouw* 1992).

A number of prison governors (a position that is equivalent to a prison warden) supported the idea of a supermax-style prison, but they did not do so unconditionally. The director of the Governors' Association, Kees Boeij, for instance, was fearful that the building of the new SSUs would be at the expense of existing building programs, thus leading to greater cell short-ages (Boeij 1992). At the same time, he and others were pointing out that although building such a prison was necessary, it was of the utmost importance that the treatment of prisoners continue to be humane. Other-wise, the prison service would release ruined people into society (*Algemeen Dagblad* 1992). A member of the Hoekstra inquiry—known for doubting the use of prison sentences longer than five years—was very clear when he described the recommendations as "cruel and horrible. . . . Yet if you do need to build prisons for extreme escape-prone prisoners, you need to do so as decently as possible. . . . An answer was needed in response to these escapes. [The proposals are] the only possible way out" (Moll 1992). While some supporters of the recommendations feared inhumane treatment, others stated that humane treatment and security were not mutually exclusive. In fact, part of humane treatment would be to confront prisoners with the effects of their own behavior. So if they tried to escape during their stay in prison, they would be transported to a prison with higher security—though they would not be subject to complete isolation since that would be inhumane (*Kommer* 1992).

There were people who completely opposed the recommendation, such as mental caretakers working in SSUs, lawyers, and representatives of prison-ers. Their fear was that if inmates were treated as escape-prone, they would actually become escape-prone thanks to the restricted conditions in which they lived (Van Almelo 1992; cf. Dobbelaar 1992; Van Harmelen 1992; De Jonge and Van Vliet 1993). Theirs, however, was a minority point of view that was overshadowed by those in favor of building the supermax to end the continuing escapes.

While the discussion continued, another SSU escape took place on October 23, 1992. This time, four prisoners managed to escape (Binnendijk 1992). In response to this incident, Junior Minister Kosto accepted the Hoekstra recommendation to build two new supermax prisons (Resodihardjo 2009, 61). When yet again inmates managed to escape from an SSU—six this time—Kosto announced that a temporary SSU would be built at Nieuw

Vosseveld Prison (Vught) so that SSU prisoners could be held in that prison until the new SSUs were operational. The temporary SSU was a refurbished World War II bunker and opened in August 1993. As it turned out, the number of SSU prisoners was so minimal that the Dutch Prison Service could suffice with a single SSU prison, which would be located in Vught as well. The SSU became operational in August 1997 (Resodihardjo 2009).

THE DUTCH SUPERMAX PRISON

As indicated by the discussion about security and humane treatment of prisoners, the supermax solution was not a decision generally supported by everyone. It was a decision forced upon policy makers as escapes continued to occur, and it was perceived that other policy options were no longer available to them (Resodihardjo 2009; King and Resodihardjo 2010). Although, as this section shows, there are similarities between the American and Dutch supermax systems, there are noticeable differences regarding the treatment of prisoners. Once the Dutch supermax system has been explained in this section, the issue of humane treatment will be addressed.

A Supermax Prison?

There is no single shared concept of supermax prisons. Instead, supermax prisons differ across and between countries. Using King's (1999) definition, however, it becomes clear that the Dutch SSU is a supermax prison. King defines a supermax prison as a physically separate unit where staff and inmates are physically separated from one another and where prisoners are sent following an administrative process and based on their own behavior (King 1999, 171). The Dutch supermax corresponds to all three characteristics of this definition.

The Dutch supermax is a separate unit in a prison complex. Consequently, one needs to go through security twice if one wants to enter the prison (first the parent prison, then the supermax unit). The supermax unit is constructed in such a way as to deter escapes—through either design or policy. Staff and prisoners are separated from one another by bulletproof glass walls, which makes it difficult for inmates to take someone hostage. In addition, prison staff always outnumber a prisoner and never deal with more than one inmate at the same time. In the unlikely event of a hostage taking, doors will lock automatically and cannot be opened from the inside. Other security features include a wire across the yard to make it impossible for helicopters to land and the use of sally ports (King and Resodihardjo 2010, 72). Last, prisoners enter the prison only when a special committee decides that a prisoner meets the entry criteria of the supermax (Kelk 2008, 91).

Entry and Exit Criteria

Male prisoners (Kelk 2008, 327) can be housed in the supermax if they "a) are considered extremely likely to attempt to escape from closed penal institutions and who, if they succeed, pose an unacceptable risk to society in terms of again committing serious violent crimes; or b) if they should escape, would pose an unacceptable risk to society in terms of severe disturbance of public order, the risk of escaping being, as such, of lesser importance."[3]

In order to assess whether a prisoner meets one of the criteria, a risk profile of the inmate needs to be made. A selection official will create a risk profile using the following information to assess the level of risk a prisoner poses:

"a. The characteristics and background of the offense that the prisoner is suspected of or convicted for,
 b. Information on a possible previous detention in this country or another country, and
 c. Possible other information including findings of meldpunt-GRIP,[4] after analysis of available data on the prisoner."[5]

The selection official will most likely use the prisoner's risk profile made by the public prosecutor to create his or her own risk profile of the prisoner. Any suspect brought before a public prosecutor will be assessed in terms of risk so that the Prison Service knows which prison to transport the suspect to and how to transport the suspect. The initial risk assessment will often be done by the public prosecutor, but in some instances the secretary of the public prosecution's office will do it.[6] In the initial risk assessment, the public prosecution's office will state

> the offence(s) that the prisoner is suspected of and whether (at that time) a sentence of more or less than nine months is to be expected. The public prosecutor can then tick off [one of] the following boxes: no peculiarities known; physical problems (need for special care); mental problems; suicidal behavior; addiction problems; violent behavior; escape risk; extradition request; other, namely . . . and [the box]: do not place in the same prison with . . . (danger that prisoners will collude/danger that retaliation will take place). (De Jonge and Cremers 2008, 59)[7]

Based on the combined information (initial risk assessment by the public prosecutor and the risk assessment by the selection official) plus an interview with the inmate, the selection officer will recommend whether or not to incarcerate the prisoner in the supermax. This recommendation is presented to the selection-advisory commission supermax, which will then decide what to do with the prisoner.[8] Every six months, a decision needs to be made whether to extend the inmate's stay in the supermax or not. Strict procedures rule this process as well.[9] There is no limit to the amount of time that prisoners can spend in the supermax (De Jonge and Cremers 2008, 94). But the regulations do state that a prisoner who has less than one and a half years remaining in prison needs to be placed in a less secure prison, unless, of course,

"a. the prisoner needs to (or possibly will) be extradited,
b. there is still an unacceptable societal risk if the prisoner escapes,
c. in the last year, the prisoner has escaped, has tried to escape or has seriously endangered the discipline and safety within the prison, or
d. there is still valid information from meldpunt-GRIP or the prosecutor's office that the prisoner will most likely escape."[10]

Prisoners can object to the initial decision to place them in a supermax as well as to any decision to prolong their stay in this kind of facility. The Appeals Board will consider the decision by looking at the decision from a formal point of view (whether all procedures were properly followed) and a content point of view (whether the inmate actually meets the criteria of supermax detention) (De Jonge and Cremers 2008, 94–95; cf. Kelk 2008, 329). De Jonge and Cremers (2008), editors of a book that is very popular with prisoners since it contains most if not all of the information prisoners need to know about being imprisoned, including template letters for judicial procedures and requests, point out that the Appeals Board is very critical in its assessment of the decisions that are appealed. "The board will be more critical in its assessment the longer a prisoner has spent time in the supermax. [Moreover], the board will be more likely to be lenient when the inmate is reaching the end of its sentence" (De Jonge and Cremers 2008, 95). However, they do point out that there is a danger of an unfair trial because the public prosecutor can decide that certain GRIP information is so sensitive that neither the prisoner nor the board will see it. This makes it more difficult for the board to assess whether the inmate actually meets the entry criteria (De Jonge and Cremers 2008, 274).

The Regime

The supermax is located in unit 5 at the Vught prison complex.[11] There are four wards in the unit, each consisting of six cells. Three of the four wards (so eighteen cells) have a supermax designation; as of the end of 2009, the fourth ward has a terrorist designation, with a regime that closely resembles the supermax regime (Molenkamp 2009, 47).[12] Both male suspects and male convicted prisoners can be housed in the supermax prison.[13] In recent years, the number of prisoners in the supermax has fluctuated between one and twelve.[14] All supermax inmates are subject to the same regime,[15] the so-called "extra secured regime of limited community."[16]

The supermax regime is quite restricted compared to other Dutch prison regimes (Kelk 2008, 329). For instance, prisoners are not allowed to go on leave, participate in the penitentiary program,[17] or receive visitors without any supervision (De Jonge and Cremers 2008, 126, 148; Kelk 2008, 329). Inmates can receive visitors only behind glass while under the supervision of prison officers. Once a month, the prisoner's partner and immediate family members can visit without a glass wall separating them. During this so-called open visit, touching is limited to only a handshake at the beginning and end of the visit, and the inmate and his visitors are separated by a table with a partition at chest height. Moreover, a prison officer supervises this meeting (and does so within hearing distance) (De Lange 2008, 251). All conversations (either in person or by phone) can be taped and stopped whenever necessary unless the prisoner is having a privileged conversation with, for instance, his lawyer.[18] Mail is checked, and both mail and taped conversations are translated if needed (Molenkamp 2009, 43). During all communal activities, the maximum number of inmates in a group is four.[19]

When it comes to security, the regime is quite similar to the regime in other prisons. The governor can decide that prisoners will have nonstop camera supervision in their own cell (De Jonge and Cremers 2008, 229–230; Kelk 2008, 243–244),[20]

"a. If this is necessary in order to maintain the order or security in the prison
 b. If this is necessary for an undisturbed execution of the prison sentence
 c. If this is necessary to protect the mental or physical condition of the prisoner
 d. If escape or harm to the health of the prisoner would create great societal unrest or seriously damage international relations with other countries or international organizations."[21]

Officially, a handcuff policy is in place that allows prison officers to handcuff prisoners when they are out of their cells. This policy is used for inmates who are constantly very aggressive—which rarely happens in the supermax unit (Molenkamp 2009, 43). In fact, the handcuff policy has not been used in the supermax in the past ten years or so.[22] When it comes to the use of strip search (*visitatie*), the current practice is to use it just as in all other prisons in Vught.[23] In other words, strip searches take place at least "a. when entering or leaving [the prison]; b. when being placed in a punishment cell or in isolation; c. prior to and after a visit without a glass wall; d. whenever needed in order to maintain order or security."[24] However, frisking does happen more often in the supermax than in any other regime (Molenkamp 2009, 43).

Just coming into physical contact with anyone working in the prison is sufficient cause for frisking the prisoner.[25]

Still, the regime and structure of the prison are quite prisoner-friendly
when compared to supermax prisons in other countries—especially the
United States. Prisoners are locked up in individual cells with their own
toilet, sink, and shower. The cells are 50 percent larger than standard cells
(Boin 2001, 341). Inmates are let out of their cell daily for at least one hour.
Prisoners can participate in recreational activities (such as cooking and using
a computer) for at least six hours a week in a minimum of two blocks of at
least two hours.[26] There is a kitchen that inmates can use to cook, they can
use fitness machines, and they can exercise in the recreation area while being
"supervised by a sports instructor who remains behind glass. Whenever
needed, art training and education will be given. [Prisoners] can use the
library through a catalogue" (Molenkamp 2009, 43).

INHUMANE TREATMENT?

So to what extent can the supermax be considered to be inhumane?
Supermax prisoners have complained about their treatment and have even
gone to court (De Jonge and Cremers 2008; Kelk 2008). In addition, there
has been some criticism, most notably from the European Court of Human
Rights (ECHR) and the European Committee for the Prevention of Torture
and Inhuman or Degrading Treatment or Punishment (CPT).

Prisoners have complained about how often they are strip searched. The
ECHR concurred with the inmates that they were strip searched too often.
Besides being strip searched prior to and following an open visit and following visits to the clinic, the dentist, and the hairdresser, prisoners were also
routinely strip searched after every weekly cell inspection. The latter was
inhumane and demeaning and constituted a violation of article 3 of the
European Convention on Human Rights (which reads "no one shall be subjected to torture or to inhuman or degrading treatment or punishment") since
there was no real need to do this considering the security measures already in
place and the fact that there was no indication that security had been
breached.[27] Since March 1, 2003, the regime has been changed. Instead of
routinely strip searching prisoners after every weekly cell inspection, they are
now strip searched only randomly.[28] As a result, prisoners are now searched
only about once every two weeks (De Jonge and Cremers 2008, 222; see also
De Jonge 2007, 285; Kelk 2008, 104–105, 276–277).

In its rulings, the ECHR frequently refers to the CPT reports. The CPT
visited the supermax and temporary supermax in 1997 and 2002.[29] In its 1997
report, the CPT made a number of recommendations, including changing
the regime and allowing inmates to be out of their cell more often, providing
prisoners with a broader range of activities, and discarding or relaxing the

group system where no more than four inmates could interact at the same time. In addition, the CPT recommended that searching policies and visiting policies should be reviewed and that an independent psychological study on the mental health of prisoners was needed (CPT 1997, 33). In its 2002 report, the CPT referred to a fight between prisoners that ultimately led to the death of one of the inmates in September 1999. "Apparently, guards were not in a position to prevent the prisoner's death, due to several factors: the speed with which the incident occurred; their physical separation from the exercise yard by armoured glass panels; and, finally, security regulations prohibiting them from entering into direct contact with more than one inmate at a time" (CPT 2002, 24). The CPT recommended that steps be taken so that prison officers could more easily intervene in prisoners' fights. In addition, the CPT concluded that inmates were still held in a "very impoverished regime" (CPT 2002, 26). The CPT also noted that the Dutch government had commissioned an investigation into the psychological well-being of the prisoners following its 1997 recommendation and that the CPT assumed that it would receive a copy as soon as the investigators had published their report. Furthermore, the CPT made a number of recommendations again, which included increases in out-of-cell time, more human contact, more activities, and less use of searching measures (CPT 2002, 25–26).

The report into the psychological well-being of supermax prisoners was published in 2003 (Kerkhof, Ferenschild, and Scherder 2003). The researchers concluded, for instance, that

> the supermax regime had a negative effect on the cognitive functioning of inmates . . . probably because of a lack of stimulants in the supermax regime. . . . The regime probably causes prisoners and prison officers to not trust each other. The mistrust combined with strip-searches resulted in an unsafe climate and lack of human interaction. . . . Inmates felt humiliated when strip-searched which further increased the pressure prisoners were under. (Kerkhof, Ferenschild, and Scherder 2003, 52)

In response, the minister of justice made it clear that although he felt that he did not need to abide by the recommendations made by the researchers, he was willing to carefully consider them, especially since strip searching procedures had already been changed following the ECHR ruling.[30] In the end, corridors were built alongside the areas where prisoners are able to recreate. Prison officers and mental caretakers can walk through these corridors and have informal chats with the inmates, thereby improving human interaction with the prisoners (Kelk 2008, 330). Other measures taken in response to the report included, for instance, some changes to the living conditions of inmates such as the planting of plants and prisoners receiving more encouragement to participate in activities.[31] The regime, however, was not drastically changed (De Jonge 2007, 287; De Jonge and Cremers 2008, 72).[32]

CONCLUSION

Looking back, we can see that the birth of the Dutch supermax was surrounded by controversy. The escapes and cell shortage problems created a huge crisis for the Dutch Prison Service. One of the solutions to deal with the crisis was the creation of a supermax prison. The acceptance of this solution can best be understood by a combination of factors, including the crisis with its continuing incidents and the shift toward a more punitive climate (Downes 1998; see also Resodihardjo 2009 and King and Resodihardjo 2010 for a more elaborate explanation on why the supermax solution was accepted in the Netherlands). Although the controversy surrounding the decision to build a supermax soon dwindled once the decision had been taken, the supermax regime remained a topic of discussion for quite some time. The regime was adjusted here and there to meet the demands of the ECHR and CPT for more humane treatment, though it is important to note here that the ECHR did not "[denounce] the high-security regime as whole" (De Jonge 2007, 283; cf. De Jonge and Cremers 2008, 71; for a contrasting view, see De Lange 2008, 276–290; De Lange and Mevis 2009, 403–404).[33] To quote former governor of the supermax Bart Molenkamp (2009, 46),

> A number of times, criticism of the supermax has resulted in reflection on the policy and small adjustments. The criticism did not cause any drastic changes of the regime. Now, fourteen years after the start of the temporary supermax, the dust surrounding the supermax-regime has settled. Even though the supermax still gets press coverage on a regular basis, this coverage is not so much the result of criticism of the regime, but mainly because the prisoners in the supermax receive ample attention.

Moreover, the number of prisoners in the supermax was and remains extremely small—fluctuating between one and twelve in recent years.[34] In fact, the number of cells with a supermax designation has decreased over the years. Add to this the fact that the supermax has achieved its main goal (no escapes), and the result is a prison that most people can live with (cf. Molenkamp 2009, 46).

CHAPTER 7

Supermaximum Prisons
in South Africa

Fran Buntman and Lukas Muntingh

SINCE DEMOCRATIZATION, SOUTH AFRICA has struggled
with serious crime at unprecedented levels. As Anthony Altbeker (2007, 12)
notes, "[E]very piece of reliable data we have tells us that South Africa
ranks at the very top of the world's league tables for violent crime. . . . [It is]
an exceptionally, possibly uniquely, violent society." Concern about
crime cuts across boundaries of race, class, urban-rural residence, age, religion, linguistics, and other divides in South Africa. It is therefore hard to
fathom how public calls for being tough on crime, which rose in the 1990s,
could not have affected the environment in which C-Max, the first supermaximum prison in South Africa, was developed. (Ebongweni was the
country's second supermaximum institution.) The link was not, however,
narrow or causal.

The South African history of supermaximum prisons has several dimensions. Department of Correctional Services (DCS) officials were concerned
about unacceptably high levels of prison violence and escapes, for which they
blamed a small category of severely disruptive prisoners. Democratization
and, more specifically, the establishment of the rule of law and human rights
principles (in direct challenge to apartheid's history) both facilitated the
supermaximum approaches and tried to pull this security experiment back
from its most regressive, retributivist, and harsh tendencies. The government
sent "tough-on-crime" messages at points, and C-Max and later Ebongweni
were part of that.

This chapter reviews this multidimensional history, discussing key aspects
of these two supermaximum-security prisons. Neither of these facilities is in
a healthy state. Human rights violations and security breaches have pock-
marked their history. Despite sophisticated infrastructure and detailed regimes
meant to promote both security and rehabilitation, the human factor—from

resource allocation to corruption in the DCS—emerges as the soft under-belly of these two prisons.

OVERVIEW AND PROFILE

Almost all South African correctional centers (formerly referred to as prisons) are designated one of three security levels: minimum, medium, and maximum security.[1] Two centers, however, are even more secure and restrictive than maximum-security facilities. These two supermaximum-security prisons house adult males, predominantly sentenced, who have been identified as being disruptive and violent in the general prison population.[2] C-Max, which stands for closed maximum-security prison, is the first of these. It is located in a section of Pretoria's Central Prison in the Pretoria management area, which includes a cluster of correctional centers and was opened in September 1997 (South African Institute of Race Relations [SAIRR] 1997–1998, 71).[3] C-Max was converted from the former death row following the Constitutional Court's 1995 *State v. Makwanyane* decision declaring the death penalty unconstitutional. The second is Ebongweni, situated in the remote southern KwaZulu-Natal town of Kokstad. Ebongweni was specifically created and designed as a large supermaximum-security prison.[4] It was planned before C-Max, but numerous delays in Ebongweni's planning and construction meant that C-Max became operational first.[5] The supermaximum-security prison is part of a broader complex including a medium-security prison (in part to provide labor for the supermaximum facility) and a housing complex (Sigcau 2002).

When C-Max opened in 1997, DCS said it would be used for South Africa's most dangerous and violent criminals, escapees, and prisoners who had violated prison regulations. F. J. Venter, a staff officer in the commissioner's office at the time DCS began the move to supermaximum facilities, underscored that the most important requirement for admission to supermaximum facilities was the commission of crimes in prison.[6] Prisoners who commit violent crimes against officials or whose behavior does not improve following a pattern of increased institutional control elsewhere are potential candidates for transfer to a supermaximum facility (Jali 2006, 354).[7] These criteria are important for the safety of both inmates and staff in prison and because rehabilitative programming cannot occur in a violent environment. Consequently, high-ranking members of prison gangs are also prime candidates for transfer to supermax. When addressing the Parliamentary Correctional Services Portfolio Committee, DCS added that supermaximum facilities would have a deterrent value for others in the prison system ("PMG Report" 1998).

Soon after C-Max was created, DCS estimated supermaximum prisons were needed for about 50 percent of the country's 7,000 "most dangerous"

FRAN BUNTMAN AND LUKAS MUNTINGH

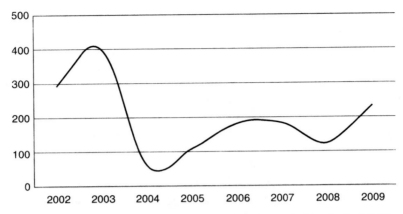

7.1. Admissions per year to Ebongweni. *Source:* Figure supplied by the Judicial Inspectorate for Correctional Services, July 2010.

inmates, mostly those who continued to commit crime in prison (SAIRR 1997–1998, 71). C-Max's capacity is for 281 prisoners; Ebongweni has space for 1,440 inmates, less than half the estimated bed space of 3,500. As of this writing, neither of those two prisons are anywhere nearly fully used. According to the Judicial Inspectorate for Correctional Services (JICS), at the end of March 2010, C-Max was 58 percent full and Ebongweni a mere 37 percent full. In contrast, most prisons in South Africa are overcrowded. As of May 31, 2010, national prison occupancy was at a 136.7 percent level of occupancy (DCS n.d.-a).

Annual admissions to Ebongweni averaged 199 new admissions per year (see figure 7.1). Figure 7.2 shows the offenders' profiles; 83 percent were convicted for violent offences and 15 percent for sexual offences.[8] Despite recent changes in the admissions profile, the overall sentence profile of prisoners at Ebongweni has remained stable (see figure 7.3). The overwhelming majority of prisoners at this facility are serving life sentences or sentences of twenty years or more. Only a small proportion of Ebongweni inmates have sentences of less than ten years. Most inmates (72 percent) are over twenty-five years of age. Only 2.5 percent are younger than twenty years, and 25 percent are between aged twenty and twenty-five. Based on the above, the typical Ebongweni prisoner is older than twenty-five years, has committed one or more violent crimes, and is serving a sentence in excess of ten years; about a third have sentences of life imprisonment.[9] This profile is consistent with the expectation that inmates in a supermaximum facility are more likely to be violent, recidivists, and career criminals.

Ebongweni and C-Max were originally intended exclusively for sentenced prisoners. Practice has deviated from this plan, and a number of high-security-risk individuals awaiting trial have been held at these two prisons.[10]

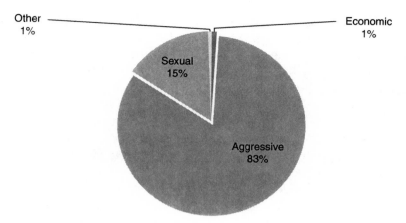

7.2. Offense profile, Ebongweni, 2005–2009. *Source:* Figure supplied by the Judicial Inspectorate for Correctional Services, July 2010.

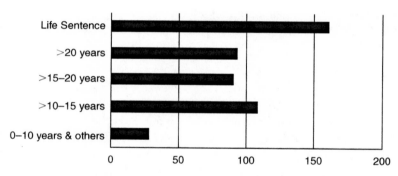

7.3. Sentence profile, Ebongweni, March 2010. *Source:* Figure supplied by the Judicial Inspectorate for Correctional Services, July 2010.

From 2002 to 2007, only two unsentenced prisoners were admitted to Ebongweni. However, between January 2008 and March 2010, the prison held eighty-eight unsentenced prisoners. This apparent shift in thinking has presumably high-risk unsentenced prisoners being placed in this remote prison. At least one resulting problem is that unsentenced prisoners have difficulties in accessing their legal representatives due to Ebongweni's location (*Star* 2010).

FEATURES OF THE SUPERMAXIMUM FACILITIES
DESIGN—SIMILARITIES AND DIFFERENCES

From physical and design perspectives, C-Max and Ebongweni have both common and different features. (In turn, South African supermaximum prisons have both similarities to and differences from various US supermaximum facilities.) In C-Max, security measures "included prisoner isolation, cordoned-off exercise yards, plastic cutlery, specially developed hand and leg irons, video surveillance, prison staff armed with stun guns, electrified riot shields, and bullet and stab-proof vests. Prisoners would not be permitted to shave or smoke" (SAIRR 1997–1998, 71). Although video surveillance was identified as a security feature in 1997, the CCTV system identified as needing upgrading in 2005 following the murder of the head of C-Max by inmates as part of a failed escape attempt (Jali 2006, 256).[11] In another similar gap between policy and practice, although C-Max inmates were allowed contact with each other only as a privilege earned through good behavior,[12] sixty-three prisoner-on-prisoner assaults were reported between September 9, 1997, and February 2, 2005. Furthermore, official reports reflect sixty-four staff-on-prisoner assaults and twenty-six of prisoners on DCS officials (Jali 2006, 359).

DCS's website explains that Ebongweni is run based on unit management, with four units for 360 offenders, six subsections per section, and ten inmates per subsection. In addition "[t]here is also a Pre-Integration Unit for 96 offenders (32 single cells and 32 double cells) and a 30 bed in-patient hospital facility" (DCS n.d.-b).[13] Ebongweni has high levels of technological controls:

> [A]n integrated security system . . . includes pneumatic sliding doors, closed circuit television, and a three-level control system with a Central Control Room, a Movement Control Room, and Section Control Rooms as well as an electrified security fence with detection and alarm systems and CCTV cameras that are fully integrated with the Security System. Access control to the centre is also managed and monitored with a turn style system supported by a swipe card and biometric finger print reading system and closed circuit television, walk-through metal detectors, and x-ray scanner. (DCS n.d.-b)

WHY SUPERMAXIMUM PRISONS IN SOUTH AFRICA?

The Ministry of Correctional Services and DCS decided to create supermaximum-security prisons in South Africa in the mid-1990s. The key policy makers (three appointed and one elected) interviewed identified three broad reasons for this innovation: the increase in the number of very long and life sentences (including due to the 1995 abolition of the death penalty), extensive prison violence, and large numbers of escapes. There were, however, significant delays in actually establishing these new prisons.

First, the sentence profile of prisoners changed following (and an important part attributable to) the abolition of the death penalty in 1995. The dismantling of the gallows began the day that the *Makwanyane* judgment (rejecting the death penalty) was delivered.[14] By the late 1990s, the number of prisoners serving very long sentences, including life sentences, was rapidly increasing. DCS was well aware that these prisoners could be very disruptive (Giffard and Muntingh 2006, 10).

Second, prison violence, sometimes fatal and including interprisoner as well as staff-prisoner assaults, had increased significantly.[15] In addition to senior officials, Sipo Mzimela, the minister of correctional services from 1994 to 1999, and Golz Wessman, Minister Mzimela's advisor at the time, emphasized that inmates who destabilize the general prison population must be separated out.[16] (The officials interviewed consistently underscored that most prisoners are not violent and not a threat to order and safety in prisons.)[17] This imperative was especially vital given the severe (and widely recognized) overcrowding in South Africa's prisons (Dissel and Ellis 2002; Fagan 2004; Muntingh 2005; Buntman 2009b).

The disruptive impact of a small group of violent prisoners in overcrowded, understaffed prisons is a legitimate and well-founded concern. The most convincing and consistent rationale for supermaximum facilities is probably the strict separation of extremely violent and disruptive inmates from the rest of the prison population, especially when such inmates facilitate and spread violence, such as through gangs. South Africa has a particularly long-standing and complex prison gang culture (Steinberg 2004/2005, 2005; Jali 2006). Strict segregation is almost certainly a necessary if not sufficient condition to challenge a dangerous and antisocial violent counterculture.[18]

Ebongweni was planned before the former death row was converted to C-Max, but C-Max was completed well before Ebongweni.[19] C-Max in Pretoria was both a response to delays in building Ebongweni and a reaction to the particular and local problems in Gauteng province, especially in the Pretoria management area. When the number of assaults in Pretoria Local Prison averaged 168 per month, then commissioner of correctional services Khulekani Sitole ordered solutions, one of which was C-Max, intended to house disruptive and violent prisoners.[20]

Construction of Ebongweni was delayed by government inaction and disagreement at the highest levels. Then minister Mzimela recalled numerous and mostly unresolved cabinet meetings concerning the uncertain sentencing status of prisoners previously sentenced to death.[21] Mzimela believed then minister of justice, the late Dullah Omar, did not appreciate the urgent security problems former death row inmates posed for DCS. Ultimately, Mzimela emphasized, DCS decided to create a supermaximum facility. The cabinet supported this decision as a departmental rather than a senior governmental decision, apparently not seeing it as a significant political issue.

Third, officials saw supermaximum facilities as a response to prisoner escapes. In 1994 alone, 1,218 prisoners escaped from custody (DCS 1994). This problem attracted significant media attention and fueled the already

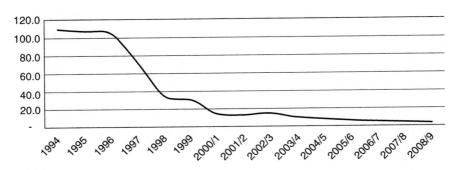

7.4. Escapes per 10,000 in custody per year. *Source:* DCS annual reports for the relevant years.

heightened public insecurity. It is important that many, perhaps most, citizens felt a sense of precariousness and vulnerability. Despite the successful negotiation of a political transition,[22] crime and especially violent crime, long-standing features of South African life, were intensified with the democratic transition. Escaping prisoners added to the pervasive fear and unease. Moreover, almost every aspect of state and society was in flux.

In 1994 there were 109.8 escapes per 10,000 prisoners in custody, but by 2008–2009 this figure had dropped to 3.9 per 10,000 prisoners in custody (figure 7.4). Although the decline in escapes somewhat correlates with the 1997 establishment of C-Max in Pretoria, there is little reason to attribute the decline in escapes to establishing this supermaximum facility. The beginning of the decline preceded C-Max, and escapes had largely stabilized at low levels when the Ebongweni supermaximum facility began to admit prisoners in 2002.

More important, escapes were widely recognized as primarily a DCS personnel problem as corruption, poor training, and lax discipline were rampant (Dissel and Ellis 2002). The Jali Commission later concluded that most escapes were facilitated by officials.[23] Earlier, DCS itself had recognized in its 2001–2002 Annual Report that "*[n]egligence by officials continues to be a major cause of escapes* whilst staff shortages and over-population also aggravate the situation" (cited by Jali 2006, 312, emphasis original). Mzimela frankly acknowledged that some prison warders facilitated escapes, by either negligence or active assistance.[24] Supermaximum prisons could make a small difference to escapes, primarily by providing greater control over staff, and also by potentially identifying inmates who were greater escape risks. But fewer escapes mostly reflected changes in DCS's approach, implemented across the country's 237 prisons (DCS Annual Reports 1994–1997) rather than, only or primarily, the establishment of C-Max (and later Ebongweni).

Indeed, two instances illustrate both the value and limits of hypersecure prisons in preventing escapes. In the first case, Casper Kruger, a convicted murderer whose death sentence was commuted to life imprisonment after *Makwanyane,* was transferred to C-Max in 1997 after he had escaped from custody twice. Kruger successfully challenged the legality of the transfer on procedural grounds and was removed from C-Max (*Nortje en Kruger v. Minister van Korrektiewe Dienste en Andere,* Case No. 213/99, March 16, 2001). After his transfer from C-Max, Kruger escaped again, only to be arrested for car hijacking. While detained at a police station, he obtained a gun, presumably smuggled in by his girlfriend, and shot two officers. He was, however, fatally shot in return fire (Laganparsad 2006). The professional assessment of Kruger as a high escape risk had been entirely vindicated.

The second example highlights the limits of the "perfect escape-proof prison" when staff members are corruptible and negligent. Annanias Mathe was a notorious criminal who was ultimately convicted of "64 charges of rape, indecent assault, attempted murder, aggravated robbery and house-breaking" (Tali and Pongoma 2009). Before his conviction, he escaped from C-Max. Initial claims were that he had escaped "Houdini-like," using Vaseline petroleum jelly to slide through a narrow window. Subsequent investigations revealed that his escape was enabled by a combination of his ingenuity, his bribing of prison staff, and negligent oversight within the prison (e.g., Hosken 2006; Bateman 2007; Daniels 2007a, 2007b). Mathe's escape was not the first from C-Max (e.g., Hosken 2008b), nor is it likely to be the last. The July 2010 murder of a C-Max official after he testified in court about a 2004 attempted escape with fatalities underscores the threat of corruption to the security of supermaximum prisons.[25]

As these two examples show, although very secure prisons are necessary for extremely dangerous and manipulative criminals, if personnel do not follow procedures, high-security approaches are irrelevant. Indeed, a gun in 2004 and cell phones and a screwdriver in 2008 were smuggled into C-Max (Hosken 2008a). Although all controls are vulnerable to inmate challenge and resistance—urine and feces "cocktails" and suicide may be examples of desperate resistance (Buntman 2009a)—successful control ultimately depends more on people than infrastructure. Supermaximum-security prisons alone, or even primarily, will never be a solution to the problem of escapes when guards set inmates free.

Broader Influences on the Decision to Adopt Supermaximum Prisons

The death penalty's end, dangerous inmates, and preventing escapes were the dominant but not the only explanations for the emergence of supermaximum-security prisons. An emerging legal emphasis on human rights, and prisoner rights in particular, interacted with the largely contrary influence of the US supermaximum model, as well as the politics of public opinion, to help set the stage for C-Max and Ebongweni. These influences were complex and often pulled in different directions.

The two South African supermaximum security facilities were strongly modeled on US supermaximum security facilities. Then minister Mzimela spent part of his years in exile (early 1960s through early 1990s) in the United States, where he met up with his future advisors, Golz Wessman and Sishi Mthabela. When Ebongweni was still at a conceptual stage, both Wessman and Mthabela returned to the United States on a study tour, including to a supermaximum security facility in Colorado.[26] Once the idea for Ebongweni was approved, a team including architects was also dispatched to the United States to study supermaximum-security prisons; Ebongweni was ultimately modeled on Marion, a supermaximum prison in Illinois.[27]

South African law and prisoner rights emphases also profoundly shaped the regime, if not the fact, of supermaximum imprisonment. In 1993 the Supreme Court of Appeal (SCA, then known as the Appellate Division) handed down an important prisoner rights judgment (*Minister of Justice v. Hofmeyr*, (3) SA 131 (A), 1993). William Hofmeyr, the plaintiff, contested his conditions of confinement when he was detained for five months in 1988 under then apartheid state of emergency regulations. Hofmeyr's central complaint was that, with two brief exceptions, he had been unlawfully separated from all other prisoners in circumstances amounting to solitary confinement. He also claimed he had been subjected to unlawful treatment in a number of other ways including insufficient exercise, no access to books, magazines, newspapers, or food from outside the prison, insufficient ability to write and receive letters, and insufficient access to radio and television broadcasts. Hofmeyr successfully sued the minister of justice, and the decision was upheld by the SCA on appeal. (At the time South Africa had not yet adopted a new constitution, and the April 1994 democratic elections had not yet taken place.)[28]

As democratic change swept the country, the SCA seized the opportunity in *Hofmeyr* to shape future jurisprudence regarding prisoners' rights under democracy. Drawing on numerous cases, dating back as far as 1912 (i.e., *Whittaker and Morant v. Roos and Bateman*, A.D. 92, 122, 1912), the court dealt extensively with prisoners' rights and in particular with solitary confinement. The judgment cites in approving terms the findings of the lower court: "[T]he segregated manner in which plaintiff was detained for the bulk of his period of detention, the fact that he was not allowed some form of indoor exercise, that he was not allowed access to books and magazines from outside the prison and that he was not allowed some form of access to radio broadcasts constitute wrongful and unlawful conduct as alleged by plaintiff." The SCA clearly stated that "The plain and fundamental rule is that every individual's person is inviolable. . . . The detention to which the plaintiff was subjected constituted an infraction of his basic rights and, in particular, of his right to bodily integrity."

When the DCS decided to establish C-Max, it was very aware of the *Hofmeyr* decision and its implications for solitary confinement, access to the media, and inmate association with other prisoners.[29] By this time, the Interim Constitution had already been adopted, and section 25(1)(b) made it clear that "[e]very person who is detained, including every sentenced prisoner, shall have the right . . . to be detained under conditions consonant with human dignity, which shall include at least the provision of adequate nutrition, reading material and medical treatment at state expense." The 1996 Constitution added "access to exercise" as an additional right (sec. 35(2)(e)).[30] The design and regime of C-Max and Ebongweni had to be guided by the Interim Constitution and the *Hofmeyr* decision.

The security and the daily regime at both prisons were designed in great detail, in particular to adhere to human rights requirements,[31] but things soon started going wrong. The Jali Commission found that the treatment of prisoners at C-Max fell far short of what the Constitution and the legislation required (Jali 2006, vol. 2, chap. 25). Several prisoners testified to the Jali Commission how they were assaulted for no reason, strip-searched in front of female staff, and given electrical shocks by warders using electric shock shields. The commission learned that electric shocks of prisoners in C-Max had become an unofficial but routine "initiation ceremony," reportedly from November 1998, soon after C-Max became operational (Jali 2006, vol. 2, chap. 25, 82). The Jali Commission clearly condemned prisoners' treatment at C-Max: "These prisoners are not treated with dignity. . . . [T]he members of the Department have no respect for prisoners' human rights" (Jali 2006, 95).

Ebongweni was not a focus of the Jali Commission, and there is consequently not the same amount of information available about this particular facility. News reports indicate, however, that all is not well. In August 2009 a fifty-nine-year-old prisoner died there under suspicious circumstances (*News 24* 2009).[32] In July 2010 it was reported that a female warder at Ebongweni was caught engaging in sexual relations with a prisoner for payment of R1,000 (US$150) (*IOL.co.za* 2010c).[33]

Although rights, laws, and the US supermaximum models were influential in the emergence of C-Max and Ebongweni, there is no evidence that terrorism, especially international terrorism, was a factor in creating South Africa's supermaximum prisons. As Mzimela put it, the word "terrorism" "did not even come up."[34] C-Max has certainly been used for political criminals like Eugene De Kock, commander of an apartheid-era South African police force counterinsurgency unit who murdered numerous anti-apartheid activists (see, e.g., Gobodo-Madikizela 2003) and members of the Boeremag, a far-right-wing Afrikaner separatist group.[35] All indications are that domestic vigilante groups like People Against Gangsterism and Drugs (PAGAD), which could be categorized as terrorists, had no or little influence on the establishment of supermaximum facilities.[36] The symbolic and political value of placing an offender like Eugene De Kock in C-Max was not, however, lost on Mzimela. Mzimela recalled that when he learned of De Kock's sentence (to two life sentences and 212 years of imprisonment), he said that C-Max "will be a home for Eugene." But Mzimela framed De Kock's incarceration in terms of the country's mood "for strong action in criminality," rather than the political transition or terrorism. As the only Inkatha Freedom Party (IFP) minister with a security portfolio in the government of national unity, Mzimela felt it was politically important for him to demonstrate he was "tough on crime" and indicate how the IFP would deal with criminals if in power. Mzimela was also concerned with his image among DCS staff members who may have regarded him as a "do-gooder" and "soft on prisoners,"[37] recognizing that, as minister, he needed support from his staff.

More broadly, this "public mood" and whether public opinion played a role in the creation of supermaximum prisons in South Africa is a complex issue to evaluate. Mzimela and Wessman unambiguously dismissed the relevance of public opinion and public pressure in establishing supermaximum facilities.[38] There is no reason to doubt the authenticity and integrity of these dismissals. Both Venter and Mzimela said, in Mzimela's words, that supermaximum facilities were "virtually a natural creation by the circumstances in South Africa." These top correctional officials saw supermaximum facilities as an organic answer to the problems their Department and Ministry confronted, not an external imposition.

Arguably, however, public opinion and politics are as much part of the "circumstances" as escapes or internal management decisions. It is impossible to envisage the pervasive—and justified—national obsession with crime, especially violent crime, *not* influencing the decision. As noted, both the quantity and the violence of crime in South Africa escalated dramatically in the 1990s. A combination of factors pressed the DCS to adopt supermaximum facilities as a solution to some of its problems. The media focus on escapes, widespread public fear about crime combined with "tough-on-crime and criminals" rhetoric from Commissioner Sitole in particular,[39] the direct and indirect influence of other countries experiences, particularly that of the United States with its own tough-on-crime rhetoric, and the advice given to Mzimela by his top advisors shaped DCS's approach toward supermaximum facilities. Although supermaximum prisons have been criticized in South Africa by the Jali Commission, the Human Rights Commission (Dissel 2002), and others, a strong pressure group against supermaximum-security prisons has not emerged in South Africa, indicative of the political acceptability of such prisons.

The tough-on-crime rhetoric and mood competed, competes, and coexists with a strong national emphasis on human rights, and an uneven emphasis on rehabilitation. The coexistence of retributive rage with a concern with rights and root causes of crime is awkward and often contradictory. Understanding this coexistence requires appreciating that post-apartheid South Africa's commitment to the rule of law is in significant part a reaction to apartheid's abuse of rights. (Moreover, apartheid helped to facilitate violent crime.)[40] As Gordon (2006, 250) notes, "The development of a culture of rights was appealing not only as a protection against the authoritarian brutality of the apartheid regime but also as a foundation for building racial, political, and social equality."

Some of the contradictions concerning the place of prison in "the New South Africa" were noted by then deputy president Thabo Mbeki when he gave a speech in 1999 at the site of what would be the Ebongweni prison in Kokstad. Not only did Mbeki analogize apartheid as a prison, but he also noted "the irony of the potential of a prison to unleash such an abundance of opportunities for so many sectors of our society" (Mbeki 1999). The opportunities he referred to were new jobs, enhanced skill development, and black economic empowerment, all intended to result from building this prison.[41]

WHY SUPERMAXIMUM? REHABILITATION, RETRIBUTION, AND SECURITY

The relationship among rehabilitation, retribution, and security in supermaximum confinement remains a persistent question both implied and stated outright by South African correctional officials and policy makers. As a matter of law, supermaximum prisons may not intend additional punishment, as the deprivation of liberty is the punishment.[42] As a matter of policy, DCS officially claims to put rehabilitation front and center of its mission. Rehabilitation efforts are considered possible and necessary even for inmates in supermaximum settings. Indeed, a three-phase program has been developed with the intention to admit inmates into the most restrictive carceral setting but then encourage and enable them to progress to less restrictive settings with greater privileges. Ebongweni's three phases are "Admission, Orientation and Assessment" (phase 1), "Normal Housing and Intervention" (phase 2), and "Preparation for Pre-Integration into Normal Open Maximum Facilities" (phase 3).[43] Providing an informed but anecdotal and cautious support of the idea of rehabilitation in supermaximum settings, Judge Erasmus, a former inspecting judge of prisons, believed inmates could be rehabilitated in supermaximum facilities. Although he was originally an opponent of supermaximum imprisonment, his experience had taught him that the model could and did work on occasion, including because inmates earned amenities to improve their situation ("PMG Report" 2006).

Although rehabilitation is supposed to be a goal of supermaximum prisons, two former ministers of correctional services, Mzimela and Balfour, were skeptical that many or all inmates sent to supermaximum facilities could be rehabilitated. Mzimela argued that a typical C-Max inmate is not capable of rehabilitation and, if given the opportunity, would commit another crime, whether inside or outside of prison.[44] Balfour reminded members of parliament that "not all offenders could be rehabilitated or corrected . . . [the DCS is] not dealing with angels." C -Max and Ebongweni were, he said, "the destination of the completely incorrigible" ("PMG Report" 2007a).[45]

The Jali Commission wanted rehabilitation in supermaximum facilities but believed that was impossible because these prisons were "merely institutions of solitary confinement" (Jali 2006, 351). It condemned supermaximum facilities, doubting that such institutions could "rehabilitate prisoners and correct their behaviour" or whether "such institutions can be defended on any constitutional basis." Rejecting most official explanations for admission to C-Max, the commission believed that the "likelihood is that C-Max Prison is being used as a form of punishment for those who attack officials . . . [rather than] correct general bad behaviour within our prisons" (Jali 2006, 381). The report noted that if the supermaximum facilities were being used as intended, there would be far more gang leaders in those facilities.

Perhaps the Jali Commission's dominant finding regarding C-Max was the enormous gulf between policy and practice.[46] Jali concluded that C-Max—and therefore, presumably Ebongweni—was likely an unconstitutional violation of inmates' rights to, among others, "dignity" and "not to be treated or punished in a cruel, inhumane or degrading way." It identified multiple occasional or routine violations of law and policy in C-Max's administration. The commission's related findings are that supermaximum confinement is unjustified in terms of policy and a violation of human rights, broadly construed. Commenting on the former, the report states, "If the major purpose of the Department [of Correctional Services] is to rehabilitate prisoners and if rehabilitation is not possible at C-Max prison, then there is no justification for the existence of an institution like C-Max Prison *or any similar institution*" (Jali 2006, 367, emphasis added). The commission's conclusion stands in contrast to assessments of Parliament, the courts, DCS, and most public opinion.

COMPARING SUPERMAXIMUM PRISONS IN SOUTH AFRICA AND THE UNITED STATES

The differences between C-Max and Ebongweni are a reminder of both continuities and discontinuities among supermaximum prisons in and beyond South Africa. These two prisons show that supermaximum facilities may be more or less technologically oriented, may be in urban or rural areas, may be large or small, and may focus on sentenced and/or unsentenced inmates. At least compared to US supermaximum prisons—to the extent these numerous state and federal institutions can be aggregated—there are some important differences worth noting.

First, except when they were first built or where there has been a scandal associated with them (e.g., escapes, human rights abuses), South Africa's super-maximum-security prisons have generated a relatively low level of interest among journalists working in various news forms. There is a comparative dearth of reportage about C-Max and Ebongweni beyond high-profile incidents. This low level of interest is surprising because South African journalism is free and assertive, and there is much public interest in crime and punishment.

In contrast, and second, the public right to know about and access to supermaximum prisons in South Africa is greater than for their US counterparts. South Africa has considerable formal oversight of prisons, including supermaximum prisons, most notably by JICS. But other internal and external groups, from a group in the South African navy to the Human Rights Commission to Amnesty International, can visit, do visit, and have visited C-Max and/or Ebongweni with greater access than is likely in the United States.[47]

Third, legal and human rights discourses are ever present for those who made, run, and oppose supermaximum prisons. To identify one of many examples, a DCS chief deputy commissioner commented that "the new generation of high-security prisons were just as secure as C-Max prisons, but much more humane" ("PMG Report" 2007b). In contrast in the United States, the discourse is arguably security first and rights (or even law) a very distant second. The reverse is true in South Africa. As noted above, in the very design of C-Max and in the conceptualization of the regimes and rules of the supermaximum prisons, the respondents interviewed for this study as well as almost all the documentation used—from parliamentary committee minutes to the Jali Commission to the DCS's own materials—put law and human rights sensibilities up front.

Despite this emphasis on rights and law, a fourth difference between South African and American supermaximum prisons is the gap, even chasm, between policy and practice. South Africa's fairly strict protections of inmates' rights in supermaximum facilities (as well as more generally) are frequently, perhaps even more often than not, ignored, as neglect, corruption, and overt abuse rule the day. In contrast, in the United States abuse is more likely to be in the limited legal and constitutional protections inmates are entitled to in the first place, rather than overt flouting of those rules. While illegal abuse certainly occurs in US prisons, including in supermaximum facilities, there is more likely to be conformity with the lax protections and rules that do apply to American inmates. Security tends to be the ultimate justification in the US context, but the same is not true in South Africa. As the Jali Commission noted, "[S]ecurity *per se* cannot justify the existence of Super Maximum Prisons like Pretoria C-Max Prison" (Jali 2006, 365).

In a similar vein, American inmates have greater formal constraints in using courts than do South African inmates. In particular, the Prison Litigation Reform Act, which the US Congress passed in 1996, uses various mechanisms "in order to restrict and discourage litigation by prisoners" (Boston 2004, 5). Despite the formal impediments, American inmates are almost certainly more likely to be able to exercise the limited rights they do have through greater inmate literacy, greater court capacity, a larger network of lawyers supportive of prisoner rights, and so on. It is not that access in the United States is good, but rather that the practical (rather than legal) constraints on inmates in South Africa, in and beyond supermaximum facilities, are so significant.

CONCLUSION

Supermaximum prisons in South Africa were established at great cost but have not lived up to the promises made by their proponents. Although violence in South African prisons in general remains at unacceptable levels, the two supermaximum-security prisons remain underutilized. The DCS has seemingly not found enough prisoners meeting the nebulous requirement of being the "worst of the worst" to fill the facilities. Despite the prisons' underutilization and thus their not being overcrowded, the Jali Commission found extensive evidence of serious human rights violations, especially at C-Max. In this regard, the commission concluded that "[n]o scientific studies nor persuasive evidence have been put before the Commission that justify the establishment of institutions like C-Max or the retention of such detention conditions in our prison system" (Jali 2006, 354). The problems reported with both facilities raise serious questions about their sustainability but also their appropriateness in a prison system that still grapples with deep-seated transformation issues. The history of C-Max, as reflected in the Jali Commission's report, clearly shows a rapid decline in discipline and the maintenance of the carefully designed regime. In many regards, the South African prison system has not yet transformed to reflect the requirements of the Constitution and, more specifically, the aims of DCS's central policy document, the White Paper on Corrections, which places rehabilitation as the core mission of the department. A prison system still struggling with such fundamental challenges seems to be an inappropriate setting for high-tech supermaximum facilities that demand staff and management of high caliber and meticulous adherence to human rights standards.

CHAPTER 8

From "Secondary Punishment" to "Supermax"

THE HUMAN COSTS OF HIGH-SECURITY REGIMES IN AUSTRALIA

David Brown and Bree Carlton

IT IS NOT CLEAR when the term "supermax" was first coined, but the lockdown at Marion prison in Illinois in 1983 is seen by many commentators as a pivotal moment (King 1999, 163). In the Australian context, we would like to draw a longer timeline, linking the emergence of supermax prisons with practices of "secondary punishment" in the early Australian penal colonies, Governor Bathurst's "culture of Salutary Terror" (Evans, 2009, 60) inflicted on convicts transported for an offense in Britain and then convicted of another offense in the colony. Secondary punishment was a form of additional punishment for further offenses such as drunkenness, insolence, refusal to work, absconding, violence, and rebellion and often involved being sent to a usually isolated, secondary punishment station where particularly harsh conditions and regimes prevailed. Governor Darling, reflecting on the reopening of the Norfolk Island penal colony by the British government as a place of detention for the worst criminals and prisoners from the New South Wales (NSW) and Tasmanian penal colonies in 1824, declared: "My object was to hold out that Settlement as a place of the extremest punishment, short of Death" (quoted in Hoare 1969, 36). Norval Morris (2002, 197, emphasis added) notes that the convicts sent to Norfolk Island were "doubly convicted convicts—in the eyes of the time, the worst of the worst, fit to live neither in their homeland nor in a convict settlement where free settlers lived; *the modern parallel is the supermax prison.*"

The key Australian sites of secondary punishment were Macquarie Harbour and Sarah Island (1821–1822), and later Port Arthur (1830) in Van Dieman's Land (Tasmania); Norfolk Island (1824); Port Macquarie (1921) in NSW; and Morton Bay (1824) in Queensland. These sites featured extreme physical isolation and practices of considerable brutality and terror, including ankle irons, extensive flogging, poor diet, spread-eagling (attaching prisoners to rings in cell walls so their arms were spread out and their feet did not touch the ground), use of a wooden gag, heavy labor in chains in inclement conditions, and inadequate clothing, and in Port Arthur, elements of the "silent system," segregation and isolation in solitary and punishment cells without any natural light, modeled on the US penitentiary system (see generally Hughes 1988; Evans 2009).

Locating the roots of supermax in longer-term penal colonial histories of secondary punishment enables a reexamination of the Maconochie reform period on Norfolk Island, which "turned the island from hell to a peaceful settlement for four of its otherwise barbarous years [1840–1844]" (Morris 2002, 192; see generally Maconochie 1845). For Morris (2002, 198), the "deep end of the prison system raises similar problems to those Maconochie confronted in 1840." Speculating on how Maconochie might manage current "dangerous and difficult to handle prisoners," Morris (2002, 201–202, emphasis added) suggests by imposing "the least afflictive control necessary in the light of the threat, and let[ting] each maximum security prison look after its own troublemakers." He argues that "there is simply *no need for a supermax prison or a supermax section of a prison* in any state prison system." While jumping a century into the mid-1900s, it is this challenge to the very existence of supermax regimes that we wish to keep alive in the following case studies of the contemporary uses, misuses, and transitions in high-security prison regimes in the Australian states of NSW and Victoria, the two most populous states in a federal system in which prisons are a state responsibility.

The case studies are of the Goulburn High Risk Management Unit (HRMU) in NSW and Barwon Acacia High-Security Unit in Victoria, the two prisons that in the Australian context are most frequently referred to as "supermax" units, and their respective predecessor high-security units: Grafton and Katingal in NSW and Pentridge H Division and Jika Jika in Victoria. This emphasis on transition enables us to chart the various shifts in the justifications for and disciplinary practices of these regimes, from state control primarily through physical brutality through to experiments with techniques of prolonged isolation and sensory deprivation, to current isolation and incentive-based regimes. This approach highlights resistance that has been mobilized by prisoners, prisoner movement and reform forces generally, against forms of unaccountable power and human rights abuses exercised in these regimes. The last section describes what is new about supermax in Australia, what role terrorism has played in the development of supermax, and the key forms of opposition and resistance to both the current practices associated with high-security units and their expansion, with particular reference to human rights concerns and the production or exacerbation of mental illness.

HIGH-SECURITY REGIMES IN NSW:
FROM GRAFTON "TRACS" TO KATINGAL
TO THE GOULBURN HRMU

Grafton: A Thirty-three-Year "Regime of Terror"

In 1942, following disturbances at a number of NSW prisons, permission was granted to use a section of Grafton gaol, a country prison, as "a special institution for the treatment of recalcitrant and intractable prisoners" (Nagle 1978, 134). The then deputy comptroller of prisons wrote to the undersecretary of justice about the need to recruit "capable, tactful and robust officers," who in light of the "arduous duties" should be paid additional remuneration, termed a "climatic allowance," despite Grafton's favorable climate compared with many other NSW prisons. The Nagle Royal Commission,[1] established after prisoners at Bathurst largely destroyed the gaol in a major riot in 1974, reported in 1978 that the "arduous duties required of these officers largely consisted of inflicting brutal, savage, and sometimes sadistic violence on the hapless group of intractables" who were "deliberately and calculatedly marked out as victims of the *regime of terror* at Grafton" (Nagle 1978, 139, emphasis added).

> The beatings were usually administered by three or four officers wielding rubber batons. . . . A former prison officer, Mr J. J. Pettit, described it: "Sometimes three, four or five of them would assault the prisoner with their batons to a condition of semi-consciousness. On occasions the prisoner urinates, and his nervous system ceases to function normally."
>
> The brutality did not end there; most prisoners were subjected to extreme violence for some days, or even weeks, after their reception at Grafton. For some it never stopped. . . . The prisoners coined their own phrases for Grafton: "S.N.T.," meaning "stark, naked terror." (Nagle 1978, 138–139)

Prisoners were locked in a separate cell for over seventeen hours a day. "The bed was two coir mats [made out of a bristly type of material from which rope is made] on the concrete floor." There was no sewage system in the cells, and prisoners were issued plastic buckets. Each evening a cell search was conducted during which further bashings would be administered "without provocation" or for an offense such as "having dust on the water" in the toilet bucket. Prisoners had to stand and face the back wall of the cell whenever the cell door was opened. No educational courses were available. There were no radios or television and until 1974 no newspapers. Visits were confined to twenty minutes per month, and "many intractables had no visits." There was twenty minutes of exercise a day. An "eyes to the ground" rule was enforced—any prisoner looking at an officer in the face was bashed.

In Grafton several prisoners committed suicide, while many others committed desperate acts of self-mutilation to get away from the place (Nagle 1978). The regime had a brutalizing effect—"one witness produced a list of prisoners who had entered Grafton for committing relatively minor offences, but who later committed extremely serious crimes of violence" (Nagle 1978, 138–144).[2]

The justification given for the Grafton regime, put forward at the Royal Commission by two of its senior officers, was that "it was necessary to inculcate fear into the prisoners from the moment of arrival, and to maintain them in a high state of fear through their stay. Otherwise they would have become uncontrollable" (Nagle 1978, 148). This view was rejected outright by the commission. The unstated argument that sustained its thirty-three-year operation was that a "regime of terror" at Grafton and the reputation and fear it engendered was a useful tool in controlling the rest of the NSW prison population.

Katingal, the "Electronic Zoo": Cost "Too High in Human Terms"

Katingal high-security unit within Sydney's Long Bay prison complex was widely regarded as a replacement for the Grafton regime of physical brutality. The Royal Commission was not able to unravel the exact rationale for Katingal, given "the secrecy with which the Katingal project has been shrouded" (Nagle 1978, 150). It is significant that the commission concluded that "it does appear that concern about containment of terrorism might well have been a substantial reason for Katingal" (Nagle 1978, 152). Nagle described the "attitude of the Department throughout the negotiations and the construction" as "narrow, obstinate, secretive, defensive and, at times, positively misleading" (Nagle 1978, 153). The building was "specifically designed not to allow 'visual access to the outside world'" (Nagle 1978, 155). There was no natural light in the building and only from enclosed exercise yards surrounded by high walls could prisoners see the sky, and then only through roof bars (Nagle 1978, 157). There were eight units with five cells each, each cell with an eyehole for observation. The commission found,

> One of the basic aims of Katingal's designers was to eliminate all possible physical contact between prisoners and officers. All doors in and round the accommodation units are operated electronically, some from a control panel on the gallery, and others from the administration office. Food is provided through a hatch at the back of the cells, and the officers need only come into direct contact with the prisoners if an emergency arises or if prisoners are taken outside their cell blocks. Whenever this happens a minimum of three officers accompany each prisoner. (Nagle 1978, 158)

The department, in its formal written submission to the Royal Commission, listed the following six categories of prisoners intended to be confined at Katingal: those violent toward other prisoners or officers, those unable to fit into the prison community because of behavioral disorders, those who were withdrawn and unpredictable in their relations with others, protection cases at risk from other prisoners, potential escapees, and habitual agitators or "stir- rers" (Nagle 1978, 153).

Programs were minimal, described by Nagle as "devised on some crude Pavlovian theory that inmates would respond to incentives by conforming," while even the superintendant admitted that they would not constitute any incentive to conform, indeed "were not really programs at all, but merely provided a system of graduated amenities" (Nagle 1978, 159). Initially at least there was no physical violence, although on prisoner accounts this changed (Matthews 2006) as relations between prisoners and officers deteriorated and there were numerous disturbances. There was one well-publicized successful escape and an attempted break-in from the outside, which came close to releasing a number of prisoners. Prisoners complained of "boredom; depres- sion; humiliation; and dulling of the mind" (Nagle 1978, 164). Social isolation and sensory deprivation were common complaints of prisoners, backed up by prison psychiatrists (Lucas 1976).

The Nagle Royal Commission recommended that "Katingal should be abandoned . . . It is clear that the cost of Katingal is too high in human terms. It was ill-conceived in the first place, was surrounded by secrecy and defen- siveness at a time when public discussion should have been encouraged. Its inmates are now suffering the consequences" (Nagle 1978, 165). Katingal was closed in 1978, three years after it was opened.[3]

Goulburn HRMU: The "Harm–U"

The Goulburn HRMU—"Harm–U" as prisoners call it—was opened in 2001 by the NSW premier, who stated that it would house "the worst [inmates] in the NSW prison system . . . these are the psychopaths, the career criminals, the violent standover man, the paranoid inmates and gang leaders" (Funnell 2006, 70). The HRMU was built primarily as a high-security unit in a climate of law-and-order politics, with the premier and government pro- claiming the unit as proof of its "tough" stand on law and order, reinforced by selective media access and a fairly constant stream of government and departmental leaks to popular media. The HRMU Management Plan states that it is designed to safely and securely hold inmates "who have been assessed as posing a high risk to the safety of the community, correctional centre staff and/or other correctional inmates or [who] present a serious threat to the security and good order of a correctional centre and a serious threat of escape" (General Purpose Standing Committee [GPSC] 2006, 71). Prisoners can be assigned from other prisons and can be held on remand at the HRMU (as is the case with prisoners charged with terrorist-related offences). The referral process from other prisons can be overridden by the commissioner or appointed delegate. There is no right of appeal against placement in the HRMU, and there is no fixed term. The current commissioner has stated that some prisoners will remain at the HRMU for the rest of their lives (GPSC 2006, 73). Prisoners have been discharged directly from the HRMU. The Department Management Plan lists the following considerations in placement decisions: "escape risk beyond the management capacity of secure correctional centres; high public interest due to extremely serious criminal activities; organising or preparing serious criminal activity whilst in custody; and extreme level of planned and strategic violence" (GPSC 2006, 70).

Upon reception at the HRMU, prisoners are subject to segregated custody and to high levels of restriction and nonassociation. All cells are single and open to a "day room" at the front and a caged yard at the rear. The administration decides whether access will be permitted to the day room and yard. Cells have some natural light through a narrow window, but all air is forced or ventilated. Prisoners not on segregation orders are permitted out of their cells for five and a half hours per day for some limited association with designated prisoners. There are seventy-five cells, and since the unit's opening prisoner numbers have usually ranged between thirty and fifty. The department produces a "behavior management plan" for each inmate, and the management regime runs on a hierarchy of sanctions based on rewards and punishment. The key rewards are access to association with other prisoners, access to exercise facilities, and an increase in access to radios, electric jugs, microwaves, and televisions. There are three levels of regime ranging from near total isolation and no amenities and belongings to restricted association and access to amenities. Prisoners move up and down these levels, increasing or losing access to association and privileges according to staff assessments of behavior. There are very high levels of security throughout the unit, and all visitors are strictly screened, controlled, and searched.

At an NSW Legislative Council Parliamentary Committee inquiry, the NSW Corrective Services Department argued that the effectiveness of the HRMU was evident in a decrease in assault rates (prisoner on prisoner and prisoner on officer) over what might be expected from the inmates contained there and that "were it not for the HRMU, there would be a higher rate of assaults in other correctional centres" (GPSC 2006, 75). The department submitted that "conditions within the HRMU are significantly more humane than those at the former Katingal" (GPSC 2006, 83).

The major complaints of prisoners have revolved around their inability to challenge assignment to the HRMU; the sterile nature of the environment and in particular the lack of natural light and air; the lack of, or limited association with, other prisoners; feelings of claustrophobia and isolation; lack of access to sufficient medical and mental health services; restrictions on and harassment and humiliation of visitors; and the claim that the HRMU operates as a de facto segregation unit while avoiding the legal accountability requirements in legislation (*Sleiman v. CCS* 2009). Some of these complaints have been echoed by outside organizations such as the NSW Council for Civil Liberties (CCL) and were discussed in an NSW Legislative Council Report (NSW Council of Civil Liberties 2008). In its "Shadow Report" prepared for the UN Committee Against Torture of July 27, 2007, the NSW CCL (2008) recommended that "the State party (Australia) invite the UN Special Rapporteur on Torture to visit the supermax prison within a prison (HRMU) at the Goulburn Correctional Centre." The UN Committee Against Torture (UNCAT) in their concluding observations in relation to Australia stated that it was "concerned over the harsh regime imposed on detainees in 'supermax' prisons" and in particular "over the prolonged isolation periods detainees, including those pending trial, are subjected to and the effect such treatment may have on their mental health" (UNCAT 2008, 8, para. 24). The committee recommended that the "State Party should review the regime imposed on detainees in supermaximum prisons, in particular the practice of prolonged isolation" (UNCAT 2008, rec. 24) and that the Australian government should advise how it has addressed this recommendation within one year (UNCAT 2008, rec. 37). It is not known what if anything has been or is being done to comply with this requirement.

HIGH-SECURITY REGIMES IN VICTORIA: FROM PENTRIDGE H DIVISION TO JIKA JIKA TO BARWON MELALEUCA

Pentridge H Division

Victoria's Pentridge Prison's H Division was opened in 1958 to house and segregate Victoria's "worst of the worst" prisoners. H Division's bluestone walls shrouded an archaic military-style regime with regulations that were stringent and dehumanizing. Prisoners wore a military-style uniform and were required to stand at attention on white crosses painted on concrete floors throughout the division. A transfer to H Division often resulted in an indefinite sentence of solitary confinement. Up until the late 1970s prisoners were assigned to breaking rocks in the labor yards while prison officers armed with rifles hovered ominously in the sentry towers above (Jenkinson 1973–1974).

H Division (which prisoners called the "slot") was feared by prisoners because one could spend an indefinite sentence under the harshness of military discipline, solitary confinement, and hard labor (Jenkinson 1973–1974, 82). In addition to the harsh conditions and solitary confinement, prisoners alleged that a daily regime of beatings by groups of prison officers, popularly dubbed the "bash," served as routine "disciplinary" practice to break violent or "difficult" prisoners into submission and compliance (Jenkinson 1973–1974). Prisoners also alleged they were subject to various forms of terror, sadistic and degrading treatment, sexual humiliation, and harassment by officers during their time in H Division (Jenkinson 1973–1974; Mooney 1982). Throughout the 1970s H Division triggered unfavorable publicity and public concern arising from protests and a series of inquiries into alleged abuses (Jenkinson 1973–1974). Also during this time, the Jenkinson Inquiry was commissioned in the early 1970s to investigate prisoner allegations of brutality. The Jenkinson report subjected the H Division to public scrutiny and did confirm there were *individual* episodes of brutality against prisoners. However, the Jenkinson report did not bring about the marked shift away from physical violence achieved in NSW by the Nagle Royal Commission through its finding of systemic violence in Grafton as Victorian prisoners reported that the regime of terror and violence continued into the late 1970s and 1980s (Minogue 1994; Edney 2006).

Jika Jika

Following a decade of prisoner resistance and staff brutality in H Division, the Pentridge Jika Jika High-Security Unit opened in 1980 to hold the system's "worst" male prisoners. In contrast to H Division, Jika Jika (also known as "Jika"), which won an architectural award, was designed to "minimize violence" through the physical separation of prison staff and prisoners and the use of remote-controlled doors and functions. A protracted period of managerial dysfunction, institutional disorder, and violence ensued. Initially dubbed an "escape-proof" and humane modern facility for high-risk prisoners, Jika was in practice geared toward total containment. Between 1980 and 1987 there were multiple escapes, escape attempts, assaults, murders, prisoner campaigns, protest actions, barricades, fires, hunger strikes, acts of self-harm, attempted suicides, and prisoner allegations of misconduct and brutality by prison staff (Carlton 2007). The impact of the harsh high-security environment on both staff and prisoners produced polarized relationships and an escalating atmosphere of tension. The pressure created exacerbated an intense sense of fear and paranoia, while giving rise to a predatory culture of psychological and physical violence between prisoners and between officers and prisoners. In October 1987 matters escalated, and in an act of desperation a group of prisoners built a barricade and lit a fire to draw attention to conditions inside. Five of the prisoners died when officers were unable to free them in time. The protest fire was preceded by two prisoner deaths (one of them a remand prisoner). Both occurred in controversial circumstances and within two days of one another in different units. During 1987, the seven deaths that occurred in Jika represented 38.8 percent of the total number of deaths in the Victorian prison system during that year, in a division that on average represented only 1.4 percent of the Victorian prison population (Office of Corrections Victoria 1987–1988).

In 1987, seven years after Jika first opened, Attorney General Jim Kennan publicly referred to Jika as a "dehumanising electronic zoo" (*Herald,* October 30, 1987). During this time, Prisoners Action Group (a prison activist group) spokesperson Jeff Lapidos publicly revealed he had obtained statistics through Freedom of Information documenting 2,500 incidents in Jika between 1985 and 1987 that were serious enough to report to the attorney general (*Herald,* January 31, 1987). The Jika protests and deaths are well documented through the campaigning and activism of a core group of prisoners housed in Jika during this time (Carlton 2007, 2009). The inquest files into the deaths of the seven men who died in Jika during 1987 document prisoner concerns about the oppressive conditions of lockdown in a sensory-deprived environment, the arbitrary and unaccountable exercise of power by authorities in classification and decision making and the meting out of discipline within the division, alleged "mind games" by prison staff, and brutal assaults by both prison staff and fellow prisoners. Jika Jika was closed in 1988 after operating for eight years.

The Barwon High-Security Wings: Acacia and Melaleuca

Jika Jika was succeeded by the High-Security Acacia Unit in Barwon prison near Geelong in Victoria. While Acacia did not have the high-tech features of Jika such as electronic doors and remote controls, it provided a high level of security and has been subject to a range of prisoner complaints about inappropriate and unaccountable prisoner placement decisions and the unmitigated use of violence, isolation, and in some cases shackles by prison staff (Derkley 1995).

In 2007, the Acacia high-security section was used to house a group of twelve unconvicted prisoners charged with preparatory-type offences connected with terrorism. They were held in Acacia for at least two years while awaiting and attending trial until a landmark Supreme Court decision led to their transfer out of high security to the Metropolitan remand center. In spite of being unconvicted remand prisoners, they were subject to an A1 security rating, the highest that can be allocated to a prisoner incarcerated in the state of Victoria, higher than the vast majority of high-security prisoners who had been convicted and classified within the system. Corrections Victoria could provide little information to justify this, and the classification decision itself was said to be informed in large part by a file of newspaper clippings (*The Australian,* March 22, 2007). The A1 rating involved lockdown in sensory deprivation conditions, constant surveillance, the use of shackles and strip searches, and the removal of privileges (*R v. Benbrika and ors,* VSC 80, 9–11, paras. 28–38). The men were confined in their cells for twenty-plus hours every day and allowed only one box visit with their families per week and one contact visit per month. In an application for bail made on behalf of the accused in 2007, Justice Bongiorno remarked that the

> conditions in Acacia Unit in Barwon prison are such as to pose a risk to the psychiatric health of even the most psychologically robust individual. Close confinement, shackling, strip searching and other privations to which the inmates at Acacia Unit are subject all add to the psychological stress of being on remand, particularly as some of them seem to lack any rational justification. This is especially so in the case of remand prisoners who are, of course, innocent of any wrongdoing. (*Raad v. DPP*, VSC 330, 3, para. 6)

An A1 security rating also resulted in stringent security procedures for the transportation of the defendants from Barwon in Geelong to court in Melbourne, a distance of seventy-two kilometers. These involved frequent strip searches at each point of transfer between van, court cells, and the courtroom. After the commencement of trial, prisoners regularly reported experiencing disorientation, travel sickness, fatigue, and confusion after their time in the van, which affected their ability to concentrate in court and thus to take part in their own defense. In 2008, Supreme Court Justice Bongiorno ruled that the Department of Corrections had failed to provide any evidence to justify a high-security classification in this case. It is significant that he ruled that the men were being subjected to an unfair trial due to the conditions of their incarceration (*R v. Benbrika and ors*, VSC 80, 25, para. 91). The Supreme Court ruling underlined the human rights implications stemming from the long-term incarceration of unconvicted prisoners in conditions of extreme hardship and the corrosive impact of these on due process, particularly the ability to receive a fair trial. The case was significant in that it was the first time that the conditions of incarceration and treatment of prisoners were linked to the right to a fair trial (Carlton and McCulloch 2008).

More recently, and in spite of Acacia's existence, the A\$8 million Melaleuca High-Security Unit was constructed and marketed by Corrections Victoria officials as a "superprison," the most secure prison in Australia, designed to hold those classified with an A1 security rating, primarily high-profile figures in the gangland wars and the state's remanded terror suspects and convicted terrorists.

LOOKING BEHIND GLOBALIZED "POLICY TRANSFER": WHAT IS "NEW" ABOUT "SUPERMAX" IN AUSTRALIA?

There are a number of difficulties in attempting to delineate what if any aspects of the series of high-security regimes in NSW and Victoria outlined above are manifestations of a US-inspired globalized convergence toward supermax regimes brought about by "policy transfer," and what aspects are simply reconfigurations of long-established local traditions in high security, punishment, and "trac" regimes, a "progression" from overt physical brutality to isolation-based sensory-deprivation regimes. One difficulty is that the definition of supermax is a "generic descriptor . . . applied to a wide variety of facilities and programs handling an equally wide variety of inmate populations" (Riveland 1999, 5), or, to put it more broadly, the term has taken on a cultural and political life of rich signification. Then there are the relatively small numbers of prisoners contained in special high-security regimes, small by US standards, as in Britain and Europe (King 1999), and minuscule compared to the estimated 25 percent of Australian convicts who endured secondary punishment. Furthermore, the justifications for supermax regimes vary widely; the reported need for supermax facilities across US states varies from 0 to 20 percent prison bed capacity. The relationship between "supermax" and disciplinary and/or administrative segregation also varies widely, as do the criteria for placement, the exact form of the regimes, the length of stay, and the terms of release (Riveland 1999, 4). Many of these issues have been demonstrated in the NSW and Victorian case studies, for example, the complaint that the HRMU classification is being used to subvert accountability mechanisms attaching to formal segregation orders, the inclusion of unconvicted remand prisoners, and the rather eclectic mix of prisoners assigned to high security, including notorious criminals and "celebrity" inmates. Such examples serve to illustrate the highly political characterization of "risk" used to classify prisoners into high-security regimes.

It is difficult to obtain information detailing specific technology, design, hardware, practices, programs, or regimes that can be shown to be recent imports into Australian high-security units directly from the United States by way of policy transfer, apart from the label "supermax" itself. The use of orange jump suits for certain high-security prisoners, the adoption of particular sorts of shackles, new classifications of prisoners, and increased electronic and other surveillance may have been influenced by US developments, although some of these may have happened anyway; some, such as the shackles, have long local pedigrees (Derkley 1995). Nor is "policy transfer" a new phenomenon. In the convict period, leading colonial governors and prison administrators were well versed in international debates in penal philosophy, the relative merits of Bentham's Panopticon, and the "silent" or "separate" systems. It is in the link between supermax and terrorism that the globalizing convergence argument gains some force.

The Influence of International and Domestic Terrorism on the "Supermax" Phenomenon

While the first mention of "terrorism" as a justification for Australian high-security prison regimes appears to be the discussion in the Nagle

Commission of the possible reasons for building Katingal, it is important to recall that "terror" has been central to our account. "Terror," often in capitals, was openly and consciously invoked by leading British politicians and colonial administrators as a conscious aim of secondary punishment. This is the "Terror" discussed by Douglas Hay and others (Hay et al. 1975; Thompson 1975), a strategy of class rule in which control was exercised over the poor through a bloody penal code, exemplary hangings, "the lessons of Justice, Terror and Mercy" (Hay et al. 1975, 63), and "the extremest punishment short of Death" inflicted in convict secondary punishment sites. State "terror" openly invoked was seen as a necessary weapon to discipline convict labor and to secure beyond it the class relations, system of ownership, wealth creation, and power upon which colonialism depended. Terror was, as we have seen, also central to the Grafton "trac" regime, described as a "regime of terror" by Royal Commissioner Nagle, and a similar characterization is arguably applicable to Pentridge H Division and Jika Jika. These units were sites of state terror, exercised largely in secret, no longer aimed at shoring up either convict labor or wider class relations but justified as necessary to keep a minority of "intractables" or the "worst of the worst" under control and to provide a deterrent to resistance in the wider prison system.

To shift to the contemporary scene, terrorism and the technologies of risk and the politics of fear it engenders have distorted domestic criminal justice processes through a marked politicization,[4] manifest in overreaching claims of executive sovereignty, lack of respect for the separation of powers, political trumping of judicial decisions, and the use of the criminal process, the courts, and the correctional system as a form of political theater.

Aside from this generalized politicization of criminal justice, the risks perceived to flow from the imprisonment of inmates charged with or convicted of terrorist-related offences has added a national security–based justification to the existence and conduct of high-security regimes. Again, evidence of specifics is very hard to uncover given the secrecy surrounding national security developments, but risks associated with terrorism seem to have affected not just the high-security end of domestic prison regimes. The design of new prisons has been influenced by the requirement that they be strengthened against *external* attack as well as internal revolts, hostage taking, and escapes, and that the capacity to seal off sections of prisons be enhanced.

New classifications have been introduced in several states; in NSW, for example, AA (men) and category 5 (women) classifications were introduced in the Crimes (Administration of Sentences) Regulation 2001 (Reg. 22): "the category of inmates who, in the opinion of the Commissioner, represent a special risk to national security (for example, because of a perceived risk that they may engage in, or incite other persons to engage in, terrorist activities) and should at all times be confined in special facilities within a secure physical barrier that includes towers or electronic surveillance equipment." Long-standing techniques such as strip searching have become more frequent and intrusive, not just in high-security sections (Minogue 2005). While this has a longer local history, particularly in relation to women (George and McCulloch 2008), it is arguable that a range of disciplinary and security practices associated with supermax are seeping into the mainstream prison system and being normalized. Strip searching of women prisoners is more common and takes on the character of "sexual assault by the state." Craig Minogue, a long-term Victorian prisoner, reports that in 2001–2002, 18,889 strip searches were conducted on the 202 women at Deer Park Prison, with one reported finding of contraband. Of 130,000 strip searches on all Victorian prisoners in 2001–2002, contraband, mainly tobacco, was discovered in 0.1 percent of searches (Minogue 2005, 70–71). Frequent urine testing has been stepped up. According to Minogue, cell extractions have taken on an increasingly militarized character, involving a team of prison officers well equipped with "protective clothing, riot gear and gas masks," ready to use handcuffs, large electrical ties, and capsicum spray, the effects of which he graphically describes (Minogue 2005). DNA samples are taken by force if prisoners are not compliant. There has been a significant upgrading of security and installation of high-tech security devices, including forms of biometric identification of visitors. Tighter restrictions are evident on access to communications, visitors, and reading matter, and there is increased concern about mobile phones and access to religious practice.

Further research is necessary to discover the extent to which there are links between these developments and US supermax practices. Probably the clearest example of "national security" and "terrorism" concerns affecting high-security prison regimes in Australia is the strengthening relationship between prison management and police, military, security, and intelligence agencies, especially in relation to concerns over "radicalization" in prison (Australian Federal Police [AFP] 2006). This has included holding a national conference on prison radicalization and the establishment of a Leadership in Criminal Intelligence Program within AFP and a Countering Violent Extremism Unit in the Federal Attorney General's Department. There has been some rather sensationalist media coverage of the issue of "conversions" of prisoners to Islam and potentially to terrorist sympathies (especially in relation to Goulburn HRMU). The tenor of some of the media concerns can be seen from the headings of articles: "Hard Men Turn to Islam to Cope with Jail, Goulburn's Super Mosque" (*Sydney Morning Herald,* November 18, 2005), "Inmates Studying al-Qaeda Manual" (*Sydney Morning Herald,* December 2, 2007), "Prisons 'Terrorist Breeding Grounds'" (*The Age,* July 26, 2006).

HUMAN COSTS OF HIGH-SECURITY REGIMES

There is a raft of evidence confirming the serious psychological and physical health effects associated with solitary confinement (Haney and Lynch
1997, 514; King 2005; Physicians for Human Rights 2005, 59). The case
studies above have been replete with the human costs of the specific NSW
and Victorian high-security regimes, including significant numbers of deaths
in custody; widespread trauma and mental illness; self-harm; suicides; brutal-
ization of prisoners and staff; killings of other prisoners and staff; and the
reproduction of a cycle of violence, some of which is later acted out on citizens after high-security inmates have been released. Bernie Matthews (a
repeat escapee who later wrote a book about his experiences at Grafton and
Katingal), while in Katingal with access to a typewriter in 1976, worked on a
much-cited submission to the Nagle Royal Commission detailing numerous
individual cases that demonstrated the ways that violence experienced by
predominantly young male property offenders in prison regimes such as the
Grafton "tracs" ("intractables"—prisoners classified by correctional authorities as escape prone, violent, troublesome, or notorious) was later recycled in
crimes of extreme violence.

The pattern that emerges from the transition from one type of high-
security regime to another is that of a cycle of resistance and violence. Prisoner
resistance to high-security regimes in prisons such as Grafton and Pentridge
H Division, marked by extreme physical brutality and deprivation that eventually become discredited and untenable, leads to the "solution" being seen
as the provision of new, modern facilities. In the name of security and control rather than hyperpunishment, the new regime seeks to minimize contact
between prison officers and prisoners; achieve high levels of security from
escape through a battery of new technology and prison design features; effect
prolonged isolation in highly artificial conditions; make prisoners dependent
on prison officers for the most basic functions and needs; prevent the classification of prisoners to the unit from being challenged or made accountable,
thereby maximizing the power of prison administrators unfettered by the
courts; and minimizing media, family, legal, and support group access to the
unit in an attempt to remove its operation from public debate and scrutiny
(Brown 2009, 165–171). The attempt to curb resistance through more strategic and differentiated control mechanisms less reliant on overt physical
violence ultimately fails as it generates new forms of resistance, some collective, some individual and inverted, as the spaces for and possible tactics of
resistance are reshaped by the new forms of power and control.

The key to breaking the cycle of resistance and violence evident in the
history of high-security units is a strategy of making any exercise of power
open to independent external scrutiny through enhanced inspection and

accountability mechanisms such as an independent prison inspector and official visitors schemes, along with a recognition that prisoners are or should be full legal subjects with access to the courts, whatever they have done to lead to their confinement or subconfinement into a high-security section; subjects capable and entitled to contest the forms of power exercised over them; entitled to exercise what one of the authors has called "discursive citizenship," an ability to take part in media, political debate, and community debate (Brown 2002, 2008, 2009). Regimes that are open to inspection, critique, and redress are reflexive in relation to their practices and are the most likely to be able to break out of or short-circuit the cycle of recrimination, hostility, protest, and violence.

CONCLUSION

The struggle is to shift high-security prison regimes from a reliance on isolation to fostering social relationships between prisoners and staff, family, visitors, lawyers, and community groups; to render the regimes routinely accountable and open to scrutiny; and to recognize their inhabitants as political subjects exercising a discursive citizenship. These endeavors are made more difficult by the invocation of risk discourses associated with terrorism and national security as justifications for the existence and practices of high-security prison regimes. To that extent, accounts of high-security regimes that emphasize novel features and see evidence of US-led policy transfer (evident in the now-ubiquitous orange Guantánamo jump suits) and globalized convergences produced by the "war on terror" have increasing purchase. And yet it is also important to dwell on continuities and transitions rather than solely on ruptures: on old conflicts like those between concentration or dispersal, legal authorization or administrative discretion, the "extremest punishment short of death" or developing human potential, the possibilities of redemption or lifelong damnation. For struggles in and against these sites of terror and abuse, to "bring power to particular account" (Thompson 1987, 167) and challenge both the production of madness, rage, and violence through isolation and the self-justifying logic that then cites this very madness, rage, and violence as reasons such regimes are necessary, are, like prison struggle generally, rarely waged at a global level. They are waged locally, where, as Maconochie showed, it is possible to bring about the transformation of a secondary punishment convict outpost like Norfolk Island, set up as the most extreme sanction (Hughes 1988, 641), or to force the closure of a Grafton, a Katingal, a Pentridge H Division, a Jika Jika (as supermax units "have been closed or significantly reduced in size in Michigan, Indiana, Wisconsin, Ohio, and Minnesota": Eisenman 2009, 11), even if such transformations are reversed, as Maconochie's was, and even if such closures are achieved at great human cost and spur the creation of yet another reconfigured high-security regime. To the extent that some of the critiques of supermax tend to locate it as one "constitutive" element in the "Statecraft of Global Americana" (Rodriguez 2008, 189, 188), they serve to obscure rather than illuminate both the variable local forces of opposition and resistance and Captain Maconochie's and Norval Morris's challenges to the very existence of supermax prisons.

CHAPTER 9

The Emergence of the Supermax
in New Zealand

Greg Newbold

IT HAS BEEN SAID THAT the era of the modern "supermax" began in 1979, when the Federal Bureau of Prisons (BOP) designated a special "level 6" security category for USP Marion, in southern Illinois (Ross 2007b). Although Marion had been constructed during a relatively liberal era in American corrections and provided a range of programs to its 350 inmates, a series of escape attempts, serious assaults, and the murders of ten inmates and two staff in the early 1980s led to a state of emergency declaration in October 1983 and general lockdown. The institution remained locked down until 2007, when it ceased to function as a maximum-security facility. During its lockdown years, Marion provided only basic services to its top-security prisoners (Haney 2005). The reasons for Marion's lockdown and the level 6 designation have been widely discussed (e.g., Consultants' Report 1985; Shalev 2009).

Six years after Marion opened, in March 1969, New Zealand commissioned a new maximum-security prison at Paremoremo, twenty miles north of its largest city, Auckland (population one million). The prison was built based on the telegraph-pole design, as the architects of what is now known as Auckland Prison East Division (colloquially termed Paremoremo Maximum or Parry Max) had used USP Marion as a model for their own design. Utilizing the most sophisticated technology available at the time, Paremoremo, when it opened, was one of the most advanced and physically secure institutions in the world.

Despite the security emphasis, for most of its first two decades Paremoremo epitomized correctional liberalism, offering a wide variety of programs, services, and facilities to its two hundred prisoners. The current author was incarcerated there during this progressive period and studied for an MA degree. After 1984, however, facilities began to decline sharply, reaching a nadir in 1989. Since this point, Paremoremo prison, like Marion, has been on lockdown status, with prisoners contained in their cells upward of 21.5 hours a day and their movement highly restricted. Security is paramount, there is no work availability for inmates, and convicts are escorted by staff whenever they leave their cell landings. The management of this maximum-security facility today is in complete contrast to what it was thirty years ago. The purpose of this chapter is to explain the decision to build Paremoremo and to show why it was gradually transformed from a liberally run exemplar of correctionalism in the 1970s to one of model custodialism in the 2000s. As will be seen, the history of the prison in many ways follows, and was influenced by, that of Marion. However, the dynamics of Paremoremo also differ from those of American supermaxes in several important respects.

ESTABLISHMENT OF PAREMOREMO

Although the building of a new maximum-security prison had been contemplated for some time, it was a destructive three-day riot at the eighty-five-year-old top-security prison at Mount Eden, Auckland, in July 1965 that prompted the New Zealand government to expedite the construction of a replacement. The new facility was designed and built during one of the most progressive decades in the nation's correctional history (Newbold 2007), and this atmosphere pervaded its planning. The philosophy behind the institution was that very high levels of physical security would permit a wide range of activities and programs within a safe perimeter. Accordingly, the prison's five cell blocks (A, B, C, D, and Classification—known as "Class") contained only forty-eight men each, in single internal cells. Bars were made of hardened cutting-tool-proof steel, cell doors were opened remotely, and access to cell blocks and other key areas was via electronic sally ports, operated from an armor-plated central control unit equipped with closed-circuit television and an intercom. Prisoners never ventured outside the cell blocks for recreation, but each block had daily access to its own concrete exercise yard, enclosed by twenty-foot-high grapple-proof walls with electric trip wires. The entire complex was surrounded by high, twin, close-mesh fences with unarmed sentry towers on each corner, manned twenty-four hours a day.

During its four years of construction, the minister of justice provided regular progress reports to the media, emphasizing the secure nature of the place and the high standard of amenities that would be provided. The cells would be light and airy, each equipped with a flush toilet, hot and cold running water, and a three-station radio. The twelve-man cell block landings would have two showers each for the men to use at will, and there would be showers in the yards as well. Six fully equipped workshops would provide training in furniture making, boot making, and tailoring. Inmates would have daily access to a modern gymnasium, with a sprung wooden floor and a fully equipped weight room to the side. A large library would be provided, as would a range of educational programs. Prisoners would be permitted contact visits for up to two hours a week in a room monitored by cameras. Everything possible would be done to address the rehabilitative needs of the country's top two hundred security risks while keeping the public safe (Newbold 1989).

The Early Years

Notwithstanding the best of intentions, the facility got off to a rocky start. The first superintendent was Edward "Ted" Buckley, who had been in charge of Mount Eden Prison at the time of the 1965 riot. Despite being supplied with clear written instructions to relax discipline and introduce programs, Buckley was nervous and insecure, opting instead to run the prison on tight rein. Believing that authority, discipline, and austerity constituted the best medicine for unruly men, he restricted freedoms by imposing numerous petty rules, blocking programs, and discouraging informal relations between inmates and staff. This, combined with inconsistent management, breakdowns in communication at all levels, and a general failure to control rising stress factors, led to rebellion. Deliberately lit fires, flood-outs, destruction of government property, strikes, and assaults on staff became endemic features of prison life. Prisoners stood together in a campaign of resistance, and several earned lengthy extensions to their sentences. Employee morale plummeted, and retaliatory inmate baiting commenced, which exacerbated tensions. Finally, a six-hour siege in 1970, during which staff hostages were threatened with death, prompted the formation of a pro-inmate pressure group in Auckland called Project Paremoremo, which in 1971 campaigned for, and finally secured, an ombudsman's inquiry. Buckley was then sidelined, and a new superintendent, Jack Hobson, took over in March 1972 (Newbold 1989).

The Liberal Era

The son of a Lancashire (England) policeman, Jack Hobson had served as a gunner in the British Navy before emigrating to New Zealand after the war. Following a brief stint in the New Zealand Army, he joined the Prison Service in 1948 and rose quickly through the ranks, becoming superintendent of Waikune Prison in 1961, of Wi Tako in 1964, and of Mount Eden in 1969. Next to Paremoremo, Mount Eden was the most secure institution in the country, and when Hobson put down a rebellion there in 1971 by ordering his men to fire pistols at inmates' legs, he was confirmed as the obvious successor to Buckley.

Hobson was an entirely different man to Buckley, and his arrival is associated with one of the most tranquil periods in the prison's history. His general philosophy was to allow as much freedom and as many programs as possible without compromising security, provided the prison ran smoothly. However, as he had demonstrated at Mount Eden, Hobson was prepared to take summary steps to keep the prison under control.

Within a few weeks of arriving, Hobson had emptied out the segregation block (D Block), and begun relaxing discipline and introducing programs. Prisoners were unlocked for thirteen hours a day and allowed to use the gymnasium every weeknight and during the day on weekends. The yards were opened at lunch hour during the week and all weekend. Prisoners were allowed to paint their cells as they wished and to decorate them with fancy curtains, bedspreads, wall hangings, and nonregulation furniture. Potted plants, canaries, and goldfish were permitted. Inmates took pride in their cell blocks and identified with them. Accordingly, brass fittings and floors were polished daily, and the toilets, showers, and dining rooms were kept spotless. Education programs started, and prisoners who showed commitment were relieved of work duties and allocated full-time study instead. On Friday evenings, inmate-organized interblock football competitions took place. Over the Christmas–New Year period, intra- and interblock sporting competitions were organized by prisoners, with prizes provided by management.

Contact visits were allowed half a day on Saturdays, and during the week, a number of official visitors ran programs and clubs. There was a Maori (indigenous) culture club, sporting clubs with outside teams competing in basketball and badminton, a weight lifting club, and a variety of night classes. There were occasional concerts from top New Zealand rock bands, and one Sunday the Harlem Globetrotters, who were touring New Zealand, visited the institution to put on a basketball display. The prison's showpiece was its debating society. Paremoremo became part of the Auckland Debating Association's annual competition, with ADA teams coming in weekly to debate. Coached by Geoff Greenbank, retired principal of King's College, an elite private school, and Don McKinnon (later Sir Donald), who went on to become deputy prime minister and then secretary general of the British Commonwealth, Paremoremo's teams succeeded on several occasions in winning the B and, later on, the prestigious A grade competitions.

Morale during this period, which lasted until the end of the 1970s, was high. Prisoners and staff were often on first-name terms, and among themselves inmates referred to Superintendent Hobson as "Uncle Jack." Assaults on staff were rare, and serious incidents were uncommon. Apart from one escape and odd confrontations, the prison ran on a predictable and even keel. There was no prisoner hierarchy to speak of; in fact, prisoners actively rejected it, denouncing inmates who attempted to dominate others as "policemen" or "screws." Thus, bullying ("standing over") was scorned, and homosexual rape was considered unspeakable. The prison held a small number of gang members, but because the inmate code banned gang identification, it was difficult to tell who was whom. Newcomers were told by residents, "In here you're not a gang member. You're an inmate." The atmosphere within the cell blocks was, for the most part, relaxed, cooperative, and benign, with the adage "do your own lag" frequently repeated. The "old lags," veterans of the rebellious "dark days" of Ted Buckley, counseled newcomers about the struggles of the past, about the importance of inmate solidarity, and about advantages of reasonable cooperation with the new regime. The quality of life at Paremoremo was such that many resisted transfer to less secure institutions and often had to be cajoled into leaving once classified to medium security.

Hobson, for his part, applied a "firm but fair" management style, which was emulated by his senior staff. He appointed nonuniformed divisional officers to each of the cell blocks to handle day-to-day governance, but his door was open to any man to discuss any issue alone and in confidence at any time. Requests were dispatched expeditiously, with explanations given in cases of refusal. Conflicts between prisoners and staff were resolved quickly and impartially. Disciplinary infractions were dealt with quickly. Serious problems brought up to two weeks of solitary confinement, and more troublesome inmates were removed to indefinite segregation in D Block. When tensions built up and threatened to boil over—as they did following a stabbing in 1975—the whole prison was locked down for several days and cells were stripped back to regulation furnishing. They remained that way until order returned. Thus, the advantages of tranquillity were reinforced (Newbold 1989).

Different Times

In spite of its obvious benefits, the entente cordiale at Paremoremo did not last. In the 1980s, conditions began to swing irrevocably for the worse. Part of the reason had to do with changes in the inmate composition. During the mid-1970s there were only about 2,600 prisoners in New Zealand, which then had a total population of about 3.1 million. Paremoremo was the country's only maximum-security facility, but because there were not enough maximum-security classifications to fill it, many of its inmates (such as the author of this chapter) were medium-security men who requested to remain at Paremoremo because of the better conditions and the opportunities on offer.

Nationally, New Zealand crime levels in the 1970s were considerably lower than, and different from, what they became later on. Illegal drugs had become recognized as a problem in the late 1960s, but the first significant heroin busts did not occur until 1975. That year, six hundred drug-dealing offenses were reported, and a number of sentences exceeding half of the maximum possible fourteen years were given for drug dealing. But overall, sentences of such length were rare: of the fifty-three hundred offenders sent to prison in 1975, only twenty-three got finite terms of seven years or more (Department of Statistics 1976). The current author, sentenced to seven and a half years in 1975 for selling heroin, was typical of these. All prisoners were eligible for automatic release on remission at two-thirds of sentence. Thirteen prisoners received life imprisonment for murder in 1975 but became parole eligible by law after seven years.

Gangs were still in their infancy (e.g., Dennehy and Newbold 2001), organized crime was virtually absent (Newbold 2009), and a good proportion of the longer drug-dealing sentences were given to young middle-class dilettantes who, like all others sentenced to two years or more, commenced their sentences in maximum security.

Levels of serious violence, which had risen during the 1960s, stabilized during the 1970s and were low compared to those in later years. For example, in 1975 there were 20 reported murders, 15 attempted murders, and 15 manslaughters in New Zealand. That year, 300 robberies were reported to the police, about 100 grievous assaults, and 258 rapes (*Appendices to the Journals of the House of Representatives* G.6 [NZ Police Annual Report] 1976, 20–21). Of the 5,300 individuals sent to prison, over 300 were jailed for drugs, 560 for nonsexual violence, 110 for robbery, and 38 for rape. The majority of those jailed (2,600) were for nonviolent crimes. Two-thirds were under the age of twenty-five (Department of Statistics 1976). No data are available for 1975, but in 1972, of 2,500 sentenced prisoners, only 552, or 22 percent, were doing time for violent or sexual crimes. The majority—more than 60 percent—were in prison for property offenses (Department of Justice 1975).

Although the maximum-security prison contained more violent and long-term offenders than the incarcerated population at large, the average prisoner in New Zealand in 1975 was younger, doing a shorter sentence, was less likely to be imprisoned for violence, and was less likely to be gang affiliated than was the situation in later decades. These factors affected the atmosphere and culture of the prisons of the day. As the profile of crime and the society in which it took place changed, so did the world of the prison.

Economic Change

During the early 1970s, unemployment was less than 2 percent of the workforce. The economy was buoyant and wages were relatively high. The period known as the postwar "long boom" began to end with upheavals in OPEC, which saw sudden escalations in oil prices in 1973 and 1979. Massive government borrowing to fund a flawed "Think Big" steel and petrochemical self-sufficiency strategy caused public debt to soar from NZ$8.6 million in 1975 to NZ$8.2 billion in 1984 (Sinclair 1988). Unemployment reached 6.8 percent by 1986. Laissez-faire economic policies introduced after a change of government in 1984 led to a brief investor boom, but failing smaller businesses caused unemployment to keep rising (Russell 1996). After the global stock market crash of October 1987, a number of large enterprises failed as well, exposing a series of multimillion-dollar frauds, assisting unemployment to peak at 11 percent of the workforce by 1993.

The era of rising unemployment and fiscal uncertainty was associated with complex changes in offending patterns in New Zealand, particularly in the area of violence. Between 1975 and 1995, reported violent offending grew by over 300 percent. Of greatest concern for prisons were increases in serious violence, with reported homicides up 50 percent, rapes up 69 percent, robberies up 460 percent, and reported serious assaults up by more than 2,000 percent.

Another change in the twenty years after 1975 was the emergence of endemic and organized drug dealing. An early foray into systematic drug importation known as the "Mr Asia" gang operated briefly in New Zealand in 1974 and 1975 but ended with the imprisonment of some members and movement of others to Australia (see Booth 1980; Hall 1981; Newbold 2004; Shepherd 2010). In the 1980s, coinciding with economic recession and rising violent crime, gang membership burgeoned, assisted by government-funded work schemes that some gangs were able to exploit at a huge profit. By this time some gangs had already begun dealing in drugs, and closure of the lucrative work schemes in 1986 boosted commercial drug activity. Initially the main focus was marijuana, but by the early 1990s methamphetamine had started becoming popular. Selling for around NZ$800 a gram, pure methamphetamine generated extraordinary profits. Observing this, gangs delved deeper into the manufacture and distribution of pure meth (known as "P"), becoming central players in the trade. Gang membership was an attractive source of money and prestige, drawing young recruits in large numbers. Many of these men ended up in prison with long sentences for violence or drug dealing (Dennehy and Newbold 2001).

SENTENCING AND PRISONS

Within the community, exploding levels of violent offending accompanied by media coverage of crimes of uncommon brutality led to calls for tougher sentencing and restrictions on early release. Thus, between 1985 and 1993, imprisonment for violence was made almost mandatory, nonparole periods for indeterminate sentences (life and preventive detention) were increased, the scope of preventive detention (imposed for serious violent and sexual offenders) was broadened, the maximum penalty for sexual offenses was extended from fourteen to twenty years, and postrelease conditions were toughened with recall to prison made easier.

This so-called violent offenses legislation (Kettles 1989) had little observable impact on crime, but it did affect sentences and prison composition.

Between 1981 and 1995 the number of prison terms given for violence grew 136 percent and the average sentence doubled. The standard nonparole period for life and preventive detention rose from seven years to ten years, and in 1993 courts were empowered to impose nonparole terms exceeding ten years. These extended minimums became increasingly popular as time went on.

Greater numbers of violent offenders serving longer terms of imprisonment impacted on prisons. Overall, musters grew from 2,600 in 1975 to 4,600 twenty years later. As noted, in the prison census of 1972, 22 percent were serving terms for crimes of violence. This increased to 42 percent in the next census of 1987 and to 59 percent in 1995. Whereas in 1972, 24 inmates were doing terms of more than seven years, in 1987 the figure was 150 and in 1995 it was 508. The number of lifers and preventive detainees grew from 55 in 1972 to 158 in 1987, to 311 in 1995.

Men with very long sentences and/or violent histories tended to begin their time at Paremoremo Maximum or to be sent there as a result of intransigence elsewhere. Due to their overrepresentation in violence statistics, a disproportionate percentage was Maori. A snapshot of the prison in 1985 is provided by Meek (1986). In 1985, 62 percent of Paremoremo prisoners were Maori or Pacific Islanders, compared to 55 percent of the general prison population. Of the prisoners, 82 percent were doing time for serious violence, 30 percent were doing finite terms of seven or more years and a quarter were doing life or preventive detention, and 20 percent were gang members.

Social Change at Paremoremo

At USP Marion, the rise in violence and disorder in the 1980s has been attributed largely to a decision in 1979 to centralize the worst federal prisoners at that institution (Consultants' Report 1985). Similarly, at Paremoremo, it was changes in the composition of prisoners that were primarily responsible for growing disorder. As the prison started filling up with young men serving long terms for violence, inmate leaders of the 1970s ended their sentences and were released or transferred. The traditions and principles they enshrined disappeared with them. Accordingly, gang identity, previously banned by prisoner mandate, became a central feature of cell block organization. By the end of the 1970s, the prison had already split into factions according to gang designation. Thus, A Block contained the Head Hunters and those acceptable to them, B Block held the Mongrel Mob and Black Power, while C Block held the weaker gangs and the unaffiliated.

The first serious gang-related incident occurred in July 1979, when Keith Hall, doing life for the torture, rape, and murder of a ten-year-old girl in 1977, had his throat cut in A Block. This was the first prison murder in New Zealand history. A member of the Head Hunters was charged with the murder but acquitted. Hereafter, internecine inmate violence became increasingly visible. Between 1978 and 1984, although the incidence of violence on staff remained low, inmate assaults grew almost threefold. In the early 1970s protective custody was almost unheard of. By 1978 it had become a permanent feature of prison life, and between 1978 and 1984 the number of inmates on protective segregation doubled. At the end of 1980, after a serious attack on a sex offender, a landing in Classification had to be set aside for protective custody. Soon after that, the whole block was taken over, for protective segs and classification services were transferred to Mount Eden.

Until now, prisoners still congregated at work and in the gym, but at the end of 1984 tensions exploded. On Christmas Eve, as the men gathered in the gymnasium for a movie, an attack by the Head Hunters on the Mongrel Mob left two Mobsters stabbed and several with serious head injuries. The prison was locked down, and seven Head Hunters were transferred to D Block. Two weeks later, there was another stabbing in the Classification Block (Newbold 1989).

The Security Clamp

Hobson had retired early in 1984, but his temporary successor, former deputy Sid Ward, was a man of similar persuasion. Realizing that Mob retaliation was inevitable and that a gang war was likely, Ward was left with little choice but to segregate the cell blocks completely. Although USP Marion had commenced its lockdown phase just the year before, also as a result of rising violence, the decision to segregate the blocks at Paremoremo was unrelated. Like Marion's, Paremoremo's security clamp began as a purely practical response to a local problem. Here, all interblock communion now ceased and prisoners were confined to their units most of the time. This had a huge impact on prison life. Visits now had to take place on different days, often during the week when many visitors could not come. Access to the gymnasium was restricted to once a week, and all interblock sporting competitions ceased. No more outside teams or concert parties came in. The Maori culture, education, and debating programs ended. The prison workshops closed.

The impact of gangs on routine at Paremoremo was thus immense, and it severely eroded the quality of life. Inactivity and chronic boredom became problems in themselves. Gang members bullied nonmembers and self-mutilations and suicides grew common. Before 1980 there had been no suicides at the prison, but between 1980 and 1987 there were fifteen, thirteen of them between 1984 and 1987 (Newbold 2007, 186). An upgrading of psychiatric services in 1987 reduced the problem.

Meanwhile, the gang situation continued to deteriorate. Much of the problem was in B Block, dominated by the Mongrel Mob, who in 1985 decided the block should be reserved exclusively for them. In a deliberate campaign, nonmembers were assaulted and terrorized, with increasing numbers requesting segregation. By mid-1985, eighty-one inmates were in protective segs, and in addition to the former Classification Block, half of D Block now had to be taken over to accommodate them. Because prisoners refused to go to B Block for fear of their safety, twenty of its forty-eight cells were empty.

Ward had retired by this time, and his successor Les Hine, who had run medium-security prisons in Wellington and Whanganui, was completely out of his league. He attempted to appease the Mob by conceding to their demands, but this only emboldened them, and attacks on staff, which had doubled in 1985, doubled again in 1987. In September 1987 staff threatened to strike unless something was done, and a few days later Hine was pulled out and replaced by Max Hindmarsh, a fifty-one-year-old former police sergeant who had been one of the officers whose life was threatened in the hostage crisis of 1970. Like Hobson, Hindmarsh was levelheaded and decisive, and by transferring troublesome Mobsters to D Block, he soon had the prison back under control. The policy of allowing gangs to congregate in separate blocks now ended. Hereafter the gangs were mixed, and those who refused to coexist were moved to D Block. Hindmarsh held his post until 1991, and although block segregation and its disadvantages remained, the prison stabilized. The relaxed situation of the 1970s never returned, but in 1988 assaults on staff and inmates reduced by over 60 percent, while self-mutilations fell by 80 percent. That year there were no suicides (Newbold 2007, 187).

Trouble Returns

After Hindmarsh departed, the prison was run by a succession of superintendents of varying caliber. The stability that Hindmarsh brought declined again as long-term violent prisoners accumulated and staff morale eroded. In 1991, while a tower sentry slept, lifer Dean Wickliffe, who in 1976 had pulled off the institution's first escape, absconded again, followed by a blaze of publicity. He was out a month before being recaptured. Two years later lifer Mike Bullock and Brian Curtis, a well-known career criminal doing eighteen years for importing LSD, broke out from the A Block yard. They remained free for six and eight years, respectively, before recapture. Following the Bullock-Curtis incident, razor wire was fitted on and between the two perimeter fences, making traverse almost impossible.

During the 1990s, not only at Paremoremo but at other prisons as well, the rising flow of violent offenders and gang members caused aggression to escalate to unprecedented levels. In 1993 the second death in New Zealand prison history occurred when double-murderer Steve Matchitt was stabbed to death in A Block. This was followed by killings at other prisons. Between 1990 and 2010, nine inmates were murdered in New Zealand, two of them at Paremoremo. In May 2010 the first corrections officer was killed on duty when former US Marine Jason Palmer died following an assault by a gang member at a new medium-security prison at Spring Hill.

At Justice's head office, a scheme known as *He Ara Hou* had been introduced in 1990, which set about reducing authoritarianism and emphasizing welfare, rehabilitation, and personalized treatment of inmates (Newbold and Eskridge 2003). At the end of 1993, however, a series of embarrassing scandals involving escapes, staff corruption, and brutality toward inmates caused the scheme to be officially abandoned (Newbold 2007), but the liberal philosophy behind it continued. At Paremoremo, within the austerity of the blocks, control now became uncommonly relaxed. An atmosphere of libertarianism prevailed where inmates were left to do their time with a minimum of interference. When I visited on a research project in 1995, the blocks were run down, unkempt, and poorly maintained. Block pride had disappeared with the segregation policy of ten years before. Hours of unlock had not changed, but prisoners lounged around the landings most of the day with little to do. The men I knew marveled at how easily available drugs were these days and at the lively trade they enjoyed with illegal items such as coffee, alcohol, and smuggled food. Staff seemed happy to let things go as long as there was no trouble.

But such laxness is a recipe for trouble; prisons require steady and firm governance (McCorkle 1970; Di Iulio 1987; Useem and Kimball 1991). Boredom, drinking, gambling, and trade in illegal items led to serious fights between inmates who sometimes refused to be locked up. A lockdown in 1996 revealed an array of contraband, including alcohol, drugs, and weapons. In 1996, an officer was stabbed in the lung and spleen. In September 1997 a young lifer was stabbed in the lungs, and three weeks later an officer was stabbed in the stomach and legs. In April 1997, a D Block man almost died after setting himself alight, and ten months later another D Block inmate was asphyxiated after setting fire to his cell.

Nationally, the scandals associated with *He Ara Hou,* a rise in escapes and suicides in the late 1990s, the prison homicides, a doubling of inmates in protective custody between 1990 and 1995, and a hostage incident at Christchurch Prison in late 1997 led to a general tightening of security. From 1998 onward, razor wire began appearing around the perimeters of all correctional institutions, and the same year compulsory random drug testing commenced. Early in 1998, national dietary and cell standards were introduced, which led to deterioration in the quality of food and reduced the amount of equipment and reading material permitted in cells. At Paremoremo this meant that goldfish and canaries, which had previously been allowed because of their pacifying effect, were now banned (Newbold 2007).

A Marion-Style Regime

It was at Paremoremo that the greatest changes were planned. In 1997 a new management team had started, which attributed recent problems to shoddy management and a climate of fear among staff, leading them to a

policy of appeasement. Prominent within the new team was security manager Bryan Christy, a tall, athletic former soldier who had worked at
Paremoremo since the early 1970s. He had firm ideas about how to remedy
a situation that many agreed was getting out of control. Christy told me that
the new strategy was initially influenced by information about USP Marion,
which had been downloaded from the Internet. Planning documents and
early discussion papers contain reference to Paremoremo as a "supermax,"
and to USP Marion. A Marion-type behavior modification system was envis-
aged for Paremoremo. Accordingly, the Auckland Prison Business Plan for
1997–1998 revealed an intention to divide the East Division (Parry Max)
into a progressive privilege regime. The objective was to deter disruptive
conduct in the standard blocks (A, B, C) by introducing a new order of
"Precautionary Segregation" in D Block. The unit was known as the "Unit
for Reducing Disruptive Behavior" (RDB Unit), and a "Development
Program" involving zero tolerance with high austerity would see the men
pass through four conduct-based phases of escalating privilege before gradu-
ating to the standard blocks.

By March 24, 1998, the RDB regime was in place, and a further system
of graduated privilege called the Sentence Management System (SMS) was
ready for the standard blocks. Here, in a similar fashion to the RDB Unit,
SMS would see prisoners pass through C, B, and A Blocks before transferring
to a lower-security prison. In the standard blocks, inmates got wind of what
was about to happen. Already smarting from the new dietary and cell standards, and fearing further reduction in freedoms, they decided to take action.
The bulk of activity occurred in A Block.

The 1998 Riot and Its Aftermath

On March 26, the day before the restrictions were to take effect, an
orchestrated protest took place. At 3:00 P.M. inmates jammed the A Block
sally port shut with a piece of wood, isolating the unit. Trapped, four duty staff
locked themselves in their office before escaping through a trap in the roof.
Now in control of the block, prisoners began burning and smashing equipment, including bedding and most of the cell toilets, joined soon afterward by
their neighbors in B Block, with whom they communicated by shouting across
the yard. As armed police surrounded the perimeter wire, A Block men
smashed holes through their cell walls, accessing the service tunnels behind.

From outside, water and electricity were cut off, and crisis squads moved
in to regain control. A negotiation team was sent to A Block, and at
7:45 P.M. the men surrendered. Several cells were now uninhabitable, however, and twelve rioters had to be transferred to Mount Eden. In D Block,
where further trouble was feared, a preemptive "softening up" process commenced. On June 26, 1998, lifer Dean Wickliffe wrote me a letter describing

what had happened. The day after the riot, he said, despite a promise from inmates that they would not resist, staff entered the block dressed in riot gear and ordered prisoners to stand at the backs of their cells with their hands against the wall. Those who hesitated had their cells opened and were subdued with batons, handcuffed, and dragged to empty cells in the Classification Block.

From this point, SMS came fully into effect. At its lowest phases (in D Block), prisoners were given almost nothing: twenty-three- to twenty-four-hour lockup with even toothbrushes and combs prohibited in cells. In Phase 6 (A Block), prisoners were allowed to eat communally in the dining room, were unlocked four hours a day, and had limited access to educational programs and the gymnasium. Throughout the prison, however, contact visiting ceased.

Due to the practical difficulties of transferring inmates between cell blocks as they went up or down in phases, there were inherent problems with SMS, which I commented on when I visited soon after its introduction. Accordingly, within twelve months SMS had been replaced by a modified regime called the "Behavior Management Regime" (BMR). BMR operated only in D Block and had four graduated phases as before. In the standard blocks conditions were fairly uniform. Inmates were unlocked five hours a day and largely confined to their landings (containing twelve men each) or released twelve at a time to the block yards, which had been fenced in two. All meals were taken in cells. The exception was upper A Block, where inmates were granted dining room privileges and access to the gym and were permitted to associate in groups of twenty-four. There, a few hobbies and educational activities were permitted, but there was no meaningful work. On March 12, 2003, Arthur Taylor, doing fifteen years for armed robbery and escape, and a leader in the March 1998 riot, wrote to me, "The place is now basically a concrete warehouse . . . the whole of Maxi life is just an existence, mate. One day is the same as the next, it's everything, and worse, that I would expect a third world prison to be."

THE NEW MILLENNIUM

The trends that have driven corrections in New Zealand since the 1980s continued with the new millennium. Between 2000 and 2008, reported violence nationwide grew by 44 percent, with the biggest leap occurring in grievous assaults (up 89 percent). A major law change in 2002 toughened sentencing and parole even further. Murder committed with certain aggravating circumstances now carries a seventeen-year minimum, and judges have begun to use discretionary nonparole minimums more often. In 2002, automatic release on remission was abolished for all sentences over two years, and minimum parole eligibility was set at one-third of sentence. However, a number of high-profile parole breaches since then have caused the board to become extremely cautious about giving parole and quicker to recall parolees for violation.

The result has been longer sentences, an exploding prison population, and associated costs, longer hours of lockup with food, program, and service cutbacks in an attempt to control these costs, doubling up in cells, conversion of shipping containers into prison cells, and, of course, a rise in prison tensions. The last prison census was in 2003 (Department of Corrections, Policy Development 2004). Since then, Corrections Department *Offender Volumes Reports* (Harpham 2010) have supplied limited information. From these sources we find that between 1995 and 2010, prison populations grew by one-third, to 8,500 (202 per 100,000 population). Between 1995 and 2003, the number of inmates serving finite terms of more than seven years grew from 508 to 965. Lifers and preventive detention detainees grew from 311 in 1995 to 679 in 2009. In 2009, 1 percent of inmates in the New Zealand prison system were classified as maximum security and 23 percent as high security. Approximately 60 percent of all prisoners were doing time for violent or sexual crimes, 27 percent were gang members, and almost two-thirds were Pacific Islanders or Maori. As a measure of growing tension, it is significant that the number of inmates in protective custody rose from 790 in 1995 to 2,334 in 2009, that is, to 28 percent of the total muster. Of the twelve prison homicides committed since 1979, seven occurred after 2000, and three of the twelve have been at Paremoremo Maximum.

PAREMOREMO TODAY

In July 2002, nine men who had been subjected to D Block's BMR sued the prison, the Department of Corrections, and the attorney general for psychological torture and gratuitous punishment. In 2004, the High Court found the regime unlawful and awarded compensation of NZ$325,000. By that time BMR had already been disbanded, but in the meantime the prison itself has changed little. It remains fundamentally a lockup facility for the most dangerous 1 to 2 percent of inmates in the New Zealand correctional system. All maximum-security prisoners (classified CB—i.e., high management/ escape, and high external risk potential) are sent to Paremoremo. In July 2010, 107 of Paremoremo's 241 inmates were CB. The remainder were high security (classified BB—i.e., with moderate management/escape potential, and high external risk) awaiting placement elsewhere. Of these, 73 percent were incarcerated for violent or sexual crimes, 35 percent were serving seven years or more, and 13 percent were doing nonfinite terms of life or preventive detention. Also, 70 percent were Maori or Pacific Islander.

When I visited Paremoremo in December 2009, a new manager, Neil Beales, had just arrived from Britain. I was given a full tour of the institution. The place was sterile, lifeless, and run down. Paintwork was chipped, brass was tarnished, the floors were dull and grimy. Prisoners, all locked in their cells, stared blankly as I walked past. Thinking I was a police or justice official, some shouted abuse. The dining rooms are still closed, and meals are served in cells. The men are allowed two-hour visits once a week but are separated from their visitors by a steel and Perspex wall that has small voice holes drilled in it. However nowadays, few get visits. It is not surprising, therefore, that positive drug tests are low—3 percent—compared to about 18 percent elsewhere in the system.

D Block and part of C is now used for "requested [voluntary] segregation," and the remainder of C Block is "directed segregation" for highly disruptive inmates or those requiring protective custody. The old Classification Block is now a "Special Needs Unit" for psychiatric cases and those at risk of self-harm. My old block, A Block, and B Block are both "mainstream" units, containing CB and BB prisoners. In December 2008, Graeme Burton, serving life and preventive detention with a minimum of twenty-six years for murder and attempted murder committed while on parole for another murder, stabbed a member of the Head Hunters twenty-seven times in A Block. The victim survived, but after this a security revision called the "Safer in the East" project saw steel grilles constructed half way down the cell landings, dividing all the blocks into groups of six. Polycarbonate shields were placed over the barred fronts of all cells to protect patrolling staff from being hit by objects. One result of the tighter regime is a reduction of inmate-on-inmate assaults. These fell from nineteen between July and October 2008 to five in the same period of 2009.

Today Burton is kept in virtual solitary in C Block with a four-man escort wherever he goes, but even general population men are locked up nearly all day. If staff are available, for two and a half hours in the morning or the afternoon they are let out in groups of six. Both halves of a landing are never allowed out at the same time. The yards are divided, and inmates have access to half a yard (about ten by fifteen yards) six at a time, or they may stay on the twenty-yard strip of linoleum outside their cells. Access to the gym is permitted, also six at a time, two hours a week. According to Arthur Taylor, who rang me from C Block in March 2010 to discuss a legal matter, because budget cuts no longer permit callbacks, if the prison is short staffed, inmates are locked up all day with no exercise period. Paremoremo Maximum has become little more than a warehouse where prisoners mark time until they are eventually transferred, released, or, occasionally, die.

DISCUSSION AND CONCLUSION

Paremoremo prison today thus bears no resemblance to the institution I knew over thirty years ago. From being a showpiece of late-twentieth-century correctional liberalism, the prison has become a dour example of modern custodialism. As we have seen, its early history mirrors fairly closely what happened at Marion. Marion was also run on comparatively liberal lines until ongoing incidents of serious violence forced a permanent lockdown.

Although Paremoremo's 1998 lockdown was influenced somewhat by information gleaned from the Internet, the strategy of suppression was already developing strongly as a result of local exigencies. The way the supermax of New Zealand currently operates is thus similar to that of many American examples, but there are a number of significant differences.

First, Paremoremo is now an aging institution. While advanced for its time, it was not designed for its current use, and it lacks the technological sophistication of the newer purpose-built American supermaxes. The extra grilles, the razor wire, and the Perspex cell shields, for example, are all recent innovations necessitated by the separation/lockdown strategy. Second, with a complement of about 240, Paremoremo is much smaller than American institutions of similar type. Even Marion, at its opening the smallest federal penitentiary in the United States, originally had 525 men (BOP 1972). The small size of Paremoremo makes running it less complicated than its larger American counterparts. Third, the restrictions imposed at Paremoremo did not occur all at once but appeared incrementally over a period of twenty-five years. These changes were not a result of any national strategy, and they have aroused little public comment or interest. Since 1984 the media have largely ignored Paremoremo. The majority of floor staff, like New Zealanders as a whole, are unfamiliar with the term "supermax" or the controversies surrounding it. Journalists frequently confuse Paremoremo Maximum (the East Division) with the medium-security facility next door (the West Division) and seem unaware that they are two entirely different institutions. Fourth, New Zealand does not have a terrorist or a major illegal immigrant problem. Thus, all of Paremoremo's inmates have been classified as dangerous to the public or to institutional security after committing civil, not political, offenses. Unlike the situation in the United States, there are no political prisoners in New Zealand, and national security is not a factor in prison management. Finally, although New Zealand prison sentences have increased markedly since 1985, they are still short by American standards (see Newbold 2003). Even at Paremoremo, 65 percent of the 240-odd prisoners are serving less than seven years and of the 31 lifers and preventive detainees, the longest nonparole period is thirty years. Most lifers and PDs will serve less than twenty years. The vast majority will be released well before they die.

So the emergence of the supermax in New Zealand is different from its counterpart in the United States in a number of important respects. As demonstrated, the reasons behind the transformation in New Zealand are complex but can be reduced to several intersecting factors:

1. *The gangs.* We have seen that it was a major gang confrontation in 1984 which resulted in the initial decision to segregate the cell blocks. Hereafter, services, programs, movements, and activities were

heavily restricted. The gangs introduced internecine conflict and broke down inmate solidarity. Concerted action, such as that which had Buckley removed, was impossible when the inmate community was factionalized through internal conflict.

2. *Violent offenders.* Boosted somewhat by declining economic conditions, escalations in violent offending rates have affected prison populations. As Paremoremo began to be filled—and to some extent be dominated—by men with a propensity to violence, its atmosphere changed. Where in the mid-1970s Paremoremo held 8 percent of the nation's prisoners—many of whom were there voluntarily—now it contains the most dangerous 2 percent. In the past there were violent men in Paremoremo too, but they were few and their behavior was mitigated by the general ambience of the inmate community. As more violent offenders entered and this ambience gave way, an atmosphere of tension and oppressiveness replaced it. Suicides, homicides, and the growth of protective custody were the result.

3. *Longer sentences.* Longer prison sentences in recent years that offer no hope of early release have created frustration and fatalism in prisoners. Tensions build when men are locked in such conditions under close confinement, particularly when there is little to do. Thus, violent outbreaks over minor matters have become more common and tighter control over association has been required.

4. *Rising prison populations and costs.* Rising musters, caused largely by longer sentences, have put great pressure on correctional facilities nationwide. Cost hikes have forced administrators to cut expenditures. This has been achieved by pruning programs, reducing rations, and increasing hours of lockup.

5. *Public antipathy.* In the liberal years of the 1970s, various antiwar and liberationist movements, dedicated to easing the plight of the underdog, proliferated. Project Paremoremo was an example. From the late 1970s onward, however, fear of violent offending, combined with horror stories of men committing serious crimes while on bail or parole, led to strident calls for harsher sentencing and harder prisons. A national referendum in 1999 received 92 percent support for a proposal for tougher sentences. In May 2010, in a populist move, the New Zealand parliament passed a version of the American "three strikes" laws, which will lead to even longer sentences of imprisonment for repeat violent and sexual offenders. A Research New Zealand poll taken a few weeks later found 81 percent support for the legislation, although only 61 percent of supporters thought it would actually deter offending. Thus, today there is considerable public support for punitiveness and little concern for inmate welfare.

If asked, the majority of New Zealanders would probably say that
prisoners are too well treated anyhow.

As is the case in the United States, given the above conditions, it is probable
that the regime currently in place at Paremoremo will endure. As the American
public, the New Zealand public demands protection from criminal predation
and sees prison security as fundamental to that end. Although it might be
possible to begin reintroducing work and reform programs for a proportion
of Paremoremo inmates, current staff are used to a system that has now been
in place for twenty-five years and would be loath to support it. If the experiment were successful, it is unlikely that anyone would notice. However, if,
for whatever reason, the experiment were to fail, its architects would be pil-
loried for wasting public money on an enterprise that critics would say had
little merit in the first place.

CHAPTER 10

The Rise of the Supermax in Brazil

José de Jesus Filho

IN 1985, the state government of São Paulo created a separate annex to a psychiatric penitentiary hospital, establishing the Penitentiary Rehabilitation Center of Taubaté, commonly called the "Piranhão," for the incarceration of the most violent inmates of the state. Before its creation, the only previous disciplinary penitentiary to house high-risk inmates had been located on Anchieta Island, off the São Paulo coast, which was closed in 1952 after a bloody mass escape. The reasons for placing inmates in Taubaté ranged from locking down escape-prone and disruptive inmates to deterring inmate-staff violence, murders, and active participation in riots. Other undefined notions, such as the labeling of some inmates as highly dangerous, served as further justifications for the regimen pursued at the Rehabilitation Center (Teixeira 2009).

At Taubaté, the inmates spent over twenty-three hours a day in solitary confinement, having at most one hour of out-of-cell time. Despite the absence of rules to regulate the treatment in Taubaté, all the witnesses, even the warden, confirmed that the inmates were kept totally isolated for twenty-three hours a day and were taken out of their cells in groups of seven to ten inmates for thirty minutes a day. Beatings, torture, and ill treatment occurred on a daily basis (Teixeira 2009). No radio, television, magazines, or newspapers were allowed. The prisoners were subjected to cold showers and disgusting food, while others were not allowed to see their families. Whenever prisoners became desperate and cried out, the guards would beat them senseless with iron pipes. In tiny cells that contained only a bed and a toilet, it was common to find excrement all over the walls. Some prisoners became so psychologically impaired that they would eat their own excrement. Others became so despondent that they committed suicide (Caros Amigos Revista 2006).

On September 2, 1992, in the aftermath of a riot in the House of Detention Carandiru, the largest prison facility in Brazil located in São Paulo, 111 inmates were slaughtered by the state military police in what became known as the Carandiru Massacre. This brutal episode inspired the film *Carandiru*. Less than a year later, in August 1993, Ismael Pedrosa, the warden from Taubaté who was known for being excessively tough, allowed his inmates to compete in a soccer tournament. The competition included members of the prison gangs Countryside Command and Capital Command (which later became PCC, Primeiro Comando da Capital—First Command of the Capital). The two teams exchanged threats, saying things like "I am going to drink your blood." When they came into the prison yard, verbal threats escalated into acts of reciprocal violence, which resulted in most of the leaders of Countryside Command being killed. After the conflict, "Geleião" (Big Jam) became the founder of the PCC. He was worried about a reprisal by the warden and the correctional officers and called fellow prisoners to join in what would come to be the PCC, claiming publicly, "We are from the PCC; whoever hurts one of us will have to deal with all of us" (Caros Amigos Revista 2006).

The PCC founders created what became known as the Self-Protection Code, based on the motto "Nobody touches our syndicate." For them, the most common "touches" were torture, abuse, and beatings by correctional officers. Quickly, the prison population came to respect the wishes of the organization. New members were "baptized" by the founders in a set ritual, and through this process hierarchical authority was established. The baptized were forbidden from making decisions without their godfathers' approval.

Besides fostering closeness among its members, this behavior also facilitated the identification of the gang leaders, which led to the State Correctional Department's decision to divide them throughout several prisons statewide, in a dispersion model approach (Riveland 1999; Pizarro and Stenius 2004; King 2007b). This action inadvertently escalated the rapid spread of the gang across the state. The gangs began by organizing themselves in small groups through "pilots" (i.e., the main cell block leaders), who spoke on behalf of the cell block groups and reported to the "towers," who in turn reported to the "generals," a small group of five or six leaders. The leaders made agreements with drug dealers from the poor areas of various cities, and the dealers helped establish other cells for the organization. Within a few years, the organization was very well established. Authorities, however, refused to acknowledge its existence publicly.

In February 2001, another crisis erupted in São Paulo, when thirty prison facilities experienced simultaneous riots. In the conflict, twenty-nine thousand inmates took over part of the state prison system, and twenty-nine inmates died. The events shook the law enforcement and penitentiary systems. For the first time, the authorities publicly recognized the existence of the PCC. By this time, however, it was too late to stop its growth, for the organization was well articulated. It had cells established all over the state, which used mobile phones to communicate among themselves and had implemented a complex distribution of roles among its members. "Generals," "pilots," "towers," "brothers," "sisters," "brothers-in-law," and "cousins" were terms used by the PCC to distinguish its members' functions. With the help of attorneys, family members, former inmates, and so on, the PCC became a cell organization, organizing crime on the streets, including drug dealing and bank robbery. The die was cast. There was nothing the state could do to suppress, in the short term, the spread of the organization.

Unlike in other countries, such as the United States, where gangs are primarily based on racial or ethnic identities and/or linked to historical immigration patterns, in Brazil members of gangs in prisons come from common social and criminal backgrounds. And the conditions of incarceration are shared equally by all inmates (Salla 2008). The PCC consolidation and legitimation within the prison population are based on the conflicting net of "solidarity" among the inmates, which combined the imposition of violence and fear with the building of membership identity, expressed by its own members as a "brotherhood" (Salla 2008).

The PCC has made headlines in Brazil and abroad. When the PCC came out of hiding and started "showing off" to the general society (e.g., burning buses and killing inmates, and claiming responsibility), the government's repeated failure to handle the prison population became apparent. Caros Amigos Revista (2006) has suggested that the PCC both won and lost. It won because it received news media coverage and, on that account, consolidated its power in prisons and expanded out of them (the prisons had become too small, in every sense). The PCC lost because the government started strengthening its enforcement mechanisms: the prisoners were transferred and held responsible for the deaths during the prison rebellions, and the government restricted visitation privileges and announced the building of new prisons following the Taubaté model in order to segregate the gang leaders in these institutions and isolate them from other inmates.

Regime Disciplinar Diferenciado

In May 2001, through a regulatory rule of the State Department of Corrections, SAP 091/01, later reaffirmed in December 2003 as law 10,792, the controversial Regime Disciplinar Diferenciado (RDD), or Differentiated Disciplinary Regimen, was established. This procedure allows for a prisoner to be placed in an individual cell for 360 days, subject to further sanction for misconduct, up to one-sixth of a sentence. The benefits under this law are limited: two hours of out-of-cell time in small groups, according to gang affiliation, and weekly visits for two hours, during which the inmate and visitors (up to two, not counting children) are separated by grids and screens. The inmates are also allowed to read in their cells.

The RDD is not a facility but rather a regimen, a culture steeped in disciplinary punishment. In some states, inmates serve their time in stand-alone supermax facilities called Centros de Reabilitação Prisional (CRP), or Prison Rehabilitation Centers.

For many experts, RDD is interpreted as a move by the state to retake control of the prison system. Because of the growing awareness of the human rights issues tied to state punishment, some observers consider RDD to be unconstitutional since it violates the fundamental rights ensured by Article 5, III, of the Brazilian Constitution, whereby no one shall be subject to torture or to inhuman or degrading treatment (Weiss 2003; Caros Amigos Revista 2006; Delmanto 2006).

In defense of the law, the former head of the São Paulo State Department of Corrections, Nagashi Furukawa, who drafted the legislation, asserted, "For a person sentenced to 300, 400, years of imprisonment, the length of sentence has no meaning. So he committed atrocities—such as beheading enemies—and was isolated 30 days, the maximum allowed by law at the time. Now he will think twice before committing a similar action" (Caros Amigos Revista 2006). Under RDD, it is as if inmates are locked in a vault, with a small vent for breathing. They are monitored by video cameras and have no contact with the outside world except through written correspondence. Radios and televisions are banned. Inmates have only a bed, a toilet, and a shower in their cells. The prison has cell phone blockers. Steel plates on the floor prevent the digging of tunnels. Steel wire ropes circle the building and the exercise yard and are covered with steel wire mesh. The visitation room, a place where inmates can meet with their lawyers, is separated by bars and tempered glass. Communication is by intercom.

In the RDD system, both pretrial and convicted inmates might be regarded as high-risk offenders, especially if there is suspected involvement with criminal organizations. Prisoners put under RDD include those who, because of their reputation, history, and leadership, have a real chance to escape or rescue and those who might disrupt prison discipline. All past and present leaders of the PCC have been under RDD, some for over two years. Today there are two stand-alone CRPs: one in the city of Presidente Bernardes and CRP Taubaté (the latter was designated for female inmates, but it was recently deactivated).

The RDD has been the subject of all sorts of criticism by experts (Franco 2003; Weiss 2003) because it does not properly define who can be placed under its rules. Instead of outlining a type of conduct that qualifies inmates for the regime, the drafters of the policy chose to adopt a resolution with open clauses, porous concepts, and vague expressions of general principles. The known targets of the law were the leaders and members of criminal gangs and prisoners whose behavior required special treatment. The conceptual flexibility needed to cover these types of prisoners is unquestionable, and in fact almost all prisoners could fall within one of the two categories. Any inmate could be considered as a member of a criminal group, and almost every prisoner might demonstrate behavior that requires special treatment (Franco 2003).

In May 2006, 765 inmates were transferred to a maximum-security facility in the city of Presidente Venceslau in the western region of the state of São Paulo. A small group, including Marcola, the PCC's top man at that time, was sent to the lockdown in the RDD. These events created rumors that on Mother's Day, May 13, the inmates would retaliate against the state.

On May 12, a small number of prisons experienced riots, while two police officers were shot outside of the prisons and a community-based police station was bombed. These events, however, did not disturb the state public safety department until the next day, when several police and correctional officers were killed, a variety of public buildings and banks were bombed, and messages written by PCC members were left behind. The third day was even worse, when riots occurred simultaneously in eighty-one prisons, resulting in 351 hostages being taken; seventy people were killed and over sixty buses burned, while several bank agencies and public buildings were hit by Molotov cocktails. The city of São Paulo simply went into turmoil. The police hit the streets during that week, killing over one hundred people including criminals and non-criminals (Jesus Filho 2006). Some observers equated the events with a civil war and attributed the actions to the establishment of the RDD (Delmanto 2006).

According to Adorno and Salla (2007), immediately after these events, more time was needed for an in-depth analysis of the social and political reasons behind the violence. Certainly, its roots were complex and conflicted. The authors claim that the emergence of organized crime in Brazil cannot be disconnected from the existing conditions and trends in contemporary society in the post–1970s period. Changes in the wake of the neoliberal introduction of the so-called economic globalization era and the disintegration of the nation-state have also been contributing factors. These developments, promoted and implemented in a short period of time, included the deep deregulation of the markets, particularly the financial markets, triggering an ordered sequence: changes in traditional national borders; fostering of capital flow; opening of space for illegal activities by making stakeholders anonymous; and currency circulation free of institutional constraints on tax havens, simplifying the funding of operations such as drug and human trafficking, arms trafficking, tax evasion, and the counterfeiting of goods and drugs. Adorno and Salla affirm that none of this would have been successful if it had not been for spectacular technological development, especially that linked to the computer and telecommunication fields.

Adorno and Salla (2007) argue that in Brazil, this backdrop is further aggravated by the public security crisis, which has lasted at least three decades.

During this period, the crime rate has escalated, and as society has became more violent, organized crime has spread. This has affected economic activities far beyond the traditional crimes against property, increasing homicide rates, particularly among juveniles and young adults, and disrupting livelihoods and social patterns inside and between social classes. Despite this shift, public security policies have continued to be formulated and implemented in conventional ways, unable to mirror the social and institutional changes within the broader societal context. Criminals have adopted modern technologies, but the law enforcement field has remained cloistered in the old police model of chasing known crooks and relying on networks of informants. And this is true despite the huge investment in public security, supported by either the federal or the state government for the expansion of staff and training opportunities as well as equipment upgrades.

The changes in criminal activities led the federal government to begin what it had delayed for a long time: the building of a federal penitentiary system. Besides the spread of internal gangs in the prisons, scholars are not certain about all the reasons that inspired the state of São Paulo to create the lockdown regimen (RDD) and the federal government to build the federal facilities. Even after interviewing two former National Department of Corrections directors and their then advisers for the purpose of answering this question, only one response was forthcoming: "[B]y the time, there was a public demand for that." Supermaxes in Brazil were conceived at the same time as the proliferation of supermaxes in the United States and other countries, but it is not clear how these time lines are correlated. The United States's get-tough and zero-tolerance policies with criminals in the 1980s played a major role in the minds of the public and influenced the work of legislators in Brazil. Thus, we believe that Brazil shared with other countries the same culture of fear of crime, and in consequence, as Ross (2007b, 61) has argued, "a punitive agenda took hold of criminal justice and led to a much larger number of people being incarcerated."

The Brazilian criminal justice system is based on federal laws. Generally, states cannot pass criminal laws (especially those that affect penitentiaries), as these are limited by federal regulatory norms for the better management of the penitentiary system. Nonetheless, traditionally the judicial and penitentiary systems have been state-based institutions, and except for a minority of federal charges, which are tried by the federal courts, most cases and all prisoners fall under the auspices of state authorities.

ROLES AND OBJECTIVES OF THE
FEDERAL PENITENTIARY UNITS

According to the Sentence Processing Law, reformed by federal law 10.792/2003, article 86, §1, federal facilities should house prisoners only as a measure to promote public safety or for the personal interests of an inmate directly. On the other hand, the federal prison internal rule, in article 3, includes the above legal text and adds to it the purpose of housing inmates subject to the RDD. In addition, law 8.072/90, or the Hideous Crimes Law, adds other goals to be achieved by the federal units:

> Article 3. The Federal Union will maintain penal high-security facilities, for the enforcement of sentences imposed on highly dangerous convicts, whose stay in state prisons endangers public order or safety.

In an explanatory booklet distributed in the city of Catanduvas in 2006 to the local population, the National Department of Corrections detailed some of its goals:

> Federal prisons: organized crime in its place.
> But does Brazil really need federal prisons? Undoubtedly. To explain it better, let us remember the recent past. In recent decades, the prison population has grown more than the number of prison places.
> This increase was so large that state governments now have difficulty keeping high-risk inmates linked to organized crime away from common inmates. The emergence of the federal prisons will completely change this situation. They will house only highly dangerous criminals: offenders that offer risk to the security of regular prisons, potential victims of attacks in prison, or those under the so-called Differentiated Disciplinary Regimen (isolation).
> This way, the federal prisons will assist governments in reducing the actions of criminal gangs within state prisons.

According to the above directives, the primary purposes of federal facilities are to house prisoners to ensure public safety and security, to promote order and discipline, to increase inmate and staff security, to protect potential victims of violence, and to house those who are subject to RDD. According to the warden of the federal facility in Mossoró, there are three additional goals: to build more federal penitentiaries for high-risk prisoners, to establish architectural prison models for both state and federal departments to utilize, and to establish prison management standards for the states to follow.[1]

As opponents have pointed out (Franco 2003; Weiss 2003; Caros Amigos Revista 2006; Mears 2008), both RDD and federal facilities are controversial. Some argue that both are unconstitutional (Franco 2003; Weiss 2003; Jesus Filho 2005), and to paraphrase Mears's (2008) argument, they constitute an investment in a costly and potentially harmful policy that appears to have little evidence-based justification or prospects for substantially achieving the goals expected of them. These new approaches thus divert attention and resources away from the strategies that might more effectively and cheaply achieve similar goals.

Some experts have suggested that RDD and federal facilities reduce recidivism because the government is better able to conduct programs of social reintegration and they have an intimidating effect on the prison population in general. In addition, with the removal of disruptive and recalcitrant inmates, social programs for social reintegration can theoretically be more effectively applied (Mears 2006).

Regardless of their declared objectives, the control units have had unintended influences, as is argued later in this chapter, such as the loss of contact with family members, the absence of defense lawyers in pretrial proceedings, the loss of good-time credits for those wrongly placed in control units, the loss of opportunity to progress to later stages in the sentencing process, and the stigmatization of some prisoners, who are considered "too dangerous" to be placed with other inmates.

In fact, placement in federal facilities has stigmatized inmates as high-risk offenders in an act of self-fulfilling prophecy (King, Steiner, and Breach 2008), not only before the judicial authority, which can influence an inmate's trial, but also before other inmates from the original facility. Some inmates after returning to their original prison are received by other inmates as new leaders.

Differences between Federal Facility Placement and RDD

According to the National Institute of Corrections (1997, 1),

[A supermax] is defined as a free-standing facility, or a distinct unit within a facility that provides for the management and secure control of inmates who have been officially designated as exhibiting violent or serious and disruptive behavior while incarcerated. Such inmates have been determined to be a threat to safety and security in traditional high-security facilities, and their behavior can be controlled only by separation, restricted movement, and limited direct access to staff and other inmates.

Some scholars (e.g., Hershberger 1998) argue that administrative maximum-security operations differ from typical penitentiary operations in several ways. For example, maximum-security inmates are handcuffed whenever they come in contact with staff; this prevents violent offenders from assaulting staff and other inmates and eliminates the possibility that escape-prone inmates will attempt to take hostages or access areas of an institution that will facilitate an escape. Inmates eat and recreate individually or in small, carefully screened and supervised groups.

Those who support the supermax model (e.g., Hershberger 1998) argue that these facilities are designed to house the more violent, order-disturbing, and escape-prone inmates. Isolating the "worst of the worst," these units improve safety for correctional officers, for other inmates, and for the public.

Supermax prisons also allow inmates in other institutions to live in more stan-dardized facilities, resulting in greater freedom of movement and access to educational, vocational, and other forms of correctional treatment.

Offenders can be placed in federal facilities only by a federal sentence made by an oversight judge. It is not necessary for an inmate to have broken any law or prison rule while behind bars to be sentenced to a federal facility. From this point of view, federal facilities function more like administrative units than as disciplinary detention centers.

If Brazilian federal facilities are understood as administrative and not dis-ciplinary detention units (i.e., units in which the placement of inmates serves strategic objectives and administrative convenience goals) (Richards 2008), then inmates should retain their rights under the Constitution and the Sentence Processing Law. Even though the right of inmates to serve their sentence near their family will be inevitably violated by imprisonment in a federal facility, guaranteed privileges should include family visits, working, studying, exercise, religious programs, and out-of-cell time individually or in groups. The disciplinary aspect of the control units should be exercised pri-marily by a different disciplinary system, the RDD, whose rules are expressed by article 52 of the Sentence Processing Law and its subsections and paragraphs, the rules of which have already been discussed.

Through the rules relevant to incarceration in the RDD lockdown, placement in one-inmate cells may be based on nothing more than mere sus-picion of involvement in a criminal organization or alleged risk to the order and discipline of a prison. These limitations differentiate RDD from federal facilities. According to the law, all one needs is a punitive character to be placed in RDD. Once in RDD, restrictions are clearly greater than those imposed on inmates in the regular system of federal prisons.

Although inmates can be placed in RDD and federal facilities only by judicial decision, the São Paulo state department of corrections has opened close supervision centers (a new kind of facility designed to bypass judicial control), which supposedly have no additional restrictions other than those imposed in regular high-security facilities. By constructing these facilities, the state simultaneously sidestepped judicial intervention on its policy and public and media attention on harsh prison conditions (Bonta and Gendreau 1995; Naday, Freilich, and Mellow 2008).

Federal Penitentiary System

The financing of facilities maintained by the federal government was entered into law through federal act 7.210/1984, also called the Lei de Exe-cução Penal or Sentence Processing Law:

> Art. 86, § 1°—The Federal Union might build correctional facilities in an area far away from the sentence jurisdiction to place, through judicial

decision, offenders sentenced to over 15 years to prison, when such measure is justified by the public safety interest or on behalf of the inmate.

Thus, in its original conception, federal facilities should have housed convicted offenders serving over fifteen years in prison. Nevertheless, before the beginning of the construction of federal facilities, federal law 10.792/2003 altered the Sentence Processing Law by taking out the minimum limit of fifteen years, so that any inmate could be placed in a federal prison to safeguard the public safety or on behalf of himself or herself:

> Art. 86. The sentences to prison applied by the courts of one state can be served in another state or in federal facilities.
>
> § 10 The Federal Union might build penal facilities in an area far away from the sentence jurisdiction to place convicted offenders, when the measure to be justified is on the public safety interest or on behalf of the offender.

Later, a new law was passed reaffirming the above-mentioned terms and creating rules to transfer inmates to federal facilities. According to act 11.671/2008, in order to place inmates in federal facilities, the warden, the prosecutor, or the inmate must apply before the local judge, who after admitting the case will submit the petition and report to the federal judge in charge of overseeing the federal facility. In turn, the judge will give the final word about whether or not to place the inmate in an isolation cell.

Moreover, law 8.072/1990 permits the federal government to administer prisons for high-risk inmates:

> Art. 3°. The Union will keep maximum security facilities designated to house high-risk offenders, whose housing in state prisons places a risk to the public safety and order.

Though the building of federal prisons was first allowed by law in 1984, it was not until June 23, 2006, that the Brazilian federal government opened its first federal facility in the small city of Catanduvas in the western part of the state of Paraná. This facility was brought into operation in the immediate aftermath of the largest rebellion in the country's history. Between 2007 and 2010, four new federal facilities were opened, purposely located in four distinct geographic areas of the country, the north, south, northeast, and midwest, all of them far away from big cities. Another facility is planned for the capital city, Brasilia (Departamento Penitenciário Nacional 2010). According to arguments of the National Department of Corrections (Departamento Penitenciário Nacional 2010), the cities for the federal facilities were intentionally selected to include all of Brazil's geopolitical regions. One of the facilities is even located in a semiarid area, and both guards and inmates complain about the water shortage and the number of insects and arachnids they have to kill every day.

Despite concerns about the validity of building prisons in such remote areas and the high costs associated with transferring inmates to those areas, the federal government has justified the introduction of the federal penitentiary system as the most efficient means of tackling the criminal gangs inside state prisons. It is important to note that, besides being situated far from the big cities, the primary prisons that were under repeated violent attacks by the PCC were administered under tight disciplinary measures and held large numbers of prisoners. Unlike the state penitentiary complexes, built to house over 1,000 inmates and usually overcrowded, the federal facilities can house no more than 208 inmates in individual cells.

Compared to state units, federal facilities have higher standards when it comes to physical, human, and material conditions. Federal correctional officers are hired through public contests, and they enjoy job security and have the highest earning potential among correctional officers. Unlike at most state prisons, the rehabilitation staff is complete and sufficient to care for inmates: the staff includes physicians, dentists, nurses, psychologists, occupational therapists, social workers, and pedagogues. On the other hand, the harsh treatment administered here causes inmates, in general, to conceive of federal facility placement as a real punishment. Inmates spend twenty-two hours locked down, and family visits are very restricted. This setting differs strongly from that of the state prisons, and the monthly cost to keep inmates in a federal facility exceeds four times the average cost associated with state prisons. The federal facilities are supplied by all sorts of antihumanistic technologies (Toch 2001): closed-circuit television, video cameras, fingerprint identification scanners at every door, intercom systems, and bulletproof glass.

For all of these reasons, the federal facilities are currently regarded as the most secure units and are supposed to house the alleged "worst of the worst." This was what the members of congress wanted when they passed the legislation establishing the federal penitentiary system, and this argument justified the unprecedented financial investment to build these prisons, each one costing around 44 million Brazilian reais, or around US$20 million.

Despite these large sums of money, approximately 80 percent of the prison population in the federal facilities is very poor, relying on public defenders for legal aid. Considering the large geographic size of Brazil, the long distance from many inmates' family residences to the federal facilities makes it almost impossible for their families to visit. It is worth noting that placement in a federal facility was initially to be limited to 360 days, a sentence that could be doubled once; then inmates were to be returned to their home state. Since the initial legislation, however, the federal courts have decided that there should no longer be a time limit for prisoners in federal facilities.

TABLE 10.1

Regional distribution of federal penitentiaries in Brazil

Region	Number of facilities	Capacity	Location	Status
North	1	208	Porto Velho/RO	Working
Northeast	1	208	Mossoró/RN	Working
Midwest	1	208	Campo Grande/MS	Working
Midwest	1	208	Brasília/DF	Under plan
South	1	208	Catanduvas/PR	Working
Total	**5**	**1,040**		

Geographic Localization

According to the National Department of Corrections, the federal penitentiary system was meant to operate five correctional facilities. Their current spatial distribution is shown in table 10.1.

Federal Correctional Facilities Structure

Federal facilities have the following basic structure:

1. Penal Facility Wardenship
2. Security and Discipline Division
3. Rehabilitation Division
4. Health Care Service
5. Administration Service

Actual Conditions

Due to the absence of research to assess the impact of both federal facilities and RDD, and because of the lack of reliable newspaper reporting, most of the information below is based on the author's personal experiences visiting and working inside the prisons and interviewing the inmates, wardens, program professionals, and former inmates in federal facilities and RDD. Because of the limited scope of the research, broad, definitive conclusions cannot be made (Pizarro and Narag 2008). Instead, the goal of this study is to demonstrate the urgent need of further research.

In a recent interview, a federal facility warden described several problems he has faced in running it. Just to give a few examples, the day we arrived at the prison, one inmate was being transferred back to his initial facility after attempting suicide. According to the warden, the prisoner is mentally ill, and the confinement worsened his mental condition. Three other inmates had threatened to commit suicide after varying periods in isolation. The warden also reported that he noticed how some officers changed their behavior (e.g., became more aggressive) within a few months of starting work in the facility. Furthermore, the warden and two other correctional officers expressed regret that in the facility there was no provision for inmate programming. Despite hiring staff to conduct rehabilitation programs, these employees were prevented from starting the programs by officers who always found a pretext to strengthen security measures to the detriment of rehabilitative programs.

In April 2010, two indigenous inmates were locked down in the Mossoró federal facility. Unless the prison system regarded their indigenous tribe as a criminal organization, there were no grounds to transfer them to this facility. The reason behind putting two indigenous prisoners in isolation was never explained. We suspect that they were placed there to distance them from their clan in order to prevent demonstrations. In June 2010, a group of forty-one inmates from Rondonia was sent to Mossoró, contradicting the viewpoint that these prisons are to exclusively house inmates who pose a threat to public security. Such collective placement shows how easily the Brazilian prison system diverges from its stated purpose. As further evidence of this, in June 2011, a petty bike thief was placed in a federal prison (Moura 2011). This drew the attention of prison authorities to the criteria used in the placement of inmates into federal facilities, and many of the authorities are now calling for scrutiny of these facilities.

Some wardens have claimed that when they are asked about who is eligible to be sent to maximum-security facilities, they think immediately about the mentally or physically ill inmates. This is confirmed in various research studies and court cases (*Madrid v. Gomez* 1995; Toch 2001; Naday, Freilich, and Mellow 2008). For these wardens, the troublemakers are the sick ones, not the high-risk ones, since the latter help them to control the masses in understaffed prison facilities. The former are placed in the general prison population in the absence of penitentiary hospitals to care for them (King 2007a). It is quite common for inmates to be transferred to federal prisons with conditions that fall short of the requirements required by the law.

There are occasions, such as after a riot in a state prison, when a large number of inmates is placed in one of the federal prisons. In 2010, twenty inmates were sent to the Campo Grande facility. One of those who was placed in Campo Grande had recently been granted permission to be moved to a medium-security facility, where he could work outside of the prison and have furlough rights five times a year. However, because of the riot, which he did not cause, he was transferred to Campo Grande. In addition, we have witnessed mentally and physically ill inmates who were sent to federal facilities. One of them was shot in the abdomen by federal police. Though he was not receiving medical treatment, the federal judge, in an ex officio manner, sent him to the federal facility. Another inmate was once placed in a federal facility by a federal judge on the accusation of participation in a criminal organization along with twenty other inmates, but the fact is that he had been granted a pretrial release by a state judge only days before this decision. Thus, someone who should have been free at the time was sent far away from home and faced total confinement.

Several inmates in the federal facilities complained that they were placed there because of political conflicts with the wardens from their original facilities. Three such inmates in the Campo Grande federal unit had grievances against their warden in Espirito Santo state prison that they had presented to the State Human Rights Commission. Another inmate was accused of attempted homicide against judges, prosecutors, and chiefs of police. Based on our discussions, it is hard to identify whether these inmates were placed in federal facilities because of their threat to public security or because of other reasons, such as political differences, collective punishment in the aftermath of riots, or individual punishment. Anyway, what is true is that most of the inmates placed within control units are low-income offenders who do not have even the resources to hire attorneys for their defense. These common social conditions challenge the claims that these inmates actually represent a tangible threat to public security.

Despite the harsh conditions at federal facilities, some inmates claim that they would elect to stay there if not for the distance from their families. The reasons for this are the quality of the services provided, the better educational programs, the food, medical, and ontological programs, and the decreased risk of being attacked by other inmates.

One common trend among inmate families is their occasional relocation to the cities near the control units. In order to promote "contact" with the families, in May 2010 the National Department of Corrections and Federal Union of Public Defense Department introduced a virtual visit program, whereby families can contact inmates through a close-circuit connection via the Internet. Often the inmates' actions and perspectives are influenced by family issues. For example, in Campo Grande, three inmates attempted suicide in the last few months. In Mossoró, one mentally ill inmate attempted suicide, and three others threatened to do the same. In Catanduvas, we met one inmate who was conducting a hunger strike. All of them, except for the mentally ill inmate, claimed the impetus for their actions as the absence of familial contact.

Wearing uniforms, having their heads shaved all the time, lack of family contact, minimum courtyard exercise time, limited contact with the "free world" through televisions and radios, and unappetizing food—these issues have led to the identity deterioration of the inmates (Goffman 1967). We have also seen a disproportional increase in the use of legal psychotropic drugs. A high number of inmates are taking antidepressants prescribed by physicians. Some inmates have been locked down in federal facilities for almost four years now, which has raised concerns about their mental health conditions.

Several state facilities are dilapidated, making them vulnerable to violent acts and conflicts. Correctional officers are often exposed to violence. When conflicts come up, such as uprisings, riots, and mutual attacks between inmates and officers, the wardens look for help from the federal system. This reflects a desperate attitude and little concern for assessing the causes that lead to the violence. This, then, creates a vicious circle since the federal facilities become avenues of avoiding actual treatment of the emergency situations, reflecting a "need" that is more symbolic than real (Pizarro and Narag 2008). This cycle motivates the federal government to invest even more in the construction of federal facilities, which cost far more than equivalent state facilities. This, then, diverts attention and resources from the state facility system, which remains undervalued, and from investing in other strategies to achieve similar goals (Mears 2008).

Some federal facilities are clearly militarized, focusing exclusively on incapacitation, with no demonstrated concern for rehabilitation programs. Though they are supposed to have inmate rehabilitation programs and are supplied with staff for this purpose, the programs have little real chance to help the inmates. The lack of commitment to the treatment programs and to inmates' individual and social rights was expressed on our site visits. A focus on risk management and security measures has overshadowed service programs to the detriment of the inmates' interests (Sá 2007). The negative consequences of security- and incapacitation-oriented prison management models are easily detected (Pizarro and Stenius 2004; Naday, Freilich, and Mellow 2008) in the deterioration of the mental health conditions of both inmates and guards.

FINAL WORDS

The rise of the supermax in Brazil stemmed from the state's inability to control and manage violence and its failure to prevent the rapid spread of organizations inside the prisons. As Ross (2007b, 61) has rightly pointed out, "Supermaxes symbolize the failure of rehabilitation and the inability of policymakers and legislators to think and act creatively regarding incarceration."

Experts affirm that supermax reflects a new penology, whereby the rehabilitative ideal is dismissed, and these new doctrines rest upon actuarial ways of thinking about how to manage accidents and public safety. Individual culpability is replaced by social utility and management, and the management of groups, performed in an actuarial way of thinking, reflects the recent trend of the penal system to target categories and subpopulations rather than individuals (Cohen 1985; Feeley and Simon 1992; O'Malley 1992; Minhoto 2008).

But, as we have described and argued, there is no rationality in the Brazilian penitentiary policy when it comes to the rise of supermax. Control units were established to control and manage gang leaders for the purpose of ensuring public safety. Nevertheless, most of those who are actually placed in the control units are very poor inmates who do not even know why they ended up there. This inevitably leads to the inmates' perception that the system is abusive, illegitimate, and unfair (Pizarro and Stenius 2004; Mears 2008).

For example, a group of inmates was swiftly placed in federal facilities or RDD after a series of riots and without any evaluation of their individual responsibility. In this context, it is worthwhile to quote Hans Toch's (2001, 385) words with respect to the supermax: "One must keep in mind that supermax placement is not a response to anyone's violent transgression—as is sometimes wrongly implied—but a classification decision. Indiscriminate treatment of people who have transgressed and have not transgressed makes no sense. It violates principles of justice to punish a person—however reprehensible he may be—for a predisposition to misbehave."

This trend to manage and control groups has also been pointed out by other scholars: "The new penology is neither about punishing nor about rehabilitating individuals. It is about identifying and managing unruly groups. It is concerned with the rationality not of individual behavior or even community organization, but of managerial processes. Its goal is not to eliminate crime but to make it tolerable through systemic coordination" (Feeley and Simon 1992, 455).

In sum, the Brazilian federal government should support research to assess the actual effectiveness of the control unit facilities as well as the actual need for them. Thus far, the government's penitentiary policy has shown nothing but irrationality and desperation in the managing of the prison population.

CHAPTER 11

Guantánamo

AMERICA'S FOREIGN SUPERMAX IN THE FIGHT AGAINST TERRORISM

Jeffrey Ian Ross and Dawn L. Rothe

MUCH OF WHAT WE KNOW about the conditions at Guantánamo and the treatment of the detainees has been obtained through visits by US politicians, monitoring by representatives from international nongovernmental and human rights organizations, reports from individuals who have been released, statements by lawyers defending those who have been detained, books written by individuals who worked at this facility, and information from reporters.[1] Not only the decision to detain enemy combatants but also the conditions to which they have been subjected have been vigorously debated.

Many of the conditions of the detention facilities and processes at Guantánamo can also be found in a traditional American supermax prisons, where detainees are confined to their cells twenty-three out of twenty-four hours a day, movement inside the facility is very limited, if not highly controlled, access to visitors is either nonexistent or severely curtailed, and access to typical amenities is sharply curtailed (Ross 2007b). In fact, two of the camps were modeled on American supermax prisons. Moreover, supermax prisons typically house convicted gang leaders and political criminals such as spies and terrorists, and the enemy combatants at Guantánamo are suspected of committing and/or aiding in the commission of terrorism. To demonstrate the similarities, we begin by providing a brief history of Guantánamo. We then explain why the United States's choice to use Guantánamo provided the opportunity for state crime and how the classification of detainees as enemy combatants and the use of torture circumvent existing treaties to which the United States is a signatory. Finally, we provide an analysis of the US government's policies and sanctioned behaviors toward the detainees.

HISTORICAL IMPORTANCE OF GUANTÁNAMO

At the far southeastern end of Cuba is a naval base owned and operated by the US government, in particular the Department of Defense. This installation, which sits on Guantánamo Bay, consists of a number of detention camps and is now generally referred to as Guantánamo or "Gitmo." In 1903, based on the Platt Amendment (i.e., a treaty between Cuba and the United States), the American government obtained what it claimed was a perpetual lease on the forty-five square miles that compose the base. Although Fidel Castro's communist regime (1959–present) accepted (at least one) payment from the Americans, the Cuban government has virulently opposed the Americans' presence.

The Guantánamo base has historically been used as a listening post and as a hub for American military and naval activities in the Caribbean. In the 1990s, Guantánamo also housed fleeing Cuban and Haitian refugees. In 1993, largely through the work of the New York City–based Center for Constitutional Rights, US Judge Sterling Johnson Jr. (Eastern District) declared the camp unconstitutional, and the refugees were subsequently relocated.

Shortly after terrorists attacked the United States on September 11, 2001, and before the Americans started bombing operations in Afghanistan on October 7, 2001, in what was called Operation Enduring Freedom, the US government formulated plans to detain captured members of the Taliban and the al-Qaeda terrorist organization. Though officials considered housing those captured on prison ships, at the military facility at Fort Leavenworth, Kansas, in the Pacific islands, on the island of Diego Garcia, and on the infamous Alcatraz Island in San Francisco Bay, the Bush administration ultimately determined that Guantánamo would serve as the ideal destination for these prisoners.

THE GEO-STRATEGIC CHOICE OF GUANTÁNAMO TO HOUSE THE DETAINEES

Over the past decade, Guantánamo, strategically located in a legal "black hole" of US-leased land in Cuba, became home to as many as seven hundred detainees from more than forty countries, all of whom were claimed to be members or supporters of Afghanistan's Taliban regime or of the al-Qaeda terrorist organization responsible for the terrorist attacks of September 11, 2001. In a radio interview on January 6, 2002, Michael O'Hanlon, a senior fellow at the Brookings Institution (a well-known liberal think tank in Washington, D.C.), explained the underlying ideology behind choosing Guantánamo:

> We can sort of do what we want to there. It's on foreign soil, and yet the foreign government doesn't have much say in how we use the place. . . . It's close enough to the United States [that] you can imagine flying in

various intelligence experts to interview these detainees and try to get information from them. So for a number of reasons, it seems the best choice, and I think Rumsfeld is right here to have selected it.

On Jan 11, 2002, within weeks of the US war in Afghanistan and the capture of four thousand prisoners, the first detainees arrived at Guantánamo (Strasser 2004). Photographs of detainees in orange jumpsuits, hooded, some with goggles, soundproof headphones, or gas masks on, and some in chains, provoked an international outcry against the Bush administration's treatment of detainees (e.g., Council of Europe 2007). These individuals were labeled as the "worst of a very bad lot . . . devoted to killing millions of Americans" (Cheney 2002). American officials acknowledged that the prisoners' guilt was not in question; in 2003, Bush stated, "The only thing we know for certain is that these are bad people."[2]

In this initial year, the detainees were not allowed access to legal counsel, nor were they permitted visits by family or friends. Moreover, in Kafkaesque fashion, these prisoners were not informed about the formal legal charges against them. Most important, the detainees were denied the sacred right of habeas corpus, one of the important bedrocks of Anglo-American jurisprudence: "In the case brought forward by the Center for Constitutional Rights, the lower courts ruled that the detainees had no right to file a writ of habeas corpus" (Ratner and Ray 2004, 4).

ANALYZING GUANTÁNAMO: THE UNFOLDING STORY

The Bush administration's decision to use Guantánamo and its treatment of the enemy combatants housed there were motivated by a need to quickly and expeditiously bring to justice and sanction those who orchestrated and participated in the 9/11 attacks, a need to immobilize actual and potential insurgents in the larger war on terrorism, a need to aid US forces in the field by reducing casualties and deaths, and a need to achieve military goals of unseating the Taliban, capturing members of al-Qaeda, and producing a regime change in Iraq.

The US efforts in the global war on terrorism also coincided with the administration's agenda: a militaristic and nationalistic response wherein "the gloves come off." The administration also expressed a disdain for a soft military strategy and allegiance to international law. As John Yoo, a former official in the Bush administration's Justice Department, stated, "This was a new kind of war wherein we had to adapt to a war wherein the enemy was not a traditional state" (Baccus 2005). This "new kind of war" also motivated a change in military techniques to gather intelligence. There was a brutal tug-of-war occurring within the United States between the FBI and the CIA over detainees who were thought to possess high-value intelligence. The FBI had a practice of repertoire building in interrogations (i.e., building of trust), while the CIA tended to use harsh tactics and practices of rendition (i.e., the transportation of detainees to areas housing harsh interrogators or those willing to resort to torture on behalf of the United States). However, little to no actionable intelligence was being attained on the whereabouts of members of al-Qaeda or its leader, bin Laden.

This was one of the factors that motivated the administration to find ways around the Geneva Conventions. The Department of Defense lawyers' memos reflected this strategy. With the arrival of detainees at Guantánamo, the quest for actionable intelligence amplified. Senior members of the Bush administration believed that the military police (MP) at Guantánamo were coddling detainees and that a harder approach was needed. In Washington, D.C., the military command knew Rumsfeld was unhappy with the amount of usable information coming out of Guantánamo. This prompted the Pentagon to expand the interrogation tactics being used, resulting in the multiple memos discussing techniques that bypassed international law if manipulated and redefined (Baccus 2005).

As human rights organizations and other international political actors continued to press the administration on its classifications of enemy combatants and the treatment of detainees, there was further motivation to move quickly, to obtain more information before it was almost impossible in the eyes of the public to carry on in the manner in which they were operating. Moreover, international support of the US war on terror began to dwindle and was replaced with scrutiny and/or outright protests, thus prompting the administration to move quickly and enhance intelligence gathering.

As US forces were pressured to obtain actionable intelligence by any means necessary and with the murky rules regarding interrogation techniques that had been changed multiple times, there was significant pressure for those within Guantánamo to produce. In addition, reward structures were present, wherein when perceived intelligence was gathered, US personnel were praised as well as promoted. The means of obtaining the ends were also normalized, thus creating an environment in which the denial of human rights and due process, the use of torture, and a host of other violations committed by US forces were no longer seen by many as deviant or wrong.

On November 13, 2001, Bush signed an executive order authorizing military tribunals for suspected terrorists. This provided the administration with a facade of legitimacy regarding the classification of detainees as enemy combatants. It also facilitated the opportunity to continue to hold them incommunicado and without due process. Under Bush's executive order, any foreign national who had been designated as a suspected terrorist or as a terrorist's aid could be detained, tried, convicted, and executed without a public trial or counsel, without proof of guilt beyond a reasonable doubt, and without the right of appeal. Ironically, the state enacted an order that it had previously denounced. The State Department routinely criticized military tribunals, secret trials that do not adhere to "fair public trials," and omissions of due processes in similar situations around the world (Rothe and Mullins 2006a, 2006b).

On January 19, 2002, nearly a month before Bush's executive order, the US Department of Justice under Attorney General John Ashcroft proposed that Geneva Convention III on the treatment of prisoners of war "does not apply to the conflict with al-Qaeda . . . [or] with the Taliban" (Gonzales 2002, 1). Based on this, Rumsfeld sent a memo declaring that "Army regulations on the interrogation of prisoners would not be observed," leading to many detainees being held incommunicado and without an independent review mechanism (Internal Memo 5). In essence, Yoo and Haynes (former general counsel of the Department of Defense) claimed the United States could utilize whatever means necessary and ignore international or domestic law in "times of war." On February 7, Bush officially opened the door to extensive illegitimate means to carry on interrogations "to quickly obtain information from captured terrorists" when he stated that the Geneva Conventions were not applicable to the conflict with the Taliban and al-Qaeda (Gonzales 2002). Just over two weeks later, on February 26, 2002, Haynes noted in a memo that in the war on terrorism, intelligence was everything and that winning depended on it. These memos not only discussed expanding the interrogation techniques but also analyzed how laws and precedence could be reinterpreted to allow the state to use such methods without the worry of legal responsibility.

Torture, according to the administration, was now almost impossible to commit—again providing the opportunity to obtain its goals through the creation of illegitimate means. In addition, since the memos were classified, the administration had a level of concealment under which it could operate (control of information). These decisions created an opportunity (and motivation) for the systematic maltreatment of prisoners. The state (in this case the Department of Justice [DOJ] and the Office of the Legal Counsel) was in a position to "reinterpret" the rules of war, the treatment and classification of detainees, and the definition of torture previously provided by US criminal statute and international precedent (Harbury 2005).

In addition, we see that the control of information and the communication structures ensuring such control were central to the administration's ability to maintain detentions. For example, while the administration has "at various times, released information about individuals who have been detained at Guantánamo, it has always maintained ambiguity about the population of the facility at any given moment, declining even to specify precisely the number of detainees held at the base" (Wittes and Wyne 2008, 1). The result has been that obscuring or withholding the actual detainee population has provided a level of secrecy that translates into strengthening the questionable practices and holding prisoners who remain unknown.

CONDITIONS OF CONFINEMENT

The conditions of confinement at Guantánamo range from sparse chain-link cages to buildings with dormitory or communal living spaces. At one extreme are small, mesh-sided cells with no privacy with lights on twenty-four hours a day. Here, most detainees are subjected to a regime more severe than what American prisoners would receive in US supermax facilities (Ross 2007b). Murat Kurnaz (2008, 157), who was incarcerated at Guantánamo from February 2002 to August 2006, stated, "Nothing in the camp is what it seems, nothing in the way the U.S. Army says it is and as it has been reported, filmed, and photographed by journalists. There are cages and interrogation rooms specially constructed for the media. In the media reports, you often see things on the bunks that I never once had in Guantánamo a backgammon board for example, or books or a bar of chocolate. . . . The fake cells were their attempt to convince people that they respected our faith."

Although conditions have changed over time, the base contains a number of detention camps that have been given alphabetic military names. Detainees were originally housed at Camp X-Ray, opened in January 2002, but this location was closed in April 2002. Prisoners were then moved to Camps Delta, Echo, and Iguana, each of which contained a series of detention camps. X-Ray had "six cell-blocks: Alpha, Bravo, Charlie, Delta, Echo and Foxtrot. The blocks were separated by narrow corridors through the chain-link fence pens. Every block had six wings also named from Alpha to Foxtrot. A wing consisted of ten cages arranged at a right angle. Every cage had a name" (Kurnaz 2008, 99). The original conditions at Camp X-Ray were described as "cages, each eight feet by eight feet. Constructed on slabs of concrete and covered with sheets of metal and wood, the collection of cages looked like an oversized dog kennel" (Higham, Stephens, and Williams 2004). James Yee, who was a Muslim chaplain at Gitmo in 2002–2003, described X-Ray as "hundreds of cages in several rows. The cages appeared to be no larger than four feet by six feet. The only protection from the blistering sun and heat was a flimsy tin roof that covered the cages. The ground was dirt" (Yee and Molloy Malloy 2005, 50–51). Because of the porous nature of the cages, prisoners were also exposed to numerous insects (e.g., spiders, black widows, tarantulas), reptiles (e.g., frogs, snakes, scorpions, iguanas), and rats (Yee and Molloy 2005, 50–51; Kurnaz 2008, 112–113). Yee and Molloy (2005, 51) added, "The prisoners were made to sleep on a thin mat on the dirty ground and a plastic bucket was placed in each cell for use as a toilet.

Armed guards kept twenty-four hour watch from wooden towers surrounding the facility."

Upon arrival, and based not only on prisoners' accounts but also news media depictions, detainees were forced to kneel for several hours on the gravel in the sun while their wrists and ankles were shackled, their mouths were covered with surgical masks, their eyes were covered with goggles with lenses that had been spray painted black, and their ears were covered with industrial earmuffs (Yee and Molloy 2005, 63). "Authorities described the gear as necessary for security during the long plane trip from Afghanistan." Detainees would beg for water but instead of provided liquid, they were kicked by guards. "Before being allowed to enter a cell, they were thoroughly searched by guards" (Yee and Molloy 2005, 63). Many inmates were repeatedly given rectal searches. Detainees "were prohibited from speaking to each other or to the guards. Buckets were placed in the cages for use as a toilet. Seldom emptied, they'd produce a rancid odor and attract flies" (Yee and Molloy 2005, 63).

Delta, which was built by the Halliburton Corporation, was different. Construction of Delta began in February 2002, and all detainees from X-Ray were transferred there by April of that year (Margulies 2006, 66). It contained five camps, a hospital, and interrogation rooms, and each camp had cell blocks with different names. According to Yee and Molloy (2005, 52), in Delta, which had approximately 660 detainees when Yee was chaplain, "[t]he prisoners were held in small [open-air] cages in two long rows facing each other across a narrow corridor. . . . [T]here was a tin roof overhead that trapped and baked the air. It was steamy and moist with the odor of forty-eight men confined in close quarters." Yee and Molloy claimed that it was hotter inside than outside, as there was no air conditioning. "The cages measured eight feet by six feet and the prisoners shared a mesh wall with two prisoners on each side and were in plain view of the detainee in the cages across the corridor. . . . Each cage had an eastern-style toilet installed at ground level into the steel cage floor, but there was no way to have privacy while using it." Kurnaz (2008, 156) describes Delta the following way:

The blocks looked as though they were made of metal walls welded together to form a giant container. Inside the containers were the cages, but this time their sides were made of metal grille instead of chain-link fence. The prisoners could see through the lattice, and the guards could keep us under observation at all times. The grille was razor sharp. . . . [T]he mattress was no longer on the ground but rested on a bunk bed welded to the wall . . . the bunk reduced the amount of free space to around three-and-a-half feet by three-and-a-half feet. At the far end of the cage, an aluminum toilet and sink took up even more room.

According to Joseph Margulies (2006, 660),

Within Delta, prisoners are currently held in one of four camps. Camps. One, Two, and Three . . . are maximum-security facilities divided into nineteen cellblocks. Each cellblock contains forty-eight cells, with two rows of twenty-four cells running down opposite sides of a long corridor. Cell doors and walls are made of tight wire mesh. Each prisoner lives in a six foot-eight-inch by eight-foot cell twenty-four hours per day, except for twenty to thirty minutes' individuals exercise five days a week (up from two), followed by a five-minute shower. Shackled whenever they leave their cells, the prisoners exercise in a twenty-five by thirty-foot cage set on a concrete slab. Bright lights shine in the cells around the clock. Guards constantly patrol the rows, with each cell observed by a guard at least once every thirty seconds.

He adds, "Each cell is furnished with a toilet, made from a hold in the ground and a sink positioned low enough to allow prisoners to wash their feet for prayers. . . . Prisoners sleep on a shelf-bunk with a mattress. Each prisoner is given a T-shirt and boxer shorts, as well as a . . . toothbrush, toothpaste, soap, washcloth, prayer cap, two blankets, one sheet, an a copy of the Koran. . . . There is no air-conditioning in Delta" (Margulies 2006, 67).

Delta had a number of trailers that were used for "meeting areas and offices." All of them had a metal D-shaped ring in the floor to handcuff a prisoner to. Delta also had a library that contained numerous Korans in different languages. Based on Yee and Molloy's (2005, 54) account, "Everything at the camp was based on a system of rewards. . . . If detainees cooperated in their cells as well as during interrogations, which took place in the trailers located throughout Camp Delta, they would be rewarded with items such as books, chess, or permission to keep a cup and food in their cell."

In cell block Echo, "Cells of pale green steel mesh ran the length of the block on either side, with one detainee per cell and a name card affixed to each. The cells were small, six feet eight inches by eight feet, with metal beds fixed to the steel mesh walls, squatting- style flush toilets on the floor, and sinks low to the ground" (Saar and Novak 2005, 51).

Yee and Molloy (2005, 60) report that during the time that he was chaplain at Gitmo, cooperative enemy combatants at Delta were let out of their cages for only fifteen minutes every three days. "There was a small recreation area at the end of the block where they were taken. It was about twice as big as a cell and was surrounded by a chain-link fence and covered in razor wire. Sometimes the guards placed a soccer ball inside and detainees kicked it around by themselves or jogged around the small space in the hot sun. . . . It was their only opportunity to exercise, other than what they cold manage inside their cages." In terms of hygiene, detainees were allowed to shower only after their recreation time. "The individual sinks in their cages offered a limited opportunity to wash."

Camp 4, at Delta, which opened in March 2003, had conditions in stark contrast to the conditions at other camps. Based on Yee and Molloy's (2005, 91) description, "it included large rooms, where ten prisoners lived together dormitory-style. They were allowed to wear white uniforms, considered preferable to the orange prison jumpsuits. They were sometimes allowed out of their room for an hour at a time to roam freely through the dusty recreation areas that included a veranda to offer shade from the brutal sun and a place for the detainees to share meals and prayers." According to Kurnaz (2008, 210),

> Camp 4 was a dump. The cells were empty metal ship containers with only a metal slot in the door for sunlight and air. Space was cramped since each cell housed up to ten prisoners. The air was stale, and the ceiling light stayed on through the night. The generators hummed constantly just like Camps 1 and 2 it was like being in a ten-man oven. We were allowed out more often for exercise. The prison "courtyard" was a corridor three feet wide by sixty feet long, running between the barbed-wire protected containers. Several times a day, two cells—twenty prisoners in total—were allowed out for an hour.

Prisoners were given more food than those in the other camps, including a cup of milk each morning, however "it was the same kind of food as before— a couple of bitter-tasting potatoes, cold vegetables, undercooked rice" (Kurnaz 2008, 211). Based on Margulies's (2006, 67) account, camp 4 houses the most cooperative prisoners: "Prisoners sleep in dormitories, and are allowed to eat and exercise together. They also wear white, rather than orange uniforms. Camp Four has a maximum capacity of approximately 160." Camp 4 and Camp Iguana house juveniles picked up in battle.

Camp Echo consisted of cages "just like the ones in Camps 1 and 2, only smaller and more solidly built, with a single toilet-sink unit like the ones found on ships. A camera was mounted behind Plexiglas on the ceiling. The walls were made of several layers of small chain-link fence, welded together" (Kurnaz 2008, 199). Each cell had its own shower.

Camp Iguana "was Gitmo's version of the Four Seasons Hotel. When prisoners were escorted to the bathroom there, they could peer through the high fences and see the endless Caribbean Sea. . . Prisoners meeting their lawyers in Camp Iguana sat on sofas in a large room with wood floors, instead of on white plastic lawn chairs" (Khan 2008, 100).

In summary, Guantánamo currently consists of six camps. As described by the Joint Task Force Guantanamo (2009) website, camps 1 through 3 resemble a typical supermax prison. According to the website, "A small percentage of the detainee population resides here. In terms of process, most of them resemble what would be found in any medium–supermax prison in the United States." The following section highlights many of these similarities.

FROM US SUPERMAX PRISONS TO GUANTÁNAMO

Processes at Guantánamo that are similar to those used in medium-supermax prisons in the United States include cell searches and cell extractions (Yee and Molloy 2005, 70–71). For example, the camp routinely relied on the work of the Immediate Reaction Force (IRF) (similar to cell extraction teams used in American prisons), which multiple prisoners recalled was used with a great degree of frequency when rules were actually or suspected of being broken. It

> consisted of five to eight soldiers with plastic shields, breastplates, hard-plastic knee-elbow; and shoulder-protectors, helmets with plastic visors, gloves with hard-plastic knuckles, heavy boots, and billy clubs. . . . They came with pepper spray in a kind of pressurized aerosol gun that they could aim precisely at a prisoner from ten feet away. It contained oleoresin capsicum. . . . They sprayed the entire cage and waited until the prisoner was completely unable to resist. Then they stormed in [and beat the prisoner]. (Kurnaz 2008, 100)

They came into the cell and pepper sprayed the detainees, beat them, and sometimes transported them to a different part of the camp.

In terms of mental effects, detainees suffered from classic signs of depression, and some from psychosis, as is often the situation with prisoners in supermax prisons after being exposed to long-term isolation. According to Yee and Molloy (2005, 101), "The most traumatized detainees were kept in Delta Block. It was equipped like the others but its occupants seemed to constitute a psychiatric ward rather than a prison block. The prisoners here were truly mentally disturbed. At any time, at least twenty prisoners were being kept in Delta Block."

Delta had a solitary confinement section called Block Oscar. According to Kurnaz (2008, 161–162), who spent time there, "This was truly nothing more than a ship's container with a door. The walls were reinforced by corrugated metal sheeting like the one in fairground stalls. Every surface . . . was covered with it. There was no mattress or wool blanket. A toilet and a sink were sunk into the floor. . . . This cage was even smaller than the one in Block 1." He adds, "There were two slots in the door, one at knee-height for food, and another for the guards to look in. A red light on the ceiling went on when a guard came to bring food or wanted to see me."

Similar to that in US supermax prisons, food was of basic quality. At Guantánamo food varied from meals ready to eat (MREs), called eamaries by the detainees (Kurnaz 2008, 56). "Meal Ready to Eat. They were supposed to contain approximately 2,000 calories. Typically they contained food like potatoes packed in tin foil or rice, meat or chicken" (Kurnaz 2008, 56). Sometimes they contained pork, which is not allowed in the Muslim religion.

As previously noted, camps 1 through 3 at Guantánamo resemble a typical supermax prison. Detainees in these camps are housed in individual cells with a toilet and sink in each cell. "There are ten cell blocks with forty-eight cells each. Detainees wear tan uniforms and canvas sneakers. The detainees are permitted at least two hours each day in one of two exercise yards at the end of each cell block. Showers are allowed in outdoor stalls after exercise periods."

Although most of the guards followed orders, others were more humane. For example, former detainees Ahmed Adil, Adil Abdul Hakim, and Abu Bakr Qassim stated in an interview with BBC reporter Neil Arun (2007, 1) that "most of them [guards] behaved like robots. . . . There were some good ones who showed us kindness and there were others who went out of their way to offend us—throwing around our copies of the Koran, making farting noises while we prayed." Another detainee noted that while he had been tortured and beaten, his cousin and one of his brothers, who had been interrogated by a different soldier, had been treated with kindness and respect.

Nevertheless, prisoners were interrogated at all hours of the day and night, and as has been the case within the confines of US supermax prisons, there have been allegations that prisoners have been abused, intimidated, and tortured. Some detainees at Guantánamo alleged that their American captors were not opposed to torture. Reports mentioned such tactics as withholding food; providing expired food; forcing the drinking of foul water; depriving prisoners of sleep; forcing them to kneel for hours while chained to the floor; shackling prisoners up to fifteen hours at once; subjecting them to loud noise, loud music, or extreme temperatures; using cultural taboos to incite humiliation; beating them; injecting them with unknown substances; holding guns to their heads; and water boarding (i.e., forcing detainees, while lying on their back, to drink water as it is poured into their mouth) (Lewis 2004a, 2004b; Tyler 2004; Waldman 2004; Lewis and Schmidt 2005). Others have reported witnessing the desecration of religious items such as copies of the Koran.[3] Here, while similar tactics have been used in US prisons, the motivation behind such abuses remained starkly different. The War on Terror has demonized all those in US captivity, and the infallibility of the process of capture and interrogation is rarely acknowledged by those who are guarding the detainees. In Guantánamo, this kind of treatment was meant to break the detainees' will in hopes of obtaining useful intelligence for the war against terror. The following section addresses the broader issue of interrogation and torture at Guantánamo.

INTERROGATION TECHNIQUES—TORTURE

Unlike in US supermax prisons, the systematic use of torture has been a dominate aspect of the Guantánamo experience. The use of this practice was documented in a series of memos that the Bush administration produced. By February 26, 2002, senior-level personnel in the Bush administration discussed easing or redefining the application of international rules constraining techniques of interrogation against persons captured in Afghanistan. On August 1, 2002, internal memos again began to circulate that attempted to circumvent US obligations under international law pertaining to issues of torture and interrogation methods. The stage for torture was being set not only for detainees at Guantánamo and in Afghanistan but also for those held in Abu Ghraib (the large prison outside of Baghdad that was the focus of a scandal in 2004) (Rothe 2006a, 2006b).

The classification of enemy combatants resulted in several legal debates, legislation, and subsequent court rulings. In July 2004, after several legal challenges, the US Department of Defense allowed combatant status review tribunals so that the detainees could formally contest their enemy combatant status. In December 2005, Bush signed into law the Detainee Treatment Act of 2005, which eliminated habeas corpus for impending claims regarding the conditions of confinement and interrogation techniques used. Specifically, it stated that no court, justice, or judge would have jurisdiction to hear or consider an application for a writ of habeas corpus filed by or on behalf of an alien detained by the Department of Defense at Guantánamo.

In June 2006, the US Supreme Court heard the case of *Hamden v. Rumsfeld* (548 U.S. 557). The Court's ruling invalidated the administration's use of military commissions (a closed military proceeding requiring less proof) because they were not authorized by Congress and such practices violated a congressional statute that required adherence to international humanitarian law. In response, Congress passed the Military Commission Act of 2006, which included rules on interrogation, detention, and habeas corpus. Most notably, the act of 2006 allowed prosecutions in a military court and reinforced the act of 2005, which abolished habeas corpus for the enemy combatants. In August 2008, the first military commissions trial at Guantánamo ended with the conviction of Salim Hamdan, who was charged with and found guilty of providing material support to terrorists. At the time of writing, other trials continue, including that of Mohammed Jawad, accused of throwing a grenade at a passing American military vehicle in Afghanistan in 2002. In 2009, he was released from Gitmo and transferred to a prison in Afghanistan, and he is currently in the process of being released into the care of his uncle.

In order to use torture against the detainees held in Afghanistan and Guantánamo, strategic and legal manipulation of international and domestic torture laws occurred within the administration. In a memo (dated August 1,

2002) to Alberto Gonzales, then counsel to the president, addressing the CIA's request for guidance on interrogation, Jay Bybee, the DOJ's legal counsel, reinterpreted the Torture Convention and other international laws to set the stage for harsher interrogation techniques. Bybee stated that the Torture Convention "prohibits only the most extreme acts by reserving criminal penalties solely for torture and declining to require such penalties for cruel, inhumane, or degrading treatment or punishment."[4] Bybee (currently a federal appeals court judge) stated that torturing al-Qaeda detainees in captivity abroad "may be justified," and that those international laws against torture "may be unconstitutional if applied to interrogations" conducted in the war on terrorism. The memo also discussed how the doctrines of "necessity and self-defense could provide justifications that would eliminate any criminal liability" on the part of officials who tortured the al-Qaeda detainees. Consequently, Bybee provided an extremely narrow definition of which acts actually constitute torture.

In light of what key administrators of the Office of the Secretary of Defense and Joint Task Force 170 saw as "tenacious resistance . . . despite our best efforts" for gathering key intelligence, more memos circulated discussing the legality of additional techniques circulated.[5] The official stated problem was that the "current guidelines for interrogation procedures at GTMO limit the ability of interrogators to counter advanced resistance." While overtly requesting verification of the suggested techniques' legality, what was being surreptitiously sought were "exquisitely refined lawyer skills to justify some part of" or all of the expanded techniques (Weisberg 2004, 301).

It was not until April 4, 2003 (two weeks after United States started bombing Iraq, and thus the beginning of the war in Iraq) that an updated version and revision of thirty-five acceptable interrogation techniques beyond those that may be applied to a prisoner of war who is subject to the Geneva Conventions was circulated. Moreover, the report provided an in-depth discussion of legal technicalities that could be used to create a "good faith defense against prosecution." On April 16, Rumsfeld sent another memo to the commander of the US Southern Command that included a new list of approved techniques that varied significantly from his earlier approved methods and from the above-referenced report. Within a matter of months, the methods approved and/or disapproved by high officials changed, causing uncertainty and an unclear, inconsistent mandate to guide interrogators.

In short, the United States was trying to make torture legal, bringing such practices out of the closet, as had been the unofficial practice. Most, but not all, of the methods CIA agents, private contractors, and military personnel employ today, for instance, were field tested in Vietnam as part of the Phoenix program and later imported to Latin America and Asia under the guise of police training "counterterrorism" programs (Rothe 2006a, 2006b).

ATTEMPTS TO CONSTRAIN THE
EXCESSES OF GUANTÁNAMO

Nongovernmental (e.g., Human Rights Watch and Amnesty International; see Human Rights Watch 2009) and intergovernmental (e.g., International Committee of the Red Cross) organizations attempted to restrain the administration from its unlawful international positions by writing letters to the administration and creating public awareness campaigns. For example, in June 2003, Amnesty International called for an independent investigation into allegations of abuse and torture in Afghanistan and Guantánamo. The International Red Cross also conducted visits to the camps that resulted in a report that described the horrendous conditions as well as the deteriorating mental health of the detainees. In 2003, Human Rights Watch condemned the United States for its treatment of the enemy combatant detainees and for its failure to classify them as prisoners of war. Nonetheless, although these organizations garnered public attention, they were unable to muster enough outcry to outweigh the administration's policies.

Beyond these organizations, international lawyers also spoke out and called upon the international arena to act together and prevent the administration from using unlawful tactics (Sands 2005). In addition, groups such as the Citizen's International Criminal Tribunal for Afghanistan (ICTA 2004) investigated the Bush administration's practices. On March 13, 2004, their indictment, *The People v. George W. Bush,* was settled after a two-year investigation. The tribunal found Bush guilty of war crimes "resultant to U.S. attacks against Afghanistan in 2001" (ICTA 2004). The guilty verdict included charges of war crimes for the torture and killings of prisoners of war, for their detention, and for their deportation to Guantánamo. Nonetheless, the ICTA failed to act as a constraint: as an ad hoc tribunal, it lacked political power and impact.

Over the past decade, members of the US Congress have been relatively silent on restricting the administration's use of Guantánamo and subsequent policies there. Moreover, Congress tacitly supported their efforts through legislative changes. In addition when the courts did offer counterpositions, they were either ignored or appealed or their legitimacy to make such rulings was put into question. On the other hand, across the country and elsewhere, there were numerous public protests in response to the abuses and torture that occurred at Guantánamo. Nonetheless, the limited negative public reactions did not disrupt the general status quo nor pose a large enough political threat to the Bush administration to serve as an effective constraint.

Part of the government reaction occurred in 2005 when senior-level military officers investigated complaints. Their report declared that "several prisoners were mistreated or humiliated, perhaps illegally, as a result of efforts to devise innovative methods to gain information." In one instance, the report noted that a female interrogator had squeezed a man's genitals (Lewis and Schmitt 2005, 35).

CONCLUSION

Like US supermax prisoners, most enemy combatants were subject to considerably restricted movement both inside and out of their cells and were not allowed to congregate during the day. They had absolutely no personal privacy; everything the convicts did was monitored, usually through a video camera that was on all day and night. Inmates had little or no access to educational or religious materials and services. Toiletries (e.g., toothpaste, shaving cream, and razors) were strictly controlled. Inmates, when removed from their cell, were typically shackled and heavily guarded.

In addition, inmates at both Gitmo and US supermax prisons are exposed to a process through which they could be transferred to less restrictive conditions if they demonstrated good behavior (i.e., conformity and/or providing intelligence). It was clear that the government wanted to control each and every movement of both populations lest they pose either a management or flight risk. Indeed, the typical inmate at Guantánamo was not a gang leader or spy, nor had killed a correctional officer or other inmate, but many were accused of acts of terrorism or of supporting terrorism, and all were perceived as escape risks.

The parallels between American supermax prisons and Guantánamo are undeniable and remain a visual and historical reminder of how American government, particularly one that wants to reinforce its agenda, deals with those it wishes to detain. In many respects, the actions of the US government attain levels of illegality that in many ways surpass deplorable actions by government officials typically found in US supermax prisons: incarcerating individuals without due process or writ of habeas corpus, holding them incommunicado, and using torture. Moreover, as chapter 12 demonstrates, the case of Guantánamo is not an anomaly. There was a pattern of diffusion from past to future (i.e., from the Phoenix programs decades ago to the opening of Abu Ghraib).

CHAPTER 12

A Globalized Militarized
Prison Juggernaut

THE CASE OF ABU GHRAIB

Dawn L. Rothe

FROM THE TIME SADDAM HUSSEIN (the former president of
Iraq) came to power in 1979, Abu Ghraib was the symbol of death and torture. Over thirty thousand Iraqis were executed there and thousands more
were tortured and mutilated only to be returned to society as visible evidence
to others of Saddam's power (American Enterprise Institute 2004; Kupelian
2004). This included amputations of body parts, rape, the removal of tongues,
and systematic beatings. Executions were routine at Abu Ghraib. The pattern
continued through the 1990s until October 2002, when Saddam granted
amnesty to most prisoners in Iraq including those at Abu Ghraib.

Prior to the US invasion of Iraq, Abu Ghraib was completely abandoned,
leaving only the memories of executions, torture, and mutilations that
occurred under Saddam's rule. After the fall of Baghdad (March 2003), coalition forces (i.e., the United States and United Kingdom) needed a detention
center for the growing numbers of insurgents and civilians captured by US
forces. Abu Ghraib was chosen by Ambassador Paul Bremer, administrator of
the Coalition Provisional Authority. Less than one month after the invasion,
the Abu Ghraib prison complex was stripped of everything that was remov-
able. Coalition authorities had the cells cleaned and repaired, floors were
tiled, and toilets and showers were installed, all in preparation to become a
place of detention for Iraqi resisters (Danner 2004a).

Bremer's choice of Abu Ghraib as a detention operations center placed a
strict detention mission–driven unit assigned to operate in the rear of enemy
lines in the middle of a combat environment.[1] To Iraqis, the facility served in
the national imagination as a constant reminder of past abuses that coincided
with the US occupation and abuses as suspected resisters or supporters of
Saddam were taken away bound and hooded often in the middle of the night

(International Committee of the Red Cross 2004). An Iraqi translator alluded to the connection of past with present represented at Abu Ghraib when he said, "I always knew the Americans would bring electricity back to Baghdad. I just never thought they'd be shooting it up my ass" (November 2003, quoted in Hersh 2004, 29).

GLOBALIZING AMERICAN HEGEMONY:
THE SUPERMAX PHENOMENON

Abu Ghraib was not, nor does it remain, an isolated phenomenon. Negligible conditions, ill treatment, and torture of prisoners continue within the confines of many supermax prisons that have resulted from the American hegemonic spread of "supermax" mentalities and the ideology that guides the current state of a US militarized criminal justice system (Hill and Beger 2009).

After all, the use of untrained personnel and the mixing of job duties of the military police are symptomatic of what we have seen in the US policing industry including that which has been implemented in supermax prisons. Though focused primarily on the UK experience, Tony Jefferson's (1990, 16) seminal scholarly piece on paramilitary policing is quite applicable to the current US situation. He defines paramilitary policing as "the application of (quasi)-military training, equipment, philosophy and organization to questions of policing." This includes the use of military hardware (semiautomatic and automatic firearms, armored vehicles, military-style uniforms, such as jumpsuits and Kevlar vest and helmets, etc.) as well as an emphasis on intelligence gathering, reconnaissance, sharing information, and cooperation including branches of the military. Furthermore, even activity that is not legally defined as criminal but is seen as defiant, such as the insurgency in response to the invasion of Iraq, or other things deemed as potential public disturbances are accorded resources and responded to with this militarized approach (Muzzatti 2005). As Peter Kraska (1993, 1996, 1999) and his colleagues (Kraska and Kappeler 1997; Kraska and Paulsen 1997) demonstrated for several years before the 2001 terrorist attacks, the 1990s saw a rise in the number of US paramilitary police units, an expansion and escalation of their activity, and a normalization of paramilitarism into mainstream policing, with a direct link between paramilitary policing and US militarism (Muzzatti 2005). Kraska (2007, 3) defines this militarism as an ideology that "stresses the use of force as the most appropriate and efficacious means to solve problems." On the other hand, militarization is the implementation of that ideology.

As with the war on terror and the increased use of supermax detention centers to house those in opposition and the current US expansionism of the ideology and use of supermax prisons in general, militarized policing and subsequently the militarized criminal justice system reproduces itself, constantly demonstrating an ever-increasing need. This process was evident in the justification of Guantánamo and is reflected in many prisons, including those "ghost" prisons deemed necessary during the "war on terror." As the following chapter lays out, such processes were also apparent in the case of Abu Ghraib. Nonetheless, before discussing the events at Abu Ghraib, we must first have an understanding of the historical events leading to the war on Iraq and the use of Abu Ghraib—a version of a US militarized supermax prison. Furthermore, to explore the war on Iraq, we must examine the neoconservatives within the Bush administration and their underlying agenda, ideology, and roles.

HISTORICAL BACKGROUND
Neoconservatives and the Unipolar Moment

The collapse of the Soviet Union in 1991 brought the Cold War to an end and presented the United States with a new set of opportunities. With US military supremacy unrivaled, the primary means at Washington's disposal to achieve global hegemony could be used with relative impunity (e.g., invading Panama and Grenada, or using Iraq's incursion into Kuwait to establish a more permanent US military presence in the oil-rich Persian Gulf region).

The end of the Soviet Union weakened domestic political support for expanding military budgets or the permanent war economy and removed the ideological rationalization of an individual nationalistic agenda. In general, the US general population expected the end of the Cold War to produce a "peace dividend" (Zinn 1980/2003).

Economic and political elites (often the same actors) did not acquiesce to the reduction in their power that would have resulted from such a realignment of US foreign interest goals. A struggle emerged between rival factions over how to capitalize on the opportunities offered by the breakup of the Soviet Union (Kramer and Michalowski 2005). One group supported an internationalist approach, particularly the George H. W. Bush and Bill Clinton administrations, while the other, often referred to as "neoconservatives," argued for a more nationalist, unilateralist, and militarist approach. This latter group would find itself in a position to shape US policy in the middle of 2001.

The term *neoconservative*, neocons, was first used in the early 1970s by the US democratic socialist leader Michael Harrington to describe a group of political actors who had been his companions in the US Socialist Party but were moving politically to the right. Many of the original neoconservative group had been associated with Henry Jackson's faction of the Democratic Party (e.g., Irving Kristol and Norman Podhoretz). In reaction to the liberalism and anti–Vietnam War stance of the Democrats, they moved to the right, joining the Republican Party (Dorrien 2004, 9–10).

A number of neocons affiliated with the Reagan administration provided the political justification for the administration's policies of military growth and use of covert activities. Moreover, as the Soviet Union was weakening, neocons in the administration of President George H. W. Bush began vigorously promoting an aggressive neoimperialist ideology. This included staving off cuts in the military budget in response to the weakened Soviet threat and the popular expectations for peace (Kramer and Michalowski 2005).

In 1992, aides under then Secretary of Defense Richard Cheney prepared a draft document titled "Defense Planning Guidance" (DPG). The DPG was an internal classified Pentagon policy statement used to guide military officials in their planning process. The draft provides the first look at the emerging neoconservative agenda. As David Armstrong (2002, 78) notes, the DPG "depicted a world dominated by the United States, which would maintain its superpower status through a combination of positive guidance and overwhelming military might. The image was one of a heavily armed City on a Hill."

The DPG was a clear statement of the neoconservative vision of "unilaterally using military supremacy to defend US interests anywhere in the world, including access to vital raw materials such as Persian Gulf oil" (Kramer and Michalowski 2005, 457; see also Armstrong 2002; Halper and Clarke 2004; Mann 2004). Upon a firestorm of criticism that ensued after the draft was leaked to the press, President George H. W. Bush and Secretary George Cheney publicly distanced themselves from the DPG.

The election of democratic president Bill Clinton temporarily removed the neocons from political positions of power within the US government. Moreover, the rapid collapse of the Soviet Union had already revealed that the neocons had been wrong on almost every issue concerning the Soviet threat. Consequently, neoconservatism lost much of its legitimacy as a mainstream political ideology, and eventually neocons found themselves in political exile, labeled as the far right wing of the Republican Party. However, from the sidelines they continued to generate a steady stream of books, articles, reports, and op-ed pieces in an effort to influence the direction of US foreign policy (Kramer and Michalowski 2005). Many of the neoconservatives joined well-funded conservative think tanks to advocate for their agenda as well. One of the most important of these was the Project for the New American Century (PNAC).

In September of 2000, PNAC issued a report titled "Rebuilding America's Defenses: Strategy, Forces, and Resources for a New Century." This document grew out of the previously mentioned controversial draft DPG of 1992 and clearly stated the ideology that would come to guide George W. Bush's foreign policies and the war on Iraq: preemption and unilateralism (Hersh 2004).

The 2000 Election

The appointment of the Bush/Cheney ticket to the White House put the neocons in political positions near the center of power. In December 2000, after a botched election, the Supreme Court of the United States awarded the

US presidency to George W. Bush, despite his having lost the popular vote by over half a million ballots. This political debacle restored the neocons to state power, with more than twenty neoconservatives and hard-line nationalists being awarded high-ranking positions within the administration (Dorrien 2004).

Moreover, the Pentagon and the Vice President's Office became unipolarist strongholds because of the close links between neoconservatives Vice President Dick Cheney and the new secretary of defense Donald Rumsfeld (Moore 2004). Then September 11, 2001, happened. The terror attacks created a climate of fear and anxiety, which the neocons mobilized as they now found themselves in empowered positions to again promote their geopolitical strategy that included the long-time goal of invading Iraq, regime change, and the reconstruction of the Middle East to spread America hegemony and economic and military supremacy. Economic and strategic interests included the opening of a new capitalistic market for US corporate exploitation as well as the eventual political control of the Middle East.

Directly related to this was the need to respond to the changing global economic order wherein the dollar was being seriously challenged. In late 2000, Saddam Hussein switched his country's currency (for purposes of export trade of oil) from the dollar to the euro and then converted his US$10 billion reserve fund at the UN from dollars to euros. Iraq profited immensely from the switch, further motivating the administration to overthrow Saddam and put in place a US-driven economy (*Observer* 2003). The dollar-euro changeover was powerful enough to risk any economic backlash in the short term to stave off the long-term dollar crash of an Organization of Petroleum Exporting Countries (OPEC) transaction standard change. This reinforced the broader general motivation to invade Iraq. The *Observer* reported, "A bizarre political statement by Saddam Hussein has earned Iraq a windfall of hundreds of millions of euros. In October 2000 Iraq insisted upon dumping the U.S. Dollar—'the currency of the enemy'—for the more multilateral euro."

It was also reported that Iraq's UN oil for food reserve fund swelled from US$10 billion to €26 billion. As Saddam changed to the euro for oil, and with talks of OPEC following suit, the Bush administration became alarmed. They began planning to block OPEC momentum toward the euro as the currency standard as well as to return the Iraqi reserves back to the US dollar. In order to preempt OPEC, the administration needed to control Iraq and its oil reserves.

Otherwise, US economic supremacy could potentially be challenged as the situation would have presented an overarching macroeconomic threat to the hegemony of the US dollar. As William Clark (2003, 2) noted,

> The Federal Reserve's greatest nightmare is that OPEC will switch its international transactions from a dollar standard to a euro standard. The real reason the Bush administration wants a puppet government in Iraq—or more importantly, the reason why the corporate-military-industrial

network conglomerate wants a puppet government in Iraq—is so that it will revert back to a dollar standard and stay that way. While also hoping to veto any wider OPEC momentum towards the euro, especially from Iran—the 2nd largest OPEC producer who is actively discussing a switch to euros for its oil exports.

Moreover, Clark (2003, 3) suggests that the following scenario would occur if OPEC made a collective switch to euros:

Otherwise, the effect of an OPEC switch to the euro would be that oil-consuming nations would have to flush dollars out of their (central bank) reserve funds and replace these with euros. The dollar would crash anywhere from 20–40 percent in value and the consequences would be those one could expect from any currency collapse and massive inflation (think Argentina currency crisis, for example). You'd have foreign funds stream out of the U.S. stock markets and dollar denominated assets, there'd surely be a run on the banks much like the 1930s, the current account deficit would become unserviceable, the budget deficit would go into default, and so on. Your basic 3rd world economic crisis scenario.

The ultimate result could potentially be the US and the EU switching roles in the global economy; thus the United States would lose its sole status as superpower.

Post–September 11 and the War on Terrorism

On the evening of September 11, 2001, and in the days following, the Bush administration campaigned to attack Iraq immediately (Clarke 2004; Woodward 2004). They implied, on numerous occasions, that there was a strong connection between Hussein and the al-Qaeda terrorist organization that was responsible for the September 11, 2001, attacks in the United States. During the build up to the war, no major statement on Iraq by the Bush administration was made without multiple references to terrorism in general and al-Qaeda specifically (see Prados 2004). Attacking Iraq, they argued, was part of the broader war on terrorism. This campaign was highly successful, as evidenced by the fact that prior to the start of the invasion, 70 percent of US citizens believed that Iraq was responsible for 9/11 (see Corn 2003).

December 2001 was the high point of US involvement in Afghanistan as the Northern Alliance, US airpower, and special force units took Kabul, removing the Taliban from power. On December 22, Hamid Karzai was sworn in as the new leader of Afghanistan, and within a few months the most highly skilled US units and CIA paramilitary teams were diverted from Afghanistan. As Richard Clarke (2004, 2) noted, "The U.S. Special Forces who were trained to speak Arabic, the language of Al Qaeda, had been pulled out of Afghanistan and sent to Iraq."

In March 2003 President Bush remarked, "[C]oalition forces have begun striking selected targets of military importance" in Iraq (Bush 2003). While hundreds of detainees were being held in Guantánamo and Afghanistan in disarray and violence and unclear, inconsistent, and open orders for interrogation techniques continued to guide the treatment of thousands of individuals, the official war on Iraq had begun.

ABU GHRAIB IS CHOSEN
The Command Structure of Abu Ghraib

In 2003, Lane McCotter, director of business development for Management & Training Corporation, a Utah-based firm claiming to be the third largest private prison company, was picked by Attorney General Ashcroft to go to Iraq as part of a team of prison officials, judges, prosecutors, and police chiefs to rebuild the state's criminal justice system. As 80 to 90 percent of Abu Ghraib had been destroyed, McCotter was chosen to direct the rebuilding and reopening of the prison as well as to train the guards deployed to Abu Ghraib (Butterfield 2004).

In June 2003, Brigadier General Janis Karpinski was named commander of the 800th MP Brigade and was put in charge of all military prisons in Iraq. While having no experience in running a military prison, she was quickly made responsible for administering three jails, eight battalions, and 3,400 reservists (Hersh 2004). Within six months, Karpinski would be admonished and suspended, a result of the abuses that occurred under her watch. Ironically, the month prior to her suspension, December 2003, Karpinski was quoted as saying that for many of those detained in Abu Ghraib "living conditions now are better in prison than at home. At one point we were concerned that they would not want to leave" (St. Petersburg Times, quoted in Hersh 2004, 21). In June 2003, the Chain of Command was as illustrated in figure 12.1.

In the summer of 2003, the 519th Military Intelligence Battalion, headed by Captain Carolyn Wood, left Bagram (a detention facility in Afghanistan) despite an ongoing criminal investigation by the US Army into alleged cases of abuse and murder and was redeployed to Abu Ghraib. There, Wood proceeded to implement new interrogation rules that, as a Pentagon report later noted, were "remarkably similar" to those she had developed at Bagram (Hersh 2004). Specifically, the list included "the use of dogs, stress positions, sleep management, [and] sensory deprivation," according to the Fay-Jones report. Moreover, the report noted other techniques, such as "removal of clothing and the use of detainee's phobias," that had been used at Bagram were now to be fully implemented at Abu Ghraib.

On August 31, 2003, General Miller, once commander of Guantánamo, arrived in Iraq, bringing with him a team of experts to review the army's procedures and to make recommendations to aid in more effective

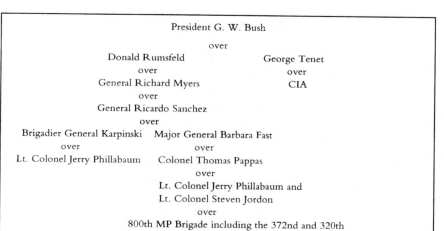

12.1. Chain of command of Abu Ghraib in 2003

information gathering (Danner 2004b; Hersh 2004; Strasser 2004). Miller filed his assessment of counter-terrorism interrogation and detention operations on September 13, 2003.[2] The report laid out his recommendations that the "detention operations function must act as an enabler for interrogation" (1). This included "setting the conditions to exploit internees to respond to questions that answer theatre commanders' critical questions" (3). In essence, Miller's intent was to "Gitmoize" the prisons in Iraq and shift the focus to interrogation and intelligence gathering (Hersh 2004).

On November 19, 2003, General Sanchez issued an order giving the 205th MI Brigade tactical control over the prison. During Miller's visit, he also met with and briefed military commanders on interrogation techniques used in Guantánamo. This included leaving behind Rumsfeld's April 2003 list of approved (though extended and meant for enemy combatants) interrogation tools. In March 2004, Miller was transferred from Guantánamo to Iraq and was named as the head of prison operations in Iraq (Karpinski's previous position).

Hidden from the official chain of command was Stephen Cambone, undersecretary of defense. Cambone answered directly to Rumsfeld and was heavily involved with the creation and implementation of the Special Access Program (SAP) enacted several weeks after the invasion of Afghanistan. Directly under Cambone was Army Lieutenant General William Boykin.[3] The SAP was composed of elite forces from the Navy SEALS and Delta Force and CIA paramilitary experts. The SAP forces were heavily involved in the operations called Black Special Access and Copper Green, which included

hiding ghost detainees during interims between interrogations and/or rendi-
tions to other states. This included utilizing the site of Abu Ghraib as a temporary holding area and for hiding ghost detainees in special dedicated
sections (including tier 1[A]). Operating in segregated parts of Abu Ghraib,
the CIA and SAP forces carried out methods of interrogation beyond the
scope of any extended authorized techniques. The protocol was also to place
detainees in Abu Ghraib secretly and undocumented.

The Taguba Report states,[4]

> The detention facilities operated by the 800th MP Brigade routinely held
> persons brought to them by Other Government Agencies (OGAs also
> known as CIA) without accounting for them, knowing their identities,
> or even the reason for their detention. The Joint Interrogation and
> Debriefing Center (JIDC) at Abu Ghraib called these detainees "ghost
> detainees." On at least one occasion, the 320th MP Battalion at Abu
> Ghraib held a handful of "ghost detainees" for OGAs that they moved
> around within the facility to hide them from a visiting International
> Committee of the Red Cross (ICRC) survey team. This maneuver was
> deceptive, contrary to Army Doctrine, and in violation of international
> law. (Taguba Report 2004)

This illustrates the existence of an entirely off-the-books detention system
within Iraq and even more importantly within the walls of Abu Ghraib, run
by the CIA and the SAP forces. Nonetheless, prior to this case, US covert
practice of rendering detainees abroad as well as interrogating them in secret
did indeed exist (e.g., Guatemala 1984–1986); however, post–September 11,
2001, the practice surged. It is now known that over one hundred individuals have been detained as ghost detainees: those being secretly detained without being recorded or identified by any MP or MI personnel, essentially
disappeared persons (Hersh 2004).

Beyond the illegalities, the US use of this practice added to the existing
quagmire of an overpopulated and understaffed detention facility. Furthermore, the interrogation tactics of these SAP forces and the CIA encouraged
and endorsed physical coercion and sexual humiliation of prisoners in an
effort to gain actionable intelligence to end the increasing Iraqi resistance
(Hersh 2004). Likewise, as military police were placed under the authority of
military interrogators, who answered to special forces, the lines of authority
at Abu Ghraib became further tangled.

Consequentially, not only was Abu Ghraib functioning with a murky chain
of command and dysfunctional SOP, there was also a general lack of resources
and staff. For example, during October 2003, there were seven thousand
prisoners in Abu Ghraib and only ninety-two MPs to keep control. When the
372 MP Company arrived at Abu Ghraib, they were but a fraction of their

company total. Their roles had already been significantly altered from prison guards to support for MI personnel and they moved right into tier 1, where CIA, SAP, and MI personnel held high-value detainees or those perceived to be of value for getting intelligence out of the insurgents. In essence, there was a general lack of role and task segregation that had devastating effects. This situation created opportunities for MPs to carry out torture and abuses that would not have existed without this intermingling of duties and lack of clearly defined roles. Moreover, the institutionalization of instrumental rationality (any means necessary to attain intelligence) that emanated from the highest levels down to the MPs played a role in an already anomic environment. Coupled with inconsistent doctrines on interrogation techniques, this had a direct impact on the organizational culture that dominated the walls of Abu Ghraib.

Private Contractors

To further complicate matters, the role of private contractors (PCs) in prisons in Iraq, specifically Abu Ghraib, was pivotal to the lack of command and inconsistent policies regarding detainee treatment. The use of PCs in the war on terrorism is unprecedented. This integration began with efforts to adapt to a downsized military through increased reliance on just-on-time privatized logistic contracts. The move to an active war following the attacks of 9/11, including the wars in Afghanistan and Iraq and the permanent "war on terror," further cemented the private-public strategy for war making by the United States (Rothe 2006a, 2006b). While many private corporations were contracted to provide logistical services (e.g., Halliburton, Bechtel, Blackwater Security, and Lord and Abbott), others were contracted for more sensitive jobs, interrogation, and interrogation assistance (Titan and CACI International) (Rothe and Ross 2010).

Both CACI and Titan employees have been implicated in torture, abuse, and murder in Iraq, more specifically Abu Ghraib. This is contrary to General Miller's testimony to Congress, when he stated, "[N]o civilian contractors had a supervisory position" (Miller 2004, 2). Of the thirty-seven "formal" interrogators at Abu Ghraib, twenty-seven belonged to CACI, and twenty-two linguists' interpreters assisting interrogators were employed by Titan.

The Detainees

By late summer 2003, thousands of Iraqis were being detained in Abu Ghraib, all loosely defined as those suspected of crimes against the coalition or common crimes against Iraqis or high-value detainees (Hersh 2004). "As the pace of operations picked up in late November–early December 2003, it became a common practice for maneuver elements to round up large quantities of Iraqi personnel (that is, civilians) in the general vicinity of a specified target as a cordon and capture technique."[5] Thousands of Iraqis were arrested as a result. This included men, women, and children, comprising a mixture of the general population. The population was nearing ten thousand (Danner 2004a). According to the ICRC, between 70 and 90 percent of the approximately eight thousand of those being detained had been arrested by mistake. For example, a former commander of the 320th MP Battalion stated in a sworn statement, "It became obvious to me that the majority of our detainees were detained as the result of being in the wrong place at the wrong time, and were swept up by Coalition Forces as peripheral bystanders during raids. I think perhaps only one in ten security detainees were of any particular intelligence value."[6] Other detainees included the "ghost detainees," to wit, those whose identities remain undisclosed to date, those allegedly linked to al-Qaeda, or individuals perceived to have intelligence of the growing insurgency movement against the United States and its allies.

Context of the Juggernaut: Abuse and Torture

From the onset of the Iraq invasion, torture and cruel and inhumane treatment were practiced by US forces. The detainees were held in their cells twenty-four hours a day, save for movement to an interrogation area or to abuse or humiliate them in front of other detainees. Conditions were overcrowded far beyond capacity, and at times there was no water or electricity for power. These conditions and practices intensified as the number of detainees continued to grow into the thousands. As noted, by late summer 2003, thousands of Iraqis were being held in Abu Ghraib. The command structure had already experienced several changes. In late August into September 2003, Major General Geoffrey Miller, the commander at Guantánamo Bay, was sent to Iraq to assess detention centers, subsequently sharing his interrogation techniques with interrogators. That same month, General Sanchez authorized expanded interrogation techniques. These quickly became standard US practice, and, according to a Human Rights Watch report, prisoners started dying during interrogation sessions almost immediately thereafter. During this same time, the number of ghost detainees being brought into the prison increased along with the presence of CIA and special forces.

During October 2003, the heaviest attacks against the US occupation occurred. At this point, several cordon and capture missions were carried out (i.e., surrounding, enclosing, and capturing individuals), significantly increasing the numbers within the confines of Abu Ghraib. Specifically, there were seven thousand prisoners in Abu Ghraib and only 92 MPs to keep control. When the 372nd MPs arrived at Abu Ghraib, they were but a fraction of their supposed company total. Their roles had already been significantly altered from prison guards to support for MI personnel, and they moved right into tier 1, where CIA, SAP, and MI personnel held high-value detainees.

By mid-November 2003, the complete takeover of MP supervision by MIs had occurred. Simply stated, the fragmentary order or "frago" stated that the 205th MI Brigade under General Thomas Pappas would have tactical control over Abu Ghraib. A report completed during this period when tactical control was handed over to the MIs by General Ryder discusses concerns over the tensions between the missions of the MPs and their new role as interrogators. The conditions in Abu Ghraib continued to deteriorate, leading to additional frustration for the already strained guard unit. The numbers of detainees increased, and the necessary staff within Abu Ghraib was lacking. In that environment, a growing brutality surfaced as MPs were overwhelmed (380 MPs to guard thousands of detainees). This was evidenced by the change in videos MPs and MIs were sending back home to loved ones that were growing more intense, filled with hostilities among each other (Baccus 2005). Moreover, the push for "actionable intelligence" and the foreign role of MPs working under MIs and SAPs significantly worsened an already hostile environment toward more extreme physical reactions as anger and frustration were growing among US forces.

Yet the numbers at Abu Ghraib continued to be in the thousands. This included numbers of ghost detainees being interrogated by CIA agents, civilian contractors, and special forces. The insurgency continued, and little to no actionable intelligence was coming from the interrogations, and most of the detainees were not linked to the insurgency in Iraq. Furthermore, techniques approved for Guantánamo detainees or "high-value terrorist targets" were used on people pulled off the streets. Abuses and torturous interrogation techniques continued, though these were not new.

The use of the expanded interrogation techniques that were fully institutionalized within the confines of Abu Ghraib was by no means unique or an anomaly that can be attributed to the expanded techniques authorized by Rumsfeld or implemented by Miller. After all, the knowledge and practice of these torture techniques by other state agencies (e.g., the CIA and SAP forces) has a long history, yet another example of the spread of militarized power. The CIA spent over fifty years trying to master effective torture methods. These tactics included sensory deprivation, forcing subjects to assume stress-inducing positions for long periods of time, and sexual humiliation. "Looking at the pictures from Abu Ghraib, it is not hard to recognize CIA research transformed into practice" (Davidson 2005). This means Abu Ghraib is not an anomaly but is in part a product of organizational diffusion. The strategies used in Afghanistan and Guantánamo were subsequently applied to prisoners in Iraq, often by members of thesame units that had abused prisoners previously (Jehl and Schmitt 2004; Taguba Report 2004; Kramer and Michalowski 2005). In essence, there was an organizational isomorphic affect where policy transcended the political boundaries of Guantánamo and Afghanistan into Iraq.[7]

Furthermore, the CIA and the military not only employed various torture techniques throughout the last half of the twentieth century but also instructed others how to do the same (e.g., Ferdinand Marcos of the Philippines, the Shah of Iran, the Contras, and right-wing dictators of Guatemala, Nicaragua, Argentina, Chile, etc.). One of the training agencies was the US Agency for International Development's Public Safety Program. In 1963, the CIA "developed a how-to guide to torture known as the Kubark Counterintelligence Interrogation manual" (Davidson 2005, 1). It was initially to be used on captured Soviet operatives, but by 1967 the agency was running forty interrogation camps in Vietnam as part of its Phoenix Program (Harbury 2005). Thousands of Vietnamese were tortured in these centers using techniques the CIA had developed.

Along the same lines as the KUBARK manual, there was the Human Resource Exploitation Manual of 1983, which was used extensively in Latin America during the Reagan era. These techniques, along with those being "perfected" by the CIA, have been part of the training at the School of Americas (SOA). The SOA also serves as a recruitment center for the CIA (Harbury 2005). There is also a program at Fort Bragg, North Carolina, known as SERE (Survival, Evasion, Resistance, and Escape), which was intended to be used to train US soldiers to resist abuses they potentially may face in enemy custody (Bloche and Marks 2005). During a June 2004 briefing, General James T. Hill reported that a team from Guantánamo went to SERE and developed a list of techniques to be used on high-value detainees. He reported that he had sent this list to Rumsfeld, who approved most of the tactics in December 2002 (recall that this was the list that was rescinded six weeks later by Rumsfeld). Furthermore, SERE trained psychologists and psychiatrists who were sent to Guantánamo and applied the techniques to detainees (along with MIs).

The process of institutional isomorphism or diffusion that occurred in Abu Ghraib can thus be traced back to clandestine practices of the CIA, instructional agencies such as the SOA and SERE. Direct diffusion can be linked with the CIA's clandestine operations and interrogations in Abu Ghraib as well as SAP forces that had knowledge of such techniques. The indirect diffusion comes from the role of the CIA and SAPs within the walls of Abu Ghraib, where these techniques were being used and occasionally witnessed. A notable example is the murder of Iraqi Abed Hamad Mowhoush by CIA forces. Mowhoush was forced into a sleeping bag, restrained with a cord, and "roughed up," a technique called the "sleeping bag technique" in CIA manuals. He died of asphyxiation and blunt trauma. There was also the iconic image of the hooded man with arms and feet spread while attached to alleged electric wires, known as the Vietnam technique. Clearly, the low-ranking soldiers did not create this technique or name it. Instead, this is a clear indication of organizational isomorphism (an indirect linkage to past institutional practices by the CIA and SAPs).

In December 2003, the Bush administration authorized an escalation of special forces designated as Task Force 121 (Army Delta members, Navy SEALs, and CIA paramilitary operatives). Their task was the neutralization of the insurgents in Iraq by capture or assassination. Many individuals captured by Task Force 121 added to the growing numbers of detainees already held at Abu Ghraib prison. The population of the US detention system in Iraq alone was nearing ten thousand (Danner 2004b).

On December 14, 2003, Saddam Hussein was found, and a general hope surfaced that the insurgency would significantly decrease. Nonetheless, the culture within the confines of Abu Ghraib was already well established, and the systematic practice of cruel and inhumane punishment continued as US military personnel, and allies, continued to capture and imprison thousands of Iraqis.

Reactions to the Abuses

On January 13, 2004, Specialist Darby handed over a copy of a CD containing photos depicting abuses and acts tantamount to torture to the Military Criminal Investigation Division (MCID) when attention focused on detainee treatment. With images that could not be denied, Combined Joint Task Force 7 (CJTF-7), the Central Command, the chairman of the Joints Chief of Staff, and the secretary of defense were all informed. Even at this point, officials did not recommend that the images be shown to more senior officials. On January 16, the Central Command issued a press release stating there was an ongoing investigation into reported incidence of detainee abuse,[8] and on January 19 Lieutenant General Sanchez requested a secret outside investigation.[9] Public accounts also began to surface yet were largely dismissed by the media and the general public. For example, on January 21, 2004, the *Washington Post* published a sworn statement released by the MCID describing a detainee's account of the abuses he faced during his time at Abu Ghraib (the MCID report was released January 28, 2004) (Greenberg and Dratel 2005).

By mid-March CBS had attained copies of some of the photographs. General Richard Myers, chair of the Joint Chiefs of Staff, asked CBS to delay the broadcast as intense fighting in Fallujah and Najaf was under way; CBS accommodated the request. While cases of abuse were making their way into the media, it was well recognized that the images themselves would be far more damaging than an occasional news story.[10]

On April 29, 2004, *60 Minutes II* on CBS aired the photos. However, until the publication of these images of abuse out of Abu Ghraib, Bush administration officials took "at best a see no evil, hear no evil approach to all reports of detainee mistreatment" (Human Rights Watch 2004, 5). Nevertheless, the images showed a reality that could not be denied.

Formal responses included several internal investigations to examine the cases of abuse and torture. These included the Taguba Report (March 2004), the Mikolashek Report (July 2004), the Schlesinger Report (August 2004), and the Fay-Jones Report (August 2004). A key problem with these investigations, however, is that public officials monitored the examination of their own behavior. As such, it should come as no surprise that the reports promote the politically tolerable view that the abuses and torture were, in effect, the result of individual misbehavior and sadism. Visible in the text of these reports, especially the Fay-Jones Report, is the "subtle bureaucratic response" dealing with the opposing interests within the state apparatus itself. Simply stated, the reports reflect the political war that erupted between agencies once the Abu Ghraib images became known. On one side were the actors (including Judge Advocate General, the Department of Justice, and the FBI) opposing expanded interrogation techniques and disregard for the Geneva Conventions, while on the other side were those in favor of such techniques and who tried to keep Abu Ghraib from becoming a political scandal (such as senior officials in the Department of Defense [DOD] and the Executive Administration). Thus, the reports, while recognizing a failure in the chain of command and the latent effects of isomorphism of techniques originally intended for the Taliban and al-Qaeda, maintain that responsibility was in no way that of the administration. As the Fay-Jones Report stated, responsibility lay with the individuals in the 800th MP Brigade night shift at tier 1 in Abu Ghraib, or as Schlesinger stated, "acts of brutality and sadism" were the result of a few who resembled "animal house on the night shift."

In addition, each investigation was limited to a specialized area. The Taguba Report (an internal investigation led by Major General Antonio M. Taguba at the request of General Sanchez) investigated the MPs and alleged cases of abuse; the Mikolashek Report investigated the detention procedures themselves; the Schlesinger Report (initiated by Secretary Rumsfeld and led by former Secretary of Defense Schlesinger) advised the DOD on the allegations; and the Fay-Jones Report (an internal army report led by Major General George R. Fay and Lieutenant General Anthony R. Jones) investigated the role of MIs. This specialization limited the investigations to the organizational components and that of individuals within specific branches of the military. This ensured that a holistic investigation did not occur, while at the same time appeasing the conflicting interests within the administration. Thus, the investigations served as an exercise in damage control. They were an attempt to maintain state legitimacy.

Beyond the internal military investigations, Senate and House committees held hearings in an attempt to assess what happened at Abu Ghraib and who was responsible for torture and other cruel, inhuman, and degrading treatment. In all, there were five Senate Armed Service Committee hearings, four House Armed Services Committee hearings, and three Public House Permanent Select Committee on Intelligence hearings.

Responses also included the suspension of Karpinski, on April 8, 2005, when she was formally relieved of command of the 800th MP Brigade. On May 5, 2005, Bush approved Karpinski's demotion to colonel. Karpinski was a high-ranking official, and the demotion was not linked to the Taguba Report or the cases of abuse and torture at Abu Ghraib. Instead, it was stated that she was demoted for "dereliction of duty, making a material misrepresentation to investigators, failure to obey a lawful order and shoplifting" (stealing less than US$50 worth of cosmetics from a military store).

Colonel Pappas was reprimanded only by being denied any further promotions and fined US$8,000, with no criminal charges or investigations pending. LTC Phillabaum is pending "relief for cause" for dereliction of duty. He has already been removed from duty. Captain Reese was simply admonished for failing to supervise his subordinates.

The only individuals being held criminally accountable are the low-ranking military personnel. Of the nine accused in the Abu Ghraib abuse and torture cases, seven have pleaded guilty. Spc. Ambuhl pled guilty to dereliction of duty, lost her rank, and was given an "honorable discharge." Spc. Cruz pled guilty and received eight months in jail along with a bad conduct discharge. SSG Fredrick also pled guilty and received eight years in jail and a dishonorable discharge. Spc. Sivits pled guilty and received one year in jail along with a bad conduct discharge. Sgt. Davis, upon a guilty plea, was sentenced to six months in jail and received a bad conduct discharge. Spc. Krol also entered a guilty plea and received ten months in jail and a bad conduct discharge. Spc. Harman was found guilty and given six months in jail and received a bad conduct discharge. Private Graner took his case to trial and was convicted and sentenced to ten years in Fort Leavenworth in January 2005. He was also reduced in rank and will be given a dishonorable discharge upon completion of his sentence. Private England was also found guilty, after her earlier plea entry of guilty was denied, and was sentenced to three years in jail and received a dishonorable discharge (*BBC News* 2005; MSNBC 2005).

To date, efforts continue to hold George W. Bush, Donald Rumsfeld, Dick Cheney, and other high-ranking officials within the administration accountable through legal channels in other countries, including the most recent effort in Switzerland, where two torture victims began the process of filing a complaint to bring charges and an arrest warrant for Bush when they found out he would be the guest speaker for an event on Switzerland's soil. Nonetheless, no other serious responses have occurred, nor have any other high-ranking officials been held responsible. In addition, Abu Ghraib was temporarily closed in mid-2006 and transformed into a parking lot for army trucks. Part of the prison reopened in early 2009 after some overhauls of the structure were completed, mainly to try to remove the collective memory of the abuses and torture that occurred within the walls at the hands of US military forces.

CONCLUSION

The conditions and events that occurred within Abu Ghraib were not the result of a few deviant soldiers as claimed by the administration. Instead, they were the result of a sociohistorical process combined with numerous key decisions and policies put in place by the Bush administration: the decision to classify prisoners as enemy combatants in Afghanistan and Guantánamo, the desire for actionable intelligence, expanded interrogation techniques, the enhanced practice of using covert forces, organizational isomorphism, a dysfunctional organizational environment at Abu Ghraib, and untrained, understaffed, and unsupervised low-ranking military personnel. Taken together, these catalysts led to the torture and abuse of hundreds of detainees at Abu Ghraib prison. However, the war on terrorism, Abu Ghraib, and even Guantánamo constitute not the beginning of the process of militarized supermax prisons or policing but instead merely more demonstrations of the continued expansion of American hegemony and power and the globalization of American ways of dealing with subpopulations that are viewed as in "need of being controlled."

CHAPTER 13

Conclusion

GLOBALIZATION, INNOVATION, OR NEITHER?

Jeffrey Ian Ross

CONTRARY TO MANY PRISON activists' beliefs, neither an insidious process, nor a conspiracy is taking place at the hands of American correctional practitioners and businessmen traveling around the world, pushing and motivating countries, in almost evangelical fashion, to build supermax prisons. Although this may be true with other criminal justice policies and practices (e.g., Jones and Newburn 2002, 2007; Wacquant 2009), American correctional practitioners, prison consultants, construction companies, and contractors do not appear to be actively promoting the benefits of supermax prisons. There is no smoking-gun scenario, as was revealed in John Perkins's *Diary of an Economic Hit Man* (2005). In truth, the manner by which each country examined in this study has adopted the supermax and/or high-security model of incarcerating their high-risk inmates is more considered than predicted. That does not mean, however, that generalizations cannot be made.

Clearly, proximity, dissemination of knowledge, training of correctional personnel in foreign countries (i.e., students and practitioners studying criminology/criminal justice in the United States or Great Britain), attending international criminology/criminal justice/corrections conferences, and the Internet all affect the dissemination of ideas, not only about crime and criminal justice but also on the correctional practices. Sometimes this leads to "policy transfer," while at other times it does not. The comparative analysis of the implementation of supermax prisons in these countries underscores the notion that, like so many things in life, context is everything, and the globalization of the supermax idea must be treated with nuance.

REASONS FOR ESTABLISHING
SUPERMAX PRISONS

The practices of supermax prisons were examined in nine countries, while two high-security correctional facilities are operated by the United States (Abu Ghraib and Guantánamo) in foreign countries. Looking at the countries that have built and/or operated supermax and high-security prisons, it is clear that they are disproportionately democratic in governmental form and neoliberal in their politics and economies (Cavadino and Dignan 2006a, 440). This structural factor has an important effect on the way that these states, their respective governments, and ministries/departments, at both the federal and state levels of corrections, perceive crime, criminals, and the roles of the criminal justice system in general and corrections in particular. This means that decisions to build one or more supermax prisons are not taken lightly. Nonetheless, the origins of the ideas are harder to detect. Indeed, in the process of suggesting the construction of supermax prisons, these countries go through similar steps, and advocates use similar justificatory rhetoric.

In many respects, it is difficult to pinpoint where exactly the ideas surrounding the construction of supermax prisons came from in each of these countries. In some cases, the source of inspiration was unequivocally the United States. New Zealand, for example, is the clearest example of this. Six years after Marion was retrofitted (1983), New Zealand's Paremoremo (supermax prison) was opened, and Marion served as the model (Newbold, this volume). In general, most of the countries have experienced the following eight factors, ordered in increased importance, that have led to the decisions to build and/or implement supermax regimes.

1. *Special teams in the prison services/departments of corrections that study the viability of supermax prisons.* During the 1980s, a group of experts in the Dutch Prison Service was assembled to examine how they could best house disruptive and escape-prone inmates. They decided upon the special security unit (SSU) model, as exemplified by US supermax prisons.

2. *Increases in reported crime.* As O'Day and O'Connor argue, the growth of the Mexican high-security prison was motivated by the government's inability to control the drug cartels and the violence they have caused. Mexico has developed its own unique, high-security institutions, although they borrow features from supermax prisons.

3. *One or more instances of brutal violence behind bars.* Many of the DOCs' decisions to build supermax prisons were prompted by one or more brutal incidents of violence by or against correctional officers, for example, Australia, Canada, the United States. Alternatively, as was

the case in the United States and Canada, numerous instances of prisoner resistance, including riots, persisted in selected correctional facilities, and/or an upsurge in gang activity, leading not only to extensive damage to the institution but also to numerous injuries and deaths of inmates and correctional officers, occurred in various locations. As a result, a decision was made at the political level and/or inside the DOC that the existing facilities were insufficient to house the perpetrators of these attacks and riots.

4. *An increase in escapes.* Some prison systems experienced an increase in the number of escapes from high-security and/or maximum-security-style prisons. This was certainly true with the Dutch Prison Service, where between the years 1991 and 1995, 186 inmates escaped from closed prison settings (Resodihardjo 2009, 58). Opposition member politicians, the media, and the public used these incidents as evidence to argue that the number of highly secure prisons in the Netherlands should be increased.

5. *Commissions of inquiry/royal commissions.* Many of the countries that constructed supermax prisons established commissions of inquiry that recommended the building of high-security prisons. In Canada, for example, after the riots at Kingston Penitentiary (1971), the Canadian government initiated a royal commission that was headed by Justice J. W. Swackhamer (1972). Among his numerous suggestions was the creation of new policies and practices that would hold inmates in more secure facilities. In Australia, the Nagle Royal Commission was established after prisoners destroyed Bathurst prison during the course of riots (1974), the cause of which was identified as a pattern of correctional officer brutality. The commission also tried to disentangle the reasons for the establishment of the Katingal prison and its high-security unit and recommended that the prison be closed (Brown and Carlton, this volume). In fact, each new successive high-security prison in Australia appears to have been opened in reaction to numerous acts of prisoner resistance that occurred in previous facilities. In the Netherlands, after various inmate escapes, the minister of justice initiated an investigation into the existing SSUs. The Hoekstra Report (1992) recommended the building of separate high-security prisons rather than the usage of ones that were extensions of closed prisons.

6. *Visits by politicians and/or heads of the ministry/department of corrections to American supermax prisons.* Before constructing the Ebongweni supermax prison (opened in 2002) in South Africa, the minister of corrections went on a study tour, which included a visit to a supermax facility in Colorado. When the decision was made to build the

institution, South African architects were sent to the United States to look at similar facilities (Buntman and Muntingh, this volume). Similarly, Paremoremo prison in New Zealand was modeled on Marion prison in Illinois.

7. *Opposition*. In almost all countries, a limited number of individuals opposed the construction of supermax facilities. This included both prison activists and political parties, whose efforts were directed against the construction of the supermax facilities. This opposition developed either at the discussion stage or after the facility was built. Political opposition was commonly in the form of protests by activist groups, or it was carried out by opposition members of parliament through public statements to the news media or during political debates. In the Netherlands, counter to what one would expect, the governor's union (akin to an organization representing prison wardens) opposed the construction of any new SSUs, arguing that it would detract from the current policies and practices of rehabilitation that existed in the Dutch Prison Service (Resodihardjo, this volume).

8. *Passage of enabling policies, practices, and/or legislation*. In many countries, the supermax facilities and control units were given the green light through the passage of enabling legislation. For example, in 2001 the Brazilian legislature passed the Regime Disciplinar Diferenciado. The policy, which was reaffirmed in 2003, "allows for a prisoner to be placed in an individual cell for 360 days, subject to further sanction for misconduct, up to one-sixth of a sentence. The benefits under this law are limited: two hours of out-of-cell time in small groups, according to gang affiliation, and weekly visits for two hours, during which the inmate and visitors (up to two, not counting children) are separated by grids and screens" (Jesus Filho, this volume). This laid the procedural and policy groundwork for the establishment of supermax prisons, first in the Penitentiary Rehabilitation Centre of Taubaté and later in different regions of the country.

In most countries, the decision to introduce supermax prisons was not clear-cut. Each state experienced "growing pains." In Canada, for example, the federal Correctional Services of Canada played a ping-pong game of constructing a high-security prison (Saskatchewan Penitentiary) as a secure handling unit and then demobilizing it, to only then construct a completely new one (Sainte-Anne-des-Plaines) (Ross, this volume).

FACTORING OUT GLOBALIZATION

As the previous review should indicate, each country had its own unique reasons for implementing a supermax prison model. And trying to factor out the influence of globalization is very difficult. With the exception of Abu Ghraib and Guantánamo, both American inventions transported to different countries, the issue of causality was more iterative (i.e., constantly evolving) than unidirectional (i.e., the United States to the foreign country). In other words, each country experimented with new procedures and practices, and when the prison officials deemed it appropriate, new facilities to house their most incorrigible criminals were constructed.

One reason to explain the adoption of the supermax relates to the relative punitiveness of the states that took the leap to build such facilities, keeping in mind that some countries (not covered in this study), while they may have officially rejected the supermax name, have for all intents and purposes constructed supermax-like structures. This is perhaps why Snacken (2010, 275) suggests that even if a state is a democracy, it will vary in its relative punitiveness and guarantees of human rights among prisoners. Also noteworthy is the fact that some of the correctional institutions in each country changed their administrative regimes so that their methods came to more closely resemble the supermaxes when comparing one prison or correctional administration to another.

The connection between globalization and Guantánamo and Abu Ghraib is not as conceptually clear as is the case with the countries analyzed in this book. In most respects, both facilities are American inventions, so it is only natural that US policies and practices that are used stateside were imported to both of these institutions (M. Brown 2005). However, in many respects, the two prisons do not completely reflect traditional correctional practices but instead utilize methods once used in navy brigs and at places like Leavenworth, the infamous American military prison.

With the exception of Abu Ghraib and Guantánamo, few of the high-security prisons have held so-called terrorists. And if current reports are accurate, the percentage of those detained at these prisons who were indeed terrorists was quite small. In 2007, Acacia Prison in Australia was unique because it held individuals who were preparing for terrorist actions. And the US supermax in Florence, Colorado, holds individuals convicted of terrorism-related crimes, but otherwise few supermax and high-security prisons have been utilized for detaining terrorists.

WHAT THE FUTURE HOLDS

Because supermax prisons are the most expensive alternative in a country's correctional system, in these times of economic restraint, many states have been forced to take an even closer look at their expenditures. The decision to build a supermax prison, no matter what its real or prospective, alleged, or actual merits are, is rarely taken lightly by a country's legislature and ministries/departments of correction. In order not to repeat the same mistakes as other jurisdictions, although it is prudent to see what other countries have done, each state must forge its own path lest it be seen as simply mimicking American criminal justice policy directions and practices. Alternatively, the solutions must be tailored to each state's own unique circumstances. It is interesting to note that in many countries reviewed in this book (e.g., South Africa and the United States), many of the supermax facilities have not been operated at full capacity. This means either that the need was overestimated or that DOCs have now found it necessary to expand the classifications of prisoners to enable them to be transferred to existing supermaxes to justify the expenditure. Furthermore, one needs to consider that many supermax prisons are underutilized. Almost all of the countries reviewed in this book have reported periods during which their high-security prisons were below capacity.

Finally, over a decade ago well-known penologist Hans Toch wrote a highly cited article, "The Future of Supermax Confinement" (2001). This piece outlined most of the negative features of American supermax prisons covered in this book. Short of suggesting their complete elimination, Toch provided a number of reforms designed to "humanize" high-security prisons. Unfortunately, despite the wisdom of the proposed reforms, over a decade later few of these changes have been implemented. Thus, it is hard to predict what the future holds for the supermax, both in the United States and elsewhere.

Notes

FOREWORD

1. Tocqueville's celebrated account of *Democracy in America* originated in a year-long mission across the republic, carried out with Gustave de Beaumont on behalf of the French government, to inquire about carceral practices in the United States. It led to the publication of the landmark study *On the Penitentiary System in the United States and Its Application in France* (1833; repr., Carbondale: Southern Illinois University Press, 1979), introduction by Thornsten Sellin.

2. The official views on penal policy circa 1968–1973 are dissected by Franklin Zimring and Gordon Hawkins, *The Scale of Imprisonment* (Chicago: University of Chicago Press, 1991). The early shock and disillusionment of penal analysts at accelerating carceral expansion after 1973 is captured by John Irwin, *Prisons in Turmoil* (Boston: Little, Brown, 1980). The hope that the United States would shepherd the planet out of the carceral impasse is expressed in Calvert R. Dodge, ed., *A World without Prisons: Alternatives to Incarceration throughout the World* (Lexington, MA: Lexington Books, 1979).

3. The fusing of these three reactionary movements into the building of a ravenous penal state is dissected in my books *Punishing the Poor: The Neoliberal Government of Social Insecurity* (Durham, NC: Duke University Press, 2009) and *Deadly Symbiosis: Race and the Rise of the Penal State* (Cambridge: Polity Press, 2012).

4. Loïc Wacquant, *Prisons of Poverty* (Minneapolis: University of Minnesota Press, 2009). See Trevor Jones and Tim Newburn, *Policy Transfer and Criminal Justice: Exploring US Influence over British Crime Control Policy* (Maidenhead, UK: Open University Press, 2006), for a complementary view from Great Britain, and Guillermina Seri, *Seguridad: Crime, Police Power, and Democracy in Argentina* (New York: Continuum, 2012), for a Latin American perspective.

5. Sharon Shalev, *Supermax: Controlling Risk through Solitary Confinement* (Cullompton, UK: Willan, 2009).

6. Michael Tonry, "Rethinking Unthinkable Punishment Policies in the United States," *UCLA Law Review* 46, no. 1 (March 1999): 1–38.

7. More so than the death penalty, whose return after the mid-1970s is a legal accident overdetermined by the deep class bias of criminal justice and which plays a decorative (and distractive) role in the overall economy of punishment in America (*pace* David Garland, *Peculiar Institution: America's Death Penalty in an Age of Abolition* [Cambridge, MA: Harvard University Press, 2010]).

8. Cheryl Marie Webster and Anthony N. Doob, "Punitive Trends and Stable Imprisonment Rates in Canada," *Crime and Justice: A Review* 36, no. 1 (2007): 297–369.

9. Rod Morgan, "Developing Prison Standards Compared," *Punishment & Society* 2, no. 3 (July 2000): 325–342.

10. As I suggested elsewhere about the diffusion of "zero-tolerance" policing and assorted devices of made-in-America punitive penality: see Loïc Wacquant, "A Global Firestorm of Law and Order," *Thesis Eleven* (forthcoming).

11. See Dario Melossi, Maximo Sozzo, and Richard Sparks, eds., *Travels of the Criminal Question: Cultural Embeddedness and Diffusion* (Oxford: Hart, 2010), and Jamie Peck, "Geographies of Policy: From Transfer-Diffusion to Mobility-Mutation," *Progress in Human Geography* 35, no. 6 (November 2011): 773–797, for stimulative reflections on this process.

12. Jeffrey Ian Ross and Stephen C. Richards, *Convict Criminology* (Belmont, CA: Wadsworth, 2003).

13. The administrative, technical, and political sources of the cumulative difficulties in defining and scoping "supermax" facilities in the United States are discussed by Alexandra Naday, Joshua D. Freilich, and Jeff Mellow, "The Elusive Data on Supermax Confinement," *The Prison Journal* 88, no. 1 (March 2008): 69–93.

14. Robert K. Merton, "Three Fragments from a Sociologist's Notebooks: Establishing the Phenomenon, Specified Ignorance, and Strategic Research Materials," *Annual Review of Sociology* 13 (1987): 1–28.

15. The philosophy of neutralization and its aporias are dissected by Franklin E. Zimring and Gordon Hawkins, *Incapacitation: Penal Confinement and the Restraint of Crime* (New York: Oxford University Press, 1995). Their central arguments can be extended and adapted to fit the meta-prison.

16. Roy D. King, "The Rise and Rise of Supermax: An American Solution in Search of a Problem?" *Punishment & Society* 1, no. 2 (October 1999): 163–186, 182; and David Garland, "Penal Modernism and Postmodernism," in *Punishment and Social Control*, ed. Thomas G. Blomberg and Stanley Cohen (New York: Aldine de Gruyter, 1995), 181–210.

17. Contrast this collective volume to another, situated at the other end of the penal spectrum spanned by advanced societies, Thomas Ugelvik and Jane Dullum, eds., *Penal Exceptionalism? Nordic Prison Policy and Practice* (London: Routledge, 2011).

18. Anne-Marie Marchetti, *Perpétuités. Le temps infini des longues peines* (Paris: Plon, 2001); Ben Crewe, *The Prisoner Society: Power, Adaptation, and Social Life in an English Prison* (New York: Oxford University Press, 2009); Joshua Page, *The Toughest Beat: Politics, Punishment, and the Prison Officers Union in California* (New York: Oxford University Press, 2010); Lisa L. Miller, *The Perils of Federalism: Race, Poverty, and the Politics of Crime Control* (New York: Oxford University Press, 2008); and Vanessa Barker, *The Politics of Imprisonment: How the Democratic Process Shapes the Way America Punishes Offenders* (New York: Oxford University Press, 2009).

19. Pierre Bourdieu, "Rethinking the State: On the Genesis and Structure of the Bureaucratic Field" [1993], *Sociological Theory* 12, no. 1 (March 1994): 1–18, and, for an adaptation of this notion to theorize penal transformation, Loïc Wacquant, "Crafting the Neoliberal State: Workfare, Prisonfare, and Social Insecurity," *Sociological Forum* 25, no. 2 (June 2010): 197–220.

CHAPTER I   THE GLOBALIZATION OF SUPERMAX PRISONS

Acknowledgments: Thanks to Rachel Hildebrandt, Peter Mickulas, Greg Newbold, Sandra Resodihardjo, Dawn L. Rothe, Loïc Wacquant, Aaron Z. Winter, and an anonymous reviewer for comments on this chapter.

1. Capital punishment in the United States is not cheap either. The cost to the state of incarcerating a person on death row, plus the numerous appeals, can be upward of US$10 million.

2. Although all supermax prisons are high-security facilities, not all high-security prisons are supermaxes.

3. Only six correctional facilities officially called supermax facilities exist outside of the United States (i.e., Special Handling Unit, Saint-Anne-des-Plaines, Québec, Canada; C-Max, Pretoria, South Africa; Al Hayer Prison, Riyadh, Saudi Arabia; Goulburn Correctional Centre, Goulburn, New South Wales, Australia; Centro de Readaptação Provisória de Presidente Bernardes, Presidente Bernardes, São Paulo, Brazil; Penitenciaría de Combita, Colombia).

4. Information about comparative incarceration rates was obtained through the International Centre for Prison Studies (http://www.prisonstudies.org/info/worldbrief/wpb_stats.php?area=all&category=wb_poprate).

5. Undoubtedly, American correctional practices and companies specializing in the design and construction of prisons have influenced the decision to build supermax/high-intensity custody facilities in other countries.

6. In no way should these be considered ethnographies or substitutes for the same.

7. Although the editor expended considerable effort trying to find an expert to write a chapter surrounding the establishment of supermax prisons in Colombia, given time limitations he was not able to achieve this goal.

CHAPTER 2 THE INVENTION OF THE AMERICAN SUPERMAX PRISON

Acknowledgments: Thanks to Miguel Zaldivar for comments on this chapter.

1. This, according to Human Rights Watch (2000). The exact current number is not available at this time.

2. Female prisoners, whom the Federal Bureau of Prisons (FBOP) deems eligible for incarceration in supermax-like facilities, are typically housed in the high-security unit at FMC–Lexington.

3. In the Federal Bureau of Prisons (FBOP), A.D. stands for administrative detention and DS for disciplinary segregation.

4. The Federal Correctional Complex in Florence has four prisons with varying levels of security, including the ADX USP, FCI, and CAMP.

5. The latest statistics collected by Bureau of Justice Statistics (BJS) on the security level of state and federal prisons date to 2000. The publication (Census of State and Federal Correctional Facilities 2000) includes a table on the security/custody levels of inmates. Unfortunately, the maximum-security level includes "super maximum," "close," and "high" (see pp. iv and v). Furthermore, the designation "supermax" is not exclusive to an individual facility but is also used to refer to a wing or unit of a particular facility. The report can be found at the following website: http://www.ojp.usdoj.gov/bjs/abstract/csfcf00.htm.

6. Based on http://www.bop.gov/locations/weekly_report.jsp#bop.

7. Sasha Abramsky (2002) puts the cost at US$50,000 for Ohio state prisoners.

8. In some cases, scholars (e.g., Rogers 1993) have advocated the use of supermax prisons, as they have believed that these facilities would eventually lead to cost reductions, lessen inmate victimization by other inmates, and enhance the possibility of rehabilitation.

9. Randy Corcoran, telephone interview, September 2008.

10. This section draws from Ross (2006b).

CHAPTER 3 HOW CANADA BUILT ITS SUPERMAX PRISON

1. This does not preclude the use of administrative segregation, which is used in provincial jails and prisons. Almost every correctional facility has a unit in which inmates are locked down because of disciplinary infractions.

2. The author recognizes the limitations of these sources and considers them sufficient for the purposes of this chapter. The conclusion specifies additional sources where more information may be obtained.

3. A series of other lesser-known reports (e.g., "Evaluation of Design for Maximum Security Prisons," 1966) buttressed the need for the construction of the SHU-like facilities, but these are not as important in the overall context of this chapter.
4. Information pertaining to the closure of this facility is not available at this time.

CHAPTER 4   SUPERMAXES SOUTH OF THE BORDER

1. Interview with Juan Escalante (pseudonym), Hidalgo County, Texas, December 2009.
2. Interview with Juan Escalante, Hidalgo County, Texas, July 2010.
3. Shortly after he took power on December 1, 2006, Mexico's president Filipe de Jesus Calderon Hinojosa ordered Don Miguel isolated in a cell in El Altiplano without so much as a telephone or even cigarettes (Stevenson 2011).

CHAPTER 6   ANALYZING THE SUPERMAX PRISONS IN THE NETHERLANDS

Acknowledgments: Parts of this chapter were previously published in Boin and Resodihardjo (2000) and Resodihardjo (2009).

1. For a historical overview of the fight between those who believed in solitary confinement and those who were in favor of social contacts, see Franke (1992, 1996).
2. An additional special security unit located in Arnhem turned out to be unsuitable and was soon used for other purposes (Hoekstra 1992, 32).
3. *Lorsé and Others v. The Netherlands,* no. 52750/99, ECHR 2003, 8. See also Regeling selectie, plaatsing en overplaatsing van gedetineerden (October 1, 2000), art. 6.
4. Meldpunt-GRIP is the prisoner detective information point of the Department of National Detective Information of the combined Dutch police forces.
5. Regeling selectie, plaatsing en overplaatsing gedetineerden (October 1, 2000), art. 22.
6. Aanwijzing formulier risiscoprofiel en executie-indicator.
7. Ibid., attachment 1.
8. Regeling selectie, plaatsing en overplaatsing van gedetineerden (October 1, 2000), art. 26.
9. Regeling selectie, plaatsing en overplaatsing van gedetineerden (October 1, 2000), art. 26, para. 4.
10. Regeling selectie, plaatsing en overplaatsing van gedetineerden (October 1, 2000), art. 26, para. 5.
11. For a couple of years, the temporary supermax functioned as a backup unit, but it is currently used to house prisoners who are difficult to control (DJI, pers. comm., March 30, 2010).
12. Terrorist units are located in Prison Vught and Prison De Schie. The main difference between the supermax regime and the terrorist unit regime is that fewer visitor restrictions apply. For instance, it is possible for prisoners to meet their visitors without bulletproof glass between them (Molenkamp 2009, 47). While the book was in production, the junior minister of safety and justice announced that a single location to hold terrorists would suffice considering the limited number of prisoners with a terrorist background. Consequently, the supermax no longer has a terrorist ward (TK 2010–2011, 29754, no. 201).
13. Model Huisregels Extra Beveiligde Inrichting, Introduction, 4.
14. DJI, pers. comm., March 9, 2010.
15. DJI, pers. comm., March 30, 2010.
16. Regeling selectie, plaatsing en overplaatsing van gedetineerden (October 1, 2000), art. 10. If needed, prisoners can be subjected to an individual regime, which

means that they will not be accompanied by any other prisoners while doing any activities such as sport (Model Huisregels Extra Beveiligde Inrichting, sec. 2.1, 6). Moreover, there used to be a distinction between regime A and regime B in the supermax. Prisoners falling under regime A could not be placed in groups bigger than three prisoners and were not allowed to use the outside recreation area. Prisoners falling under regime B could not be placed in groups bigger than four prisoners and were allowed to use the outside recreation area. After a year, it was decided to no longer use regime A. All prisoners now fall under regime B (DJI, pers. comm., March 30, 2010), though both regimes are still mentioned in the supermax house rules (Model Huisregels Extra Beveiligde Inrichting, sec. 2.1, 6–7).

17. Prisoners participating in the penitentiary program are allowed to leave the prison (before their sentence is up) and participate in work or training-related projects under the supervision of a parole officer and the governor of the prison. The aim of the program is to help prisoners resocialize, integrate in society, and get a job (De Jonge and Cremers 2008, 125).

18. Model Huisregels Extra Beveiligde Inrichting, sec. 2.1, 6.

19. Ibid.

20. Only prisoners in isolation, in a punishment cell, or in the supermax unit and prisoners under an individual regime can be observed using CCTV (Kelk 2008, 244).

21. Penitentiaire beginselenwet (June 18, 1998), art. 34a.

22. DJI, pers. comm., March 30, 2010. Former governor of the supermax Molenkamp points out that *visitatie* is not the same as an invasive internal body search. What people working in the prison service call *visitatie* is covered by article 29, paragraph 2 of the prison law (Molenkamp 2009, 43). The law states, "The search of the prisoner's body includes looking externally at the openings and cavities of the prisoner's body" (Penitentiaire beginselenwet June 18, 1998, art. 29, para. 2).

23. Vught consists of a mix of different prisons and units.

24. Model Huisregels Extra Beveiligde Inrichting, sec. 6.4, 35. Cf. Molenkamp (2009, 43).

25. Ibid., sec. 2.1, 6 and sec. 6.4, 35.

26. Ibid., sec. 3.1, 8 and sec. 3.5, 11.

27. *Lorsé and Others v. The Netherlands*, no. 52750/99, ECHR 2003, 25; *Van der Ven v. The Netherlands*, no. 50901/99, ECHR 2003, 22. Other European Court of Human Rights (ECHR) rulings include *Salah v. The Netherlands*, no. 8196/02, ECHR 2006; *Baybaşin v. The Netherlands*, no. 13600/02, ECHR 2006; and *Sylla v. The Netherlands*, no. 14683/03, ECHR 2006.

28. At first, the minister of justice continued with the routine use of strip searches. In a summary proceeding, the judge told the minister to change the strip search procedure (De Jonge and Cremers 2008, 281; cf. De Lange 2008, 287–289).

29. The temporary supermax was visited in 2002 because the supermax was being renovated and prisoners had been moved to the temporary supermax.

30. TK 2003–2004, 24587 no. 96, 2.

31. EK 2003–2004, 29200 VI, E.

32. One of the other measures taken in response to the report was the introduction of two regimes so that prisoners could go from a basic regime to a regime with more facilities if they exhibited good behavior (EK 2003–2004, 29200 VI, E). The text in the parliamentary document seems to refer to the A and B regimes previously discussed in this chapter. However, the A and B regimes lasted only for a year, and all prisoners now fall under the same supermax regime.

33. TK 2002–2003, Aanhangsel, 1789.

34. DJI, pers. comm. March 9, 2010.

CHAPTER 7   SUPERMAXIMUM PRISONS IN SOUTH AFRICA

Acknowledgments: Fran Buntman thanks Adam Dale and Annie Jackson for research assistance on this project. Both authors thank the respondents for their time and insights and Jeffrey Ian Ross for including us in this project.

1. The Correctional Services Amendment Act (25 of 2008) changed certain nomenclature from the earlier principal legislation, the 1998 Correctional Services Act 111. Prison became "correctional centre," "prisoners" became "inmates," and "sentenced prisoners" were termed "sentenced offenders."

2. The two supermaximum security prisons are distinguished from the maximum-security prisons via their design, operation, and strict security regime. As explained and discussed in the text, there is no necessary relationship between the security classification system (minimum, medium, maximum, and supermaximum) and the inmate privilege system, which also involves classifying individual inmates based on their conduct. The highest rating is an A classification, and B and C follow with lower levels of privileges. This intersection between security classification and privilege classification could mean, for example, that a C group inmate in a minimum- or medium-security prison would not be allowed a contact visit, whereas an inmate in A group in C-Max or Ebongweni would be allowed a contact visit (Department of Correctional Services [DCS] 2008). However, DCS's website suggests that no inmates in C-Max or supermaximum facilities are entitled to contact visits (http://www.dcs.gov.za/visitingoffenders/visitationprocess.aspx). DCS does not have plans to build further supermaximum facilities ("PMG Report" 2007b).

3. Pretoria is the administrative capital of South Africa. It is a city of about a million people in the dense and dominantly urban Gauteng province. DCS has divided South Africa into fifty-two management areas. Each area may include several smaller prisons or may have only one large prison.

4. Although DCS does not refer to the Ebongweni as a C-Max prison, others often refer to both supermaximum prisons as C-Max. Parliament's own Portfolio Committee on Correctional Services ("PMG Report" 1998) referred to "CMAX prisons" in March 1998. The University of South Africa, which facilitates university-level study in prisons in part by designating prisons as testing centers, refers to "Ebongweni C-Max (Kokstad)" but does not refer to C-Max at Pretoria Central, although the latter also allows testing. See http://www.unisa.ac.za/default .asp?Cmd=ViewContent&ContentID=17069.

5. F. J. "Frikkie" Venter, interview conducted by Lukas Muntingh, July 9, 2010, Johannesburg.

6. Ibid. At the time of this interview, Venter remained in the DCS in a more senior position.

7. Ibid. The Jali (2006) Report outlined the typical profile of a supermax inmate as a sentenced prisoner serving a long term of imprisonment and who has committed crimes inside prison or attempted escape.

> The criteria for admission of inmates to C-Max Prison are contained in a Departmental document, referenced 1/3/13 dated 5 November 1998. In terms of this document the following criteria are used by the Department for the transfer of prisoners to C-Max Prison:
>
> - Prisoners sentenced to longer than twenty (20) years within the last three (3) months.
> - Prisoners who have been found guilty of escaping/attempted to escape or aided an escape.
> - Prisoners who have been declared dangerous persons by the Court.

- Prisoners who have assaulted/murdered a DCS official, an SAPS [South African Police Services] official or fellow inmate.
- Prisoners who are troublesome and who do not show any improvement in their behaviour even after they have been demoted to C Group.
- Prisoners who are actively involved in prison gangsterism.
- Prisoners who have been convicted for hijackings and who have murdered/assaulted their victims, are members of notorious crime syndicates, or are serial killers/rapists. (Jali 2006, 354–355).

8. Figures supplied by the Judicial Inspectorate for Correctional Services, July 2010.
9. Under South African law, life imprisonment requires incarceration for the prisoner's natural life, but parole must be considered after twenty-five years. Inmates who are sixty-five or older and have served at least fifteen years may also be considered for parole. Children (under the age of eighteen years) may not be sentenced to life imprisonment. Correctional Services Act 111 of 1998, sec. 73(1) and sec. 73(6).
10. For C-Max, see, for example, http://www.news24.com/SouthAfrica/News/ Boeremag-judge-slams-jailers-20041203.
11. A detailed summary of the context of these murders and associated escape attempt as well as completed suicides and suicide attempt is provided at http:// www.pmg.org.za/minutes/20041116-management-hivaids-and-security-breach- pretoria-c-max-briefing-department.
12. Appropriate conduct in C-Max allows prisoners to move from phase 1 to phase 2. Inmates in phase 2 have contact with each other in the courtyard and bathrooms.
13. DCS identified Ebongweni as one of thirty-six "centres of excellence," a term used from August 2005 as part of an effort to transform the South African prisons system. It remains uncertain what this project has achieved.
14. Gideon Morris, interview conducted by Lukas Muntingh, June 10, 2010, Cape Town. During the establishment of the supermaximum prisons, Morris was the secretary to Mzimela, then minister of correctional services. At the time of his 2010 interview, Morris was the director of South Africa's Judicial Inspectorate of Correctional Services.
15. For example, in 1997 a total of seventy-five prisoners died due to unnatural causes; twenty-five of these were due to prisoner-on-prisoner violence (DCS Annual Report 1997).
16. Sipo Mzimela, phone interview conducted by Fran Buntman, July 10, 2010, Washington, D.C.; Golz Wessman, interview conducted by Lukas Muntingh, July 16, 2010, Westlake, Cape Town. At the time of these interviews, neither Mzimela nor Wessman worked in corrections.
17. Morris emphasized escape as the motivation for establishing C-Max. Both he and Wessman insisted that public perceptions of increasingly dangerous prisoners "had no role" in the prison's creation.
18. DCS increasingly had to deal with individuals who received military training as members of the liberation movements (e.g., ANC) but subsequently applied their skills to commit violent crimes, such as cash-in-transit robberies (Venter interview).
19. It took nearly two years for death row to be converted into C-Max.
20. Venter interview.
21. Mzimela interview; the Criminal Law Amendment Act (105 of 1997), which came into force in 1998, created a mechanism to deal with prisoners sentenced to death.
22. It is interesting that the highest number of escapes in one year was not in 1994. In 1975–1976, over 2,300 people escaped, and the relative number would be even greater if adjusted for the population increase (Oppler 1998). Although this history

shows that escapes were not unique to a post-apartheid South Africa, for all practical purposes such comparisons would be meaningless to a society newly exposed to an open media, a black-majority government, an extremely serious crime problem, and fundamental social change in every way.

23. In September 2001, Mr. Justice Thabane Jali was appointed by the then South African president, Thabo Mbeki, to chair a commission of inquiry into "incidents of corruption, maladministration, violence or intimidation in the Department of Correctional Services" (Jali 2006). The commission's report, known as the Jali Report, was presented to the president in December 2005 and made public in 2006. Its comments included the following: "Escapes of prisoners from prison are not a new issue. . . . What is new is the practice of members deliberately setting prisoners free. These corrupt members then escape the claws of the justice system because they are not suspended and thereby remain employed in the Department" (Jali 2006, 278).

24. "Warder" is the long-standing South African term for correctional officer (or prison guard). It should not be confused with "warden," usually a more senior prison official, a term widely used in various other countries.

25. On July 21, 2010, a C-Max official was fatally shot at home by unknown gunmen a week after he gave court testimony about an attempted escape from C-Max during which two officials were killed (Lindeque 2010).

26. Venter interview.

27. Wessman interview. In contrast, Mzimela did not believe C-Max was inspired by US trends. He emphasized C-Max was a "basic stronghold," not a high-tech prison, and that DCS studied and built it using knowledge from numerous countries that were visited, not only the United States. Venter distinguished between the regimes at Ebongweni and C-Max, and regarded Ebongweni's system as more severe and harsh.

28. The Interim Constitution (Act 200 of 1993) came into force on April 27, 1994.

29. Venter interview.

30. When C-Max was developed, new legislation to replace the 1958 Prisons Act had not yet been adopted.

31. Venter interview; Wessman interview.

32. See http://www.news24.com/SouthAfrica/News/Probe-into-prisoners-death-20090814.

33. See http://www.iol.co.za/index.php?set_id=1&click_id=13&art_id=nw20100730 145253490C61095.

34. Mzimela interview.

35. Boeremag is a white Afrikaner separatist and supremacist group. Schönteich and Boshoff (2003, 60) argue this "extreme right [group] mixes religion and politics . . . driven by a philosophy based on extreme nationalist views and a sense of God-given purpose. . . . The Boeremag [was i]nitially belittled by the media, and underestimated by the police and the intelligence community, [but] the danger posed by the organisation rapidly grew to become South Africa's primary security threat during the last quarter of 2002."

36. Morris interview; Mzimela interview.

37. Wessman interview.

38. Ibid.; Mzimela interview

39. A particularly dramatic example was then commissioner Sitole's proposal to use disused underground mine shafts as supermaximum security prisons. He equated criminals, especially violent criminals, with animals who "must never see sunlight again" (Sitole 2010).

40. "Because it was illegal and illegitimate, the apartheid state's practices eroded the moral fibre of South African society. The state relied more and more on criminal

actions to shore up its fortunes and in the process, it pulled the rest of society into a maelstrom of corruption and crime. As such, apartheid political and economic relations were not only a break on the development of the economy, they were also an albatross on the moral sensibilities of society" ("ANC Strategy and Tactics, as Amended at the 50th National Conference, December 1997," http://www .marxists.org/subject/africa/anc/1997/strategy-tactics.htm).

41. Claims that prisons help rural economies are common in the United States, although the net positive impact has been questioned and debated (see, e.g., Beale 1993, 1996; Farrigan and Glasmeier 2007). This South African context emphasized black economic empowerment (Sigcau 2002) as well as rural employment and development.

42. Correctional Services Act (111 of 1998), sec. 36.

43. The policy procedures state,

> On admission all offenders enter Ebongweni in Phase I for orientation and assessment processes. These offenders are assessed every 3 months and can be considered for promotion to Phase II after 6 months, depending on their adjustment, behavior and co-operation. Offenders in Phase II are subjected to specific Intervention and Correctional Programmes and are assessed every 3 months by a Case Review Team and every 6 months by the Case Management Committee. After a period of 24 months of good behavior and the successful completion of the identified Intervention and Correctional Programmes offenders can be considered for promotion to Phase III. Offenders in Phase III are subjected to specific pre-transfer programmes in order to facilitate their re-integration into a normal open maximum environment and transfer to the correctional centre of origin. All offenders are subjected to the mentioned three phases and applications for transfers are not entertained at this level. All applications for transfer prior to the successful completion of all three phases are referred to the National Selection Panel for consideration. A Special Care Unit for offenders with behavioral/adjustment problems has been established and forms part of the Phase I.
> (http://www.dcs.gov.za/AboutUs/COE/Centre/KZN/Documents/ EbongweniPhaseI-III/Prog-Phase.doc)

As is often the case, there is a frequent gap between policy and practice. For example, although the various programming is identified as available, a "severe shortage of Social Workers is seriously hampering the rendering of social work services and programmes" (http://www.dcs.gov.za/AboutUs/COE/Centre/KZN/ Documents/EbongweniPhaseI-III/social.doc).

44. Mzimela interview.

45. A small insight into the reality of how individual perceptions rather than supposedly neutral criteria may shape prisoner classification or placement was offered in the differing perspectives as to whether Eugene De Kock should be placed in C-Max. For Mzimela (interview), the heinous nature of De Kock's crimes and his notoriety made him a supermaximum candidate. In contrast, Wessman (interview) saw the key factors not as the awfulness of his crimes but the fact that he cooperated and showed remorse, underscoring De Kock's potential for rehabilitation. In practice, De Kock was in C-Max for a while, but not permanently.

46. This gap is arguably a consistent feature of South African criminal justice policies.

47. Examples of visits to supermaximum facilities in South Africa include the Judicial Inspectorate for Correctional Services (various), the Human Rights Commission (Dissel 2002), navy personnel to C-Max in April 2010 (as noted in a now-expired Facebook page), and Parliament's Portfolio Committee on Correctional Services to Ebongweni in May 2010 (http://www.feveronline.co.za/details.asp?Sto Num= 7019).

CHAPTER 8   FROM "SECONDARY PUNISHMENT" TO "SUPERMAX"

1. The NSW Royal Commission presided over by Justice Nagle was hugely influential, ran for three years, and had myriad implications on a range of fronts. It remains as a landmark historical event insofar as it had far-reaching national implications for prison reform agendas at the time.
2. For prisoner accounts of the Grafton regime see, for example, Matthews (2006) and Denning (1982).
3. On the struggle over Katingal and the Nagle Royal Commission recommendations generally, see Findlay (1982), Vinson (1982), and Zdenkowski and Brown (1982); and on its legacy, see Brown (2005).
4. This refers to a whole range of enhanced security screening practices, including the seizure of water bottles, toothpaste, and so on at airports, the new X-ray technology that can be used to screen people down to their bones, an increase in CCTV, public announcements to look out for unattended luggage, and so on.

CHAPTER 10   THE RISE OF THE SUPERMAX IN BRAZIL

1. Warden, interview with author, June 21, 2010.

CHAPTER 11   GUANTÁNAMO

This chapter builds upon Ross (2006a, 2007a).
1. With few exceptions, this information is critical of the conditions at Guantánamo. One exception to this state of affairs is the book by Lieutenant Colonel Gordon Cucullu (2009), which paints a sympathetic picture of the Gitmo and the job servicemen have to do.
2. George W. Bush, in a joint press conference with British prime minister Tony Blair, July 17, 2003, http://www.npr.org/templates/story/story.php?storyId= 1340091.
3. The Koran controversy originally came to public attention in a 2005 *Newsweek* magazine article. Shortly after the publication, it was determined that the story was based on false sources. Later, a US military report confirmed that actual incidents of Koran desecration had in fact taken place. All the detainees' memoirs contain similar accounts of Koran desecration.
4. Memo 14, from Jay Bybee, August 1, 2002, in Greenberg and Dratel (2005, 172–217).
5. Memo 16, from Major General Hill, October 25, 2002, in Greenberg and Dratel (2005, 223–224).

CHAPTER 12   A GLOBALIZED MILITARIZED PRISON JUGGERNAUT

1. "Schlesinger Report," August 2004, in Greenberg and Dratel (2005, 908–975).
2. "Assessment of DOD Counter-terrorism Interrogation and Detention Operations," http://www1.umn.edu/humanrts/OathBetrayed/Taguba%20Annex% 2020.pdf.
3. Boykin came under fire in the fall of 2003, when it was reported that while giving a speech in an Oregon church he equated Satan with the Muslim religion (Hersh 2004).
4. The Taguba Report, prepared by Maj. Gen. Antonio M. Taguba, is the final report of the Army Regulation military inquiry conducted in 2004 into the Abu Ghraib prisoner abuse.
5. "General Fay's Report," January 2004, in Greenberg and Dratel (2005, 987–1131).

6. "Annex to Fay Jones Report" (DOD 000415–000416), http://www.aclu.org/torturefoia/released/030905/.
7. Organizational isomorphism is a process where a specific practice is diffused through knowledge and/or contact via a network linking individuals and roles.
8. "Final Report of the Independent Panel to Review DOD Detention Operations Memo to US Central Command," January 19, 2004, in Strasser (2004, 1–165).
9. "Memo to US Central Command," January 19, 2004, in Greenberg and Dratel (2005, 552).
10. "Schlesinger Report," August 2004, in Greenberg and Dratel (2005, 908–975).

References

Abramsky, S. 2002. "Return of the Madhouse." *The American Prospect,* February 11, 26–29.

Adorno, S., and F. Salla. 2007. "Criminalidade organizada nas prisões e os ataques do PCC." *Estudos Avançados* 21 (61): 7–27.

Algemeen Dagblad. [0]1992. "Nieuw soort gevangenis moet vluchten inperken. Nog geen commentaar Kosto op plan commissie Hoekstra." September 22, 1, 4.

Altbeker, A. 2007. *A Country at War with Itself: South Africa's Crisis of Crime.* Johannesburg: Jonathan Ball.

American Enterprise Institute. 2004. "Report and Video of Saddam's Torture at Abu Ghraib." http://www.aei.org/events/2004/06/08/naming-names-event/.

Armstrong, D. 2002. "Dick Cheney's Song of America: Drafting a Plan for Global Dominance." *Harper's Magazine,* October, 76–83.

Arun, N. 2007. "Guantanamo Uighurs' Strange Odyssey." *BBC News,* January 11. http://news.bbc.co.uk/2/hi/europe/6242891.stm.

Austin, J. 2003. "The Use of Science to Justify the Imprisonment Binge." In *Convict Criminology,* ed. J. I. Ross and S. C. Richards, 17–36. Belmont, CA: Wadsworth.

Austin, J., M. A. Bruce, L. Carroll, P. L. McCall, and S. C. Richards. 2001. "The Use of Incarceration in the United States." *Critical Criminology* 10 (1): 17–41.

Austin, J., and J. Irwin. 2001. *It's About Time.* Belmont, CA: Wadsworth.

Australian Federal Police (AFP). July 2006. "National Media Release: Seminar to Address Radicalisation in Prisons." Canberra: AFP Media.

Baccus, R. 2005. "The Torture Question." *Frontline.* PBS, October 18, 2005. www.pbs.org/wgbh/pages/frontline/torture/etc/faqs.html.

Baker, E., and J. Roberts. 2005. "Globalization and the New Punitiveness," In *The New Punitiveness: Trends, Theories, and Perspectives,* ed. J. Pratt, D. Brown, M. Brown, S. Hallsworth, and W. Morrison, 121–138. Cullompton: Willan.

Barak-Glantz, I. L. 1983. "Who's in the 'Hole'?" *Criminal Justice Review* 8 (1): 29–37.

Bartollas, C. 2002. *Invitation to Corrections.* Boston: Allyn & Bacon.

Bateman, B. 2007. "Officials Suspended for Mathe's Escape." *Pretoria News,* March 28. HighBeam Research.

BBC News. 2005. "U.S. Soldier Guilty of Iraq Abuse." September 29. http://news.bbc.co.uk/2/hi/4284838.stm.

Beale, C. 1993. "Prisons, Population, and Jobs in Nonmetro America." *Rural Development Perspectives* 8 (3): 16–19.

———. 1996. "Rural Prisons: An Update." *Rural Development Perspectives* 11 (2): 25–27.

Beaumont, G. de, and A. de Tocqueville. 1833/1964. *On the Penitentiary System in the United States and Its Application in France.* Carbondale: Southern Illinois University Press.

Begg, M. 2007. *Enemy Combatant: A British Muslim's Journey to Guantánamo and Back.* New York: Pocket Books.

Bergin, T. 2010. "How and Why Do Criminal Justice Public Policies Spread throughout U.S. States? A Critical Review of the Diffusion Literature." *Criminal Justice Policy Review* 20 (10): 1–19.

Beyens, K., and S. Snacken. 1996. "Prison Privatization: An International Perspective." In *Prisons 2000: An International Perspective on the Current State and Future of Imprisonment,* ed. R. Matthews and P. Francis, 240–265. New York: St. Martin's.

Binnendijk, H. 1992. "Boze Kosto wil snel geld voor cellen. Gedetineerden gijzelen zes bewaarders bij ontsnapping in Hoogeveen." *De Volkskrant,* October 24.

Bloche, M., and J. Marks. 2005. "Doing unto Others as They Did unto Us." *New York Times,* November 14. http://www.nytimes.com/2005/11/14/opinion/14blochemarks.htm.

Bloem, D. 2006. *Judicial Inspectorate of Prisons on Human Rights and Privileges of Inmates* (South Africa, Correctional Services Portfolio Committee). Cape Town: Parliamentary Monitoring Group.

———. 2007. *Minister's Progress Report on Prison Escapes* (South Africa, Correctional Services Portfolio Committee, Department of Correctional Services). Cape Town: Parliamentary Monitoring Group.

Blunt, C. 2010. "Letter to Pauline Cryer in Response to Independent Monitoring Board Annual Report 09/10 for HMP Wakefield." London: Ministry of Justice.

Boeij, C. M. 1992. "Nieuwe extra veilige gevangenissen noodzakelijk." *Trouw,* September 30, 11.

Boin, A. 2001. "Securing Safety in the Dutch Prison System: Pros and Cons of a Supermax." *Howard Journal* 40 (4): 335–346.

Boin, A., and S. L. Resodihardjo. 2000. "Van normale incidenten tot nieuw beleid: crisis in het gevangeniswezen." In *Institutionele crises. Breuklijnen in beleidssectoren,* ed. Arjen Boin Sanneke Kuipers and Marc Otten, 59–82. Alphen aan den Rijn, Netherlands: Samsom.

Bonta, J., and P. Gendreau. 1995. "Re-examining the Cruel and Unusual Punishment of 'Prison Life.'" In *Long-Term Imprisonment: Policy, Science, and Correctional Policy,* ed. T. Flanagan, 75–94. Thousand Oaks, CA: Sage.

Booth, P. 1980. *The Mr. Asia File: The Life and Times of Marty Johnstone.* Auckland: Fontana/Collins.

Boston, J. 2004. "The Prison Litigation Reform Act." Prepared for Second Circuit Court of Appeals Staff Attorneys' Orientation. September 14. www.wnylc.net/pb/docs/plra2cir04.pdf.

Bottomley, K. 1995. *CRC Special Units: A General Assessment.* London: Home Office.

Bowden, C. 2004. *Down by the River: Drugs, Money, Murder, and Family.* New York: Simon & Schuster.

Bowden, J. 2009. "Managing the Challenging Behavior." *Inside Time,* May. http://www.insidetime.org/articleview.asp?a=473.

Briggs, C. S., J. L. Sundt, and T. C. Castellano. 2003. "The Effect of Supermaximum Security Prisons on Aggregate Levels of Institutional Violence." *Criminology* 41 (4): 1341–1376.

Brister, L. E. 1986. *In Mexican Prisons: The Journal of Eduard Harkort, 1832–1834.* College Station: Texas A&M University Press.

Brown, D. 2002. "Prisoners as Citizens." In *Prisoners as Citizens,* ed. D. Brown and M. Wilkie, 308–325. Sydney: Federation Press.

———. 2005. "Continuity, Rupture, or Just More of the 'Volatile and Contradictory'? Glimpses of New South Wales' Penal Practice behind and through the Discursive."

In *The New Punitiveness: Trends, Theories, and Perspectives,* ed. J. Pratt, D. Brown, M. Brown, S. Hallsworth, and W. Morrison, 27–46. Cullompton: Willan.

————. 2008. "Giving Voice: The Prisoner and Discursive Citizenship." In *The Critical Criminology Companion,* ed. T. Anthony and C. Cunneen, 228–239. Sydney: Hawkins Press.

————. 2009. "'Too High in Human Terms': The Costs of High Security Imprisonment." Review of *Imprisoning Resistance,* by B. Carlton, and *Intractable,* by Bernie Mathews. *Current Issues in Criminal Justice* 21 (1): 162–179.

Brown, M. 2005. "'Setting the Conditions' for Abu Ghraib: The Prison Nation Abroad." *American Quarterly* 57:973–997.

Bruton, J. 2004. *The Big House: Life Inside a Supermax Security Prison.* Minneapolis, MN: Voyageur Press.

Buntman, F. 2009a. "Imprisoning Terrorists: Human Rights, Security, and Resistance after Guantanamo Bay." Paper presented at the Law and Society annual meeting, Denver, CO, May 29.

————. 2009b. "Prison and Democracy: Lessons Learned and Not Learned, from 1989 to 2009." *International Journal of Politics, Culture, and Society* 22 (3): 401–418.

Bureau of Prisons. 1972. *US Penitentiary, Marion, Illinois: Information for Marion Residents.* Washington, DC: Bureau of Prisons, Department of Justice.

Bush, G. W. 2003. "Presidential Address to the Nation." March 19.

Butterfield, F. 2004. "Mistreatment of Prisoners Is Called Routine in U.S." *New York Times,* May 8. www.nytimes.com/2004/05/08/national/08PRIS.html.

Cairns, A. 1998. "Human Cockfighting in Prison? Jailbirds Say Guard Provoked Gladiator-Style Combat." *Toronto Sun,* May 7.

Calverley, D. 2010. "Adult Correctional Services in Canada, 2008/2009." Ottawa: Statistics Canada. http://www.statcan.gc.ca/pub/85–002-x/2010003/article/11353-eng.htm.

Campbell, H. 2009. *Drug War Zone: Frontline Dispatches from the Streets of El Paso and Juarez.* Austin: University of Texas Press.

Campbell, M. 1999. "The Canadian Approach." *Toronto Globe and Mail,* December 7, R2.

Cape Argus. 2009. "South Africa: Police Must Shoot to Kill, Worry Later—Cele." August 1.

Carlie, M. K., and K. I. Minor. 1992. *Prisons around the World: Studies in International Penology.* New York: McGraw-Hill.

Carlton, B. 2007. *Imprisoning Resistance: Life and Death in an Australian Supermax.* Sydney: Sydney Institute of Criminology, Federation Press.

————. 2009. "Proliferating Control and Crisis: The Official Uses and Abuses of Modern High-Security in Australia." *Prison Service Journal* 183 (May): 3–12.

Carlton, B., and J. McCulloch. 2008. "Contemporary Comment: R v Benbrika and Ors (Ruling No 20): The 'War on Terror,' Human Rights and the Pre-emptive Punishment of Terror Suspects in High-Security." *Current Issues in Criminal Justice* 20 (2): 287–292.

"Caros Amigos Revista." 2006. *Edição Extra,* May.

Carter, P. 2007. *Securing the Future: Proposals for the Efficient and Sustainable Use of Custody in England and Wales.* London: Lord Carter of Coles.

Castañeda, J. 2010a. "Mexico's Failed Drug War." *Cato Institute Economic Development Bulletin* 13 (May 6). www.cato.org/pubs/edb/.

————. 2010b. "What's Spanish for Quagmire? Five Myths That Caused the Failed War Next Door." *Foreign Policy.* www.foreignpolicy.com.

Cavadino, M., and J. Dignan. 2006a. "Penal Policy and Political Economy." *Criminology & Criminal Justice* 6 (4): 435–456.

———. 2006b. *Penal Systems: A Comparative Approach.* London: Sage.

Centraal Bureau voor de Statistiek (CBS). 1997. *Gevangenisstatistiek 1996.* Voorburg, Netherlands: CBS.

Cheney, D. 2002. "Rumsfeld: Afghan Detainees at Gitmo Bay Will Not Be Granted POW Status." *Fox News,* January 28. www.foxnews.com/story/0,2933,44084,00.html.

Chikunga, S. 2007. "Speech by Sindi Chikunga on the State of the Nation Address Debate, February 13." http://www.anc.org.za/caucus/index.php?include=docs/sp/2007/sp0213.html.

Christie, N. 1993/2003. *The Prison Industrial Complex.* London: Routledge.

———. 2005. "A Suitable Amount of Crime." In *Resource Material Series No. 67, 127th International Training Course,* 3–24. Tokyo: United Nations Asia and Far East Institute.

Churchill, W., and J. Vanderwall, eds. 1992. *Cages of Steel.* Washington, DC: Maissoneuve Press.

Clare, E., and K. Bottomley. 2001. "Evaluation of Close Supervision Centres: Home Office Research Study 219." London: Home Office Research, Development & Statistics Directorate.

Clark, W. 2003. "The Real Reasons for the Upcoming War with Iraq: A Macroeconomic and Geostrategic Analysis of the Unspoken Truth." www.ratical.org/ratville/CAH/RRiraqWar.html#p2.

Clarke, R. 2004. *Against All Enemies: Inside America's War on Terror.* New York: Free Press.

Cohen, S. 1985. *Visions of Social Control: Crime, Punishment, and Classification.* London: Polity.

Coid, J., M. Yang, S. Ullrich, T. Zhang, A. Roberts, C. Roberts, R. Rogers, and D. Farrington. 2007. *Predicting and Understanding Risk of Re-offending: The Prisoner Cohort Study* (Research Summary 6). London: Ministry of Justice.

Cole, D. 2005. *Enemy Aliens.* New York: New Press.

Committee for the Prevention of Torture and Inhuman or Degrading Treatment or Punishment (CPT). 1997. *Report to the Netherlands Government on the Visit to the Netherlands Carried Out by the European Committee for the Prevention of Torture and Inhuman or Degrading Treatment or Punishment (CPT) from 17 to 27 November 1997.* Strasbourg: Council of Europe.

———. 2002. *Report to the Authorities of the Kingdom of the Netherlands on the Visits Carried Out to the Kingdom in Europe and to the Netherlands Antilles by the European Committee for the Prevention of Torture and Inhuman or Degrading Treatment or Punishment (CPT) in February 2002.* Strasbourg: Council of Europe.

Consultants' Report Submitted to the Committee of the Judiciary, US House of Representatives. 1985. *The United States Penitentiary, Marion, Illinois.* Washington, DC: Government Printing Office.

Corn, D. 2003. *The Lies of George W. Bush: Mastering the Politics of Deception.* New York: Crown.

Coroner's and Justice Act. 2009. http://www.legislation.gov.uk/ukpga/2009/25/contents.

Corrections Digest. 2002. "California Cites Falling Population in Rejecting Construction of Supermax." April 26.

Council of Europe. 2007. *Guantanamo: Violation of Human Rights and International Law?* Strasbourg: Council of Europe.

Coyle, A. 2001. *The Management of Prisoners Serving Long-Term Sentences.* London: International Centre for Prison Studies.

Cucullu, G. 2009. *Inside Gitmo: The True Story behind the Myths of Guantanamo Bay*. New York: Harper.

Culhane, C. 1985. *Still Barred from Prison*. Montréal: Black Rose Books.

Daniels, L. 2007a. "C-Max Officials Face Prosecution for Gross Negligence Involved in Mathe's Escape." *Mercury* (Durban, South Africa), February 10. HighBeam Research.

———. 2007b. "Four May Get Chop after Mathe Prison Break; Probe Finds Negligence by Officials Made It Easy for Prisoner to Escape." *Star* (Gauteng, South Africa), February 21. HighBeam Research.

Danner, M. 2004a. "The Logic of Torture." *New York Review*, June 24. www.markdanner.com/nyreview/062404_Road_to_Torture.htm.

———. 2004b. *Torture and Truth*. New York: New York Review Books.

Davidson, L. 2005. "Torture in Our Time." *Logos* 4 (4). www.logosjournal.com/issue_4.4/davidson.htm.

De Borst, E. J. 1991. *Vluchten kan niet meer?* The Hague: Beleidsinfo D&J.

De Jonge, G. 2003. "Noot 26." *European Human Rights Cases* 3 (3): 208–210.

———. 2007. "European Detention Standards." In *Dutch Prisons*, ed. M. Boone and M. Moerings, 281–296. The Hague: BJu Legal.

De Jonge, G., and H. Cremers, eds. 2008. *Bajesboek. Handboek voor gedetineerden*. Breda, Netherlands: Stichting Uitgeverij Papieren Tijger.

De Jonge, G., and A. van Vliet. 1993. "Ontsnappingen en andere onrust in het gevangeniswezen." In *Crimineel jaarboek uitgave 1993*, ed. L. van Almelo, R. Van der Velden, and H. Durieux, 91–127. Nijmegen, Netherlands: Papieren Tijger.

Dekker, S., R. Jongejan, and E. Spek. 2003. "Crisis in het gevangeniswezen. Bolletjesslikkers en het cellentekort." *Bestuurskunde* 12 (2): 77–87.

De Lange, J. 2008. *Detentie genormeerd. Een onderzoek naar de betekenis van het CPT voor de inrichting van vrijheidsbeneming in Nederlandse penitentiaire inrichtingen*. Nijmegen, Netherlands: Wolf.

De Lange, J., and Paul A. M. Mevis. 2009. "De gedetineerde als rechtssubject; algemene aspecten van de rechtspositie van gedetineerden." In *Detentie. Gevangen in Nederland*, ed. E. R. Muller and P. C. Vegter, 373–420. Alphen aan den Rijn, Netherlands: Kluwer.

Delmanto, R. 2006. "Da máfia ao RDD." *Boletim IBCCRIM* (São Paulo) 14 (163): 5.

Dennehy G., and G. Newbold. 2001. *The Girls in the Gang*. Auckland: Reed.

Denning, R. 1982. *Ray Denning Diary*, Sydney: Ray Denning.

Departamento Penitenciário Nacional. 2010. "Sistema Federal."

Department of Correctional Services (DCS). 1994. *Annual Report 1994*. Pretoria: DCS.

———. 2008. *The Awarding of Inmate Privileges According to Inmate Classification in DCS*. Briefing to the Parliamentary Portfolio Committee, South Africa. June 18. from http://www.pmg.org.za/report/20080618-correctional-services-inmates-privilege-system-department-briefing.

———. n.d.-a. "Basic Information." http://www.dcs.gov.za/WebStatistics/.

———. n.d.-b. "Ebongweni Centre of Excellence." http://www.dcs.gov.za/AboutUs/COE/Centre/KZN/EbongweniMaxCC.aspx.

———. n.d.-c. "Incarceration Levels as of the Last Day of 2010/05." http://www.dcs.gov.za/WebStatistics/.

Department of Corrections, Policy Development. 2004. *Census of Prison Inmates and Home Detainees*. Wellington: Department of Corrections.

Department of Justice. 1975. *Justice Department Penal Census 1975*. Wellington: Department of Justice.

Department of Statistics. 1976. *Justice Statistics 1975.* Wellington: Government Printer.

Derkley, K. 1995. "Leg-Irons: Return to the 19th Century?" *Law Institute Journal* 69 (8): 751.

De Telegraaf. 1992. "Gekooid." September 22.

De Volkskrant. 1992a. "Commissie bepleit bouw twee speciale strafinrichtingen. Overdekte luchtplaats moet ontsnapping onmogelijk maken." September 22.

De Volkskrant. 1992b. "Elke ontvluchte gedetineerde zet rechtsstaat te kijk." September 23.

Dienst Justitiële Inrichtingen (DJI). 1999. *Feiten in Cijfers.* The Hague: Ministry of Justice.

Di Iulio, J. J. 1987. *Governing Prisons: A Comparative Study of Correctional Management.* New York: Free Press.

Dikötter, F., and I. Brown, eds. 2007. *Cultures of Confinement: A History of the Prison in Africa, Asia, and Latin America.* Ithaca, NY: Cornell University Press.

Dissel, A. 2002. "Tracking Transformation in South African Prisons." *Track Two* 11 (2). http://ccrweb.ccr.uct.ac.za/archive/two/11_2/transformation.html.

Dissel, A., and S. Ellis. 2002. *Reform and Stasis: Transformation in South African Prisons.* http://www.csvr.org.za/wits/papers/papadse.htm.

Dobbelaar, J. 1992. "Na 'superbajes' is er helemaal geen draad meer op te pakken." *Trouw,* November 30, 11.

Dorrien, G. 2004. *Imperial Designs: Neoconservatism and the New Pax Americana.* New York: Routledge.

Dowker, F., and G. Good. 1993. "The Proliferation of Control Unit Prisons in the United States." *Journal of Prisoners on Prisons* 4 (2): 95–110.

Downes, D. 1988. *Contrasts in Tolerance: Post-war Penal Policy in the Netherlands and England and Wales.* Oxford: Oxford University Press.

————. 1998. "The Buckling of the Shields: Dutch Penal Policy 1985–1995." In *Comparing Prison Systems: Towards a Comparative and International Penology,* ed. R. P. Weiss and N. South, 143–174. Amsterdam: OPA.

DSPD Programme. 2011. "High Secure Sites." http://www.dspdprogramme.gov.uk/high_secure_sites.html.

Edney, R. 2006. "Contested Narratives of Penal Knowledge: H Division Pentridge Prison and the Histories of Imprisonment." *Current Issues in Criminal Justice* 17 (3): 362–379.

Eisenman, S. F. 2009. "The Resistible Rise and Predictable Fall of the U.S. Supermax." *Monthly Review* 61 (6): 1–11.

Ekstedt, J. W., and C. T. Griffiths. 1988. *Corrections in Canada: Policy and Practice.* 2nd ed. Toronto: Butterworths.

El Universal. 2010. "Será el penal de Guasave de máxima seguridad: SSP." March 31. www.eluniversal.com/mx.

Equality and Human Rights Commission. 2010. "High Court Ruling on Prison Service Compliance with Race and Disability Laws." February 17. http://www.equalityhumanrights.com/news/2010/february/high-court-ruling-on-prison-service-compliance-with-race-and-disability-laws/.

Evans, R. 2009. "19 June 1822 Creating an Object of Real Terror: The Tabling of the First Bigge Report." In *Turning Points in Australian History,* ed. M. Crotty and D. A. Roberts, 42–61. Sydney: UNSW Press.

Fagan, H. 2004. "Curb the Vengeance: Laws on Minimum Sentencing and Parole Spell Worsening Prison Conditions." *South Africa Crime Quarterly* 10 (1–5). http://www.issafrica.org/pubs/CrimeQ/N0.10/1Curb.pdf.

Farrigan, T. L., and A. K. Glasmeier. 2007. "The Economic Impact of Prison Development Boom on Persistently Poor Rural Places." *International Regional Science Review* 30 (3): 274–299.

Feeley, M., and J. Simon. 1992. "The New Penology: Notes on the Emerging Strategy of Corrections and Its Implications." *Criminology* 30 (4): 449–470.

Fick Inquiry. 1947. *Rapport van de commissie voor de verdere uitbouw van het gevangeniswezen.* The Hague: SDU.

Fihla, N. 2005. *Correctional Services Act Workshop.* Pretoria: Correctional Services Portfolio Committee. South Africa.

Findlay, M. 1982. *The State of the Prison.* Bathurst, Australia: Mitchellsearch.

Flynn, N. 1998. *Introduction to Prisons and Imprisonment.* Winchester: Waterside Press.

Foreign Prisoner Support Service. 2006. "Mexican Army Urged to Take Over Prisons." In *Mexican Prisons.* West End, Queensland, Australia: Foreign Prisoner Support Service. www.foreignprisoners.com.

Foucault, M. 1977/1995. *Discipline and Punishment: The Birth of the Prison.* 2nd ed. New York: Vintage.

Franco, A. S. 2003. "Meia ilegalidade." *Boletim IBCCRIM* (São Paulo) 10 (123): 2–3.

Franke, H. 1992. "The Rise and Decline of Solitary Confinement: Socio-Historical Explanations of Long-Term Penal Changes." *British Journal of Criminology* 32 (2): 125–143.

———. 1996. *De macht van het lijden: Twee eeuwen gevangenisstraf in Nederland.* Amsterdam: Uitgeverij Balans.

Franklin, R. H. 1998. "Assessing Supermax Operations." *Corrections Today* 60:126–128.

Funnell, N. 2006. "Where the Norm Is Not the Norm: The Department of Corrective Services and the Harm-U." *Alternative Law Journal* 31 (2): 70–74.

Garland, D. 1990. *Punishment and Modern Society: A Study in Social Theory.* Chicago: University of Chicago Press.

———. 2001. *The Culture of Control.* Chicago: University of Chicago Press.

Gazette (Montreal). 1995. "Canvar Building Prison Extension." December 16.

Gendreau, P., and J. Bonta. 1984. "Solitary Confinement Is Not Cruel and Unusual Punishment: People Sometimes Are!" *Canadian Journal of Criminology* 26 (4): 467–478.

General Purpose Standing Committee. 2006. *General Purpose Standing Committee No. 3, NSW Legislative Council: Issues Relating to the Operations and Management of the Department of Corrective Services.* Sydney: NSWGPS.

George, A., and J. McCulloch. 2008. "Naked Power: Strip Searching in Women's Prisons." In *The Violence of Incarceration,* ed. P. Scraton and J. McCulloch, 107–123. New York: Routledge.

Gibbons, J. J., and N. de B. Katzenbach. 2006. *Confronting Confinement: A Report of the Commission on Safety and Abuse in America's Prisons.* http://www.prisoncommission.org/report.asp.

Giffard, C., and L. Muntingh. 2006. *The Effect of Sentencing on the Size of the South African Prison Population.* Cape Town: Open Society Foundation for South Africa.

Gilmore, R. W. 1999. "Globalization and U.S. Prison Growth." *Race and Class* 40 (2–3): 171–188.

Glaze, L. E. 2009. *Correctional Populations in the United States, 2009. Bureau of Justice Statistics Bulletin* (NCJ 231681). Washington, DC: Bureau of Justice Statistics.

Gobodo-Madikizela, P. 2003. *A Human Being Died That Night: A Story of Forgiveness.* Claremont, South Africa: David Philip.

Goffman, E. 1967. *Asylums: Essays on the Social Situation of Mental Patients and Other Inmates.* New York: Penguin.

Goldberg, E., and L. Evans. 1998. *The Prison Industrial Complex and the Global Economy.* Berkeley, CA: Agit Press.

Gonzales, A. 2002. "Memorandum for the President: Decision re Application of the Geneva Convention on Prisoners of War to the Conflict with Al Qaeda and the

Taliban." *MSNBC News.* http://www.american-buddha.com/911.memopres1 .25.02.htm.

Gordon, D. R. 2006. *Transformation and Trouble: Crime, Justice, and Participation in Democratic South Africa.* Ann Arbor: University of Michigan Press.

Grassian, S. 1983. "Psychopathological Effects of Solitary Confinement." *American Journal of Psychiatry* 140 (11): 1450–1454.

Grassian, S., and N. Friedman. 1986. "Effects of Sensory Deprivation in Psychiatric Seclusion and Solitary Confinement." *International Journal of Law and Psychiatry* 8 (1): 49–65.

Grayson, G. 2001. *Mexico: Changing of the Guard.* New York: Foreign Policy Association.

———. 2009. *Mexico: Narco-Violence and a Failed State.* New Brunswick, NJ: Transaction.

Greenberg, K. J., and J. L. Dratel, eds. 2005. *The Torture Papers: The Road to Abu Ghraib.* New York: Cambridge University Press.

Hall, R. 1981. *Greed: The "Mr Asia" Connection.* Sydney: Pan Macmillan.

Hallinan, J. T. 2003. *Going Up the River.* New York: Random House.

Halper, S., and J. Clarke. 2004. *America Alone: The Neoconservatives and the Global Order.* Cambridge: Cambridge University Press.

Haney, C. 1993. "'Infamous' Punishment: The Psychological Consequences of Isolation." *National Prison Project Journal* 8:3–7, 21.

———. 2003. "Mental Health Issues in Long-Term Solitary and 'Supermax' Confinement." *Crime & Delinquency* 49 (1): 124–156.

———. 2005. "Supermax Prisons." In *Encyclopedia of Prisons and Correctional Facilities,* ed. M. Bosworth, 938–944. Thousand Oaks, CA: Sage.

Haney, C., and M. Lynch. 1997. "Regulating Prisons of the Future: A Psychological Analysis of Supermax and Solitary Confinement." *New York University School of Law Review of Law and Social Change* 23 (4): 477–570.

Harbury, J. 2005. *Truth, Torture, and the American Way.* Boston: Beacon.

Harpham, D. 2010. *Offender Volumes Report 2009.* Wellington: Department of Corrections.

Harris, K. 2001a. "Canada's Most Dangerous Cons; Profiles of 5 SHU Inmates." *Toronto Sun,* November 26.

———. 2001b. "The SHU: In a Special 2-Part Report the Sun Goes Inside the Special Handling Unit-Home to Canada's Most Dangerous Criminals." *Toronto Sun,* November 25.

———. 2005. "'Magical World' for Female Cons; Union Slams Double Standard, Calls for Special Handling Unit." *Toronto Sun,* October 15, 18.

Hartman, K. E. 2008. "Supermax Prisons in the Consciousness of Prisoners." *The Prison Journal* 88:169–176.

Hay, D., E. P. Thompson, P. Linebaugh, and J. G. Rule. 1975. *Albion's Fatal Tree.* London: Allen Lane.

Hayward, S. 2004. "Infamous Prison Holds Few Clues as to the Past." *Miami Herald,* September 2.

Hersh, S. 2004. *Chain of Command: The Road from 9–11 to Abu Ghraib.* New York: HarperCollins.

Hershberger, G. L. 1998. "To the Max: Supermax Facilities Provide Prison Administrators with More Security Options." *Corrections Today* 60:54–57.

Higham, S., J. Stephens, and M. Williams. 2004. "Guantanamo—A Holding Cell in the War on Terror." *Washington Post,* May 2, A01.

Hill, S., and R. Beger. 2009. "A Paramilitary Policing Juggernaut." *Social Justice* 36 (1): 25–40.

HM Chief Inspector of Prisons. 2006. *Extreme Custody: A Thematic Inspection of Close Supervision Centres and High Security Segregation.* London: HM Inspectorate of Prisons.

————. 2008a. *An Inspection of the Category a Detainee Unit at HMP Long Lartin.* London: HM Inspectorate of Prisons.

————. 2008b. *Report on an Announced Inspection of HMP Wakefield, 1–5 December 2008.* London: HM Inspectorate of Prisons.

————. 2009a. *Report on an Announced Inspection of HMP Long Lartin, 14–18 July 2008.* London: HM Inspectorate of Prisons.

————. 2009b. *Report on an Announced Inspection of HMP Manchester, 27–31 July 2009.* London: HM Inspectorate of Prisons.

————. 2009c. *Report on an Unannounced Full Follow-Up Inspection of HMP Belmarsh, 27 April–1 May 2009.* London: HM Inspectorate of Prisons.

————. 2010a. *Muslim Prisoners' Experiences: A Thematic Review.* London: Ministry of Justice.

————. 2010b. *Report on an Unannounced Full Follow-Up Inspection of HMP Woodhill, 16–20 November 2009.* London: HM Inspectorate of Prisons.

————. 2011a. *Report on an Unannounced Full Follow-Up Inspection of HMP Frankland, 9–19 November 2010.* London: HM Inspectorate of Prisons.

————. 2011b. *Report on an Unannounced Full Follow-Up Inspection of HMP Full Sutton, 27 October–5 November 2010.* London: HM Inspectorate of Prisons.

HM Chief Inspector of Prisons for England and Wales. 1999. *Close Supervision Centres: A Thematic Review.* London: Home Office.

————. 2000. *Inspection of Close Supervision Centres: August–September 1999.* London: Home Office.

————. 2010. *Annual Report, 2008–2009.* London: Stationery Office.

HM Prison Service. 1996. *Management of Disruptive Prisoners: CRC Review Project Final Report* (Spurr Report). Unpublished report.

————. 2009. *Equality Impact Assessment National Policy: Close Supervision Centre Procedures.* http://www.justice.gov.uk/downloads/publications/noms/2009/noms-single-equality-scheme.pdf.

————. 2011a. *Monthly Bulletin—February 2011.* http://www.justice.gov.uk/downloads/statistics/hmps/10004C6Apop_bull_feb_11.doc.

————. 2011b. *Wakefield Regime.* http://www.justice.gov.uk/contacts/prison-finder/wakefield/regime.

Hoare, M. 1969. *Norfolk Island.* Brisbane: University of Queensland Press.

Hoekstra, R. J. 1992. *Rapport Evaluatiecommissie Beveiligingsbeleid Gevangeniswezen, deel I, II and III.* The Hague: Ministry of Justice.

Home Office. 1968. *Report of the Advisory Council on the Penal System: Regime for Long-Term Prisoners in Conditions of Maximum Security* (Radzinowicz Report). London: HMSO.

————. 1984. *Managing the Long-Term Prison System* (Control Review Committee Report). London: HMSO.

————. 1987. *Special Units for Long-Term Prisoners: Regimes Management and Research: A Report by the Research and Advisory Group on the Long-Term Prison System.* London: HMSO.

————. 1991a. *Custody, Care, and Justice* (White paper). London: HMSO.

————. 1991b. *Prison Disturbances April 1990: Report of an Enquiry* (Woolf Report). London: HMSO.

————. 1994. *The Escape from Whitemoor Prison on Friday 9th September 1994: The Woodcock Enquiry.* London: HMSO.

———. 1995. *Review of Prison Service Security in England and Wales and the Escape from Parkhurst Prison on Tuesday 3rd January 1995* (Learmont Report). London: HMSO.

———. 1999/2010. *Prison Rules Consolidated 2010—Statutory Instruments 1999(728).* London: HMSO.

Home Office and Department of Health. 1999. *Managing Dangerous People with Severe Personality Disorder: Proposals for Policy Development.* London: Home Office.

Hosken, G. 2006. "Only 8 Guards on Duty in C-Max." *Pretoria News,* December 9. HighBeam Research.

———. 2008a. "C-Max Prison Used to Plan Criminal Activities." *Pretoria News,* September 1. HighBeam Research.

———. 2008b. "Criminal Houdini Almost Escapes." *Saturday Star* (Gauteng, South Africa), June 7. HighBeam Research.

Howard, J. 1777. *The State of the Prisons in England and Wales with Preliminary Observations and an Account of Some Foreign Prisons.* Warrington: William Eyres.

Hughes, R. 1986. *The Fatal Shore: A History of the Transportation of Convicts to Australia 1787–1868.* New York: Knopf.

———. 1988. *The Fatal Shore: The Epic of Australia's Founding.* New York: Vintage.

Human Rights Watch. 1997. *Cold Storage, Super-Maximum Security Confinement in Indiana.* New York: Human Rights Watch.

———. 2000. "Out of Sight: Supermaximum Security Confinement in the United States." Vol. 12. www.hrw.org/reports/2000/super-max.

———. 2004. "Iraq." http://www.hrw.org/world-report-2005/iraq.

———. 2009. "Guantanamo." http://www.hrw.org/en/category/topic/counterterrorism/guantanamo.

Independent Monitoring Board. 2009. *"A Prison Within a Prison": Summary of the Conditions Reported in Segregation Units in Prisons in England and Wales.* London: HM Prison Service.

Independent Monitoring Board—Belmarsh. 2010. *HMP Belmarsh: Annual Report of the Independent Monitoring Board, 2009–2010.* London: HM Prison Service.

Independent Monitoring Board—Frankland. 2010. *HMP Frankland: Annual Report, 1st December 2009–30th November 2010.* London: HM Prison Service.

Independent Monitoring Board—Full Sutton. 2010. *HMP Full Sutton: Annual Report for the Year Ending 30th November 2009.* London: HM Prison Service.

Independent Monitoring Board—Long Lartin. 2010. *HMP Long Lartin Annual Report of the Independent Monitoring Board, 1 February 2009–21 January 2010.* London: HM Prison Service.

Independent Monitoring Board—Manchester. 2010. *Independent Monitoring Board Annual Report, March 1, 2008—February 28, 2010.* London: HM Prison Service.

Independent Monitoring Board—Wakefield. 2010. *HMP Wakefield: Annual Report of the Independent Monitoring Board, 1 May 2009–30 April 2010.* London: HM Prison Service.

Independent Monitoring Board—Whitemoor. 2010. *Annual Report 2010: 1 June 2009–31 May 2010.* London: HM Prison Service.

Independent Monitoring Board—Woodhill. 2010. *HMP Woodhill: Annual Report of the Independent Monitoring Board, June 2009-May 2010.* London: HM Prison Service.

International Committee of the Red Cross. 2004. "Report." www.globalsecurity.org/military/library/report/2004/icrc_report_iraq_feb2004.htm.

International Criminal Tribunal for Afghanistan at Tokyo. 2004. "The People versus George Walker Bush." http://www.ratical.org/radiation/DU/ICTforAatT.html.

IOL.co.za. 2010c. "Warder 'Had Sex with Inmate for R 1 000.'" July 30. http://www.iol.co.za/index.php?set_id=1&click_id=13&art_id=nw20100730145 253490C610957.

Jackson, M. 1983. *Prisoners of Isolation: Solitary Confinement in Canada.* Vancouver: University of British Columbia Press.

————. 2002a. *Justice Behind Walls: Human Rights in Canadian Prisons.* Vancouver: Douglas and McIntyre.

————. 2002b. *Justice Behind the Walls: A Site Dedicated to Protecting Human Rights in Canadian Prisons.* http://justicebehindthewalls.net/book.asp?cid=203.

Jali, T. 2006. *Commission of Inquiry into Alleged Incidents of Corruption, Maladministration, Violence, or Intimidation in the Department of Correctional Services.* http://www.info .gov.za/otherdocs/2006/jali/.

Jefferson, T. 1990. *The Case against Paramilitary Policing.* Bristol: Open University Press.

Jehl, D., and E. Schmitt. 2004. "Afghan Deaths Linked to Unit at Iraq Prison." *New York Times,* May 24, 1.

Jenkinson, K. 1973–1974. *Report of the Board of Inquiry into Allegations of Brutality and Ill Treatment at H.M. Prison Pentridge.* Melbourne: Government Printer.

Jesus Filho, J. 2005. "O RDE: nova punição administrativa." *Boletim Ibccrim* (São Paulo) 13 (157): 14–15.

————. 2006. "Prisões brasileiras e colombianas na mesma margem." In *Margem Esquerda—ensaios marxistas,* no. 8. São Paulo: Boitempo Editorial, 2006.

Joint Task Force Guantanamo. 2009. http://www.jtfgtmo.southcom.mil/xWEBSITE/ index.html.

Jones, D., ed. 2006. *Humane Prisons.* Abingdon, UK: Radcliffe.

Jones, T., and T. Newburn. 2002. "Learning from Uncle Sam? Exploring U.S. Influences on British Crime Control Policy." *Governance: An International Journal of Policy, Administration, and Institutions* 15 (1): 97–119.

————. 2007. *Policy Transfer and Criminal Justice.* Maidenhead, UK: Open University Press.

Joseph, R.L.W. 1983. "A Description of the Development of Special Handling Units in Canada." Research paper, Department of Criminology, University of Ottawa.

Kaiser, G. 1982. *Prison Systems & Correctional Laws: Europe, the United States, and Japan: A Comparative Analysis.* Dobbs Ferry, NY: Transnational.

Kelk, C. 2008. *Nederlands detentierecht.* 3rd ed. Deventer, Netherlands: Kluwer.

Kerkhof, A.J.F.M., K.C.M.P. Ferenschild, and E.J.A. Scherder. 2003. *De psychische conditie van gedetineerden in de Extra Beveiligde Inrichting en de afdeling voor Beperkt Gemeenschapsgeschikte Gedetineerden in PI Nieuw Vosseveld in Vught.* The Hague: WODC.

Kettles, S. 1989. *The Violent Offences Legislation (Parts I and II).* Wellington: Department of Justice.

Khan, M. R. 2008. *My Guantanamo Diary: The Detainees and the Stories They Told Me.* New York: Public Affairs.

King, K., B. Steiner, and S. R. Breach. 2008. "Violence in the Supermax: A Self-Fulfilling Prophecy." *The Prison Journal* 88:144–168.

King, R. D. 1999. "The Rise and Rise of the Supermax: An American Solution in Search of a Problem." *Punishment & Society* 1 (2): 163–186.

————. 2001. Symposium, Best Practices and Human Rights in Supermax Prisons: A Dialogue conference, Seattle, WA, September.

————. 2005. "The Effects of Supermax Confinement." In *The Effects of Imprisonment,* ed. A. Liebling and S. Maruna, 118–145. Cullompton: Willan.

———. 2007a. "Imprisonment: Some International Comparisons and the Need to Revisit Panopticism." In *Handbook on Prisons,* ed. Y. Jewkes, 99–122. Portland, OR: Willan.

———. 2007b. "Security, Control and the Problems of Containment." In *Handbook on Prisons,* ed. Y. Jewkes, 329–355. Portland, OR: Willan.

King, R. D., and S. L. Resodihardjo. 2010. "To Max or Not to Max: Dealing with High Risk Prisoners in the Netherlands and England and Wales." *Punishment and Society* 12 (1): 65–84.

King's College London. 2007. *Prison Populations.* http://www.prisonstudies.org.

Kirby, S. 2010. "What Is the Meaning of Segregation for Prisoners: Creating a Space for Survival by Reframing Contextual Power." PhD diss., Teesside University. http://tees.openrepository.com/tees/handle/10149/118046.

Kommer, M. 1992. "Resocialisatie blijft mogelijk. Strenge beveiliging en humane behandeling geen tegenstelling." *Trouw,* October 2.

Kramer, R., and R. Michalowski. 1995. "The Iron Fist and the Velvet Tongue: Crime Control Policies in the Clinton Administration." *Social Justice* 22 (2): 87–100.

———. 2005. "War, Aggression, and State Crime: A Criminological Analysis of the Invasion and Occupation of Iraq." *British Journal of Criminology* 45 (4): 446–469.

Kraska, P. B., ed. 1993. *Altered States of Mind: Critical Observations of the Drug War.* New York: Garland.

———. 1996. "Enjoying Militarism: Personal/Political Dilemmas in Studying U.S. Police Paramilitary Units." *Justice Quarterly* 13:405–429.

———. 1999. "Militarizing Criminal Justice: Exploring the Possibilities." *Journal of Political and Military Sociology* 27 (Winter): 205–215.

———. 2007. "Militarization and Policing: Its Relevance to 21st Century Police." *Policing* 1:1–13.

Kraska, P. B., and V. E. Kappeler. 1997. "Militarizing American Police: The Rise and Normalization of Paramilitary Police Units." *Social Problems* 44 (1): 1–17.

Kraska, P. B., and D. J. Paulsen. 1997. "Grounded Research into US Paramilitary Policing: Forging the Iron Fist Inside the Velvet Glove." *Policing and Society* 7:253–270.

Kruger v. Minister of Correctional Services and others, CN.7117/2002, High Court of South Africa, March 2, 2005.

Kupelian, D. 2004. "Saddam's Daily Horrors Make America's Abu Ghraib Abuses Seem Almost Trivial." June 21. http://www.worldnetdaily.com.

Kurki, L., and N. Morris. 2001. "The Purpose, Practices, and Problems of Supermax Prisons." In *Crime and Justice: A Review of Research,* ed. M. Tonry, 385–422. Chicago: University of Chicago Press.

Kurnaz, Murat. 2008. *Five Years of My Life: An Innocent Man in Guantanamo.* New York: Palgrave Macmillan.

Lacey, N. 2008. *The Prisoners' Dilemma: Political Economy and Punishment in Contemporary Democracies.* Cambridge: Cambridge University Press.

Laganparsad, M. 2006. "Court Sequel to Hostage Drama." *Daily News* (Durban, South Africa), April 20, 5. IOL.co.za.

Larsen, M., S. Harkat, and M. Harkat. 2008. "Justice in Tiers: Security Certificate Detention in Canada." *Journal of Prisoners on Prison* 17 (2): 31–46.

Larsen, M., and J. Piché. 2009. "Exceptional State, Pragmatic Bureaucracy, and Indefinite Detention: The Case of the Kingston Immigration Holding Centre." *Canadian Journal of Law and Society* 24 (2): 203–229.

Lawrence, S., and D. P. Mears. 2004. *Benefit-Cost Analysis of Supermax Prisons: Critical Steps and Considerations.* Washington, DC: Urban Institute.

Levasseur, R. L. 1998a. "From USP Marion to ADX Florence (and Back Again): The Fire Inside." In *The Celling of America: An Inside Look at the U.S. Prison Industry,* ed. D. Burton-Rose, with D. Pens and P. Wright, 200–205. Monroe, ME: Common Courage Press.

———. 1998b. "Trouble Coming Everyday: ADX, One Year Later." In *The Celling of America: An Inside Look at the U.S. Prison Industry,* ed. D. Burton-Rose, with D. Pens and P. Wright, 206–211. Monroe, ME: Common Courage Press.

Levinson, S. 2004. *Torture: A Collection.* New York: Oxford University Press.

Lewis, A. 2004a. "A President Beyond the Law." In *Guantanamo: What the World Should Know,* by M. Ratner and E. Ray, x–xi. White River Junction, VT: Chelsea Green.

———. 2004b. "U.S. Military Describes Findings at Guantanamo." *New York Times,* March 21, 8.

Lewis, N. W., and E. Schmidt. 2005. "Inquiry Finds Abuses at Guantanamo Bay: Pentagon's Report Follows FBI Complaints about Practices." *New York Times,* May 1, 35.

Lindeque, M. 2010. "C-Max Prison Official Shot Dead." *East Coast Radio,* July 21 [Television broadcast]. http://www.ecr.co.za/kagiso/content/en/east-coast-radio/east-coast-radio-news?oid=836529&sn=Detail&pid=5882&C-max-prison-official-shot-dead.

Lippke, Richard L. 2004. "Against Supermax." *Journal of Applied Philosophy* 21 (2): 109–124.

Lovell, D., K. Cloyes, D. Allen, and L. Rhodes. 2000. "Who Lives in Super-Maximum Custody?" *Federal Probation* 64 (1): 33–38.

Lowman, J., and B. MacLean. 1991. "Prisons and Protest in Canada." *Social Justice* 8 (3): 130–154.

Lucas, W. E. 1976. "Solitary Confinement: Isolation as Coercion to Conform." *ANZ Journal of Criminology* 9 (1): 153–167.

Luhnow, D., and J. de Córdoba. 2009. "Mexico's Most Wanted Man." *Wall Street Journal,* June 13.

Lynch, J. 1987. *Imprisonment in Four Countries: Bureau of Justice Statistics Special Report.* Washington, DC: US Department of Justice.

———. 1988. "A Comparison of Prison Use in England, Canada, West Germany, and the United States: A Limited Test of the Punitive Hypothesis." *Journal of Criminal Law & Criminology* 79 (1): 180–217.

MacGuigan, M. 1977. *Sub-Committee on the Penitentiary System in Canada: Report to Parliament.* Ottawa: Ministry of Supply and Service.

Maconochie, Alexander. 1845. *Principles of the Mark System: Now Sought to Be Introduced into Transportation, Imprisonment, and Other Forms of Secondary Punishment.* London: n.p.

Madrid v. Gomez, 1995 W.I. 17092 (N.D. Cal 1995).

Mahmood, M. 2004. "Collateral Consequences of the Prison-Industrial Complex." *Social Justice* 31 (1–2): 31–35.

Makin, K. 1984. "Is New Super Penitentiary a Giant Step Backward?" *Toronto Globe and Mail,* November 3.

Malarek, V. 1980. "'Supermax': It's a Solitary Life of Misery for Convicts in Special Unit." *Toronto Globe and Mail,* September 12.

Mallory, J. 2006. "Globalization, Prisons, and the Philosophy of Punishment." *Women's Studies* 35 (6): 529–543.

———. 2007. "Mass Incarceration, Democracy, and Inclusion." *Socialism and Democracy* 21 (1): 97–122.

Mann, J. 2004. *Rise of the Vulcans: The History of Bush's War Cabinet.* New York: Viking.

208 References

Margulies, J. 2006. *Guantanamo and the Abuse of Presidential Power*. New York: Simon & Schuster.

Martinson, R. 1974. "What Works? Questions and Answers about Prison Reform." *Public Interest* 35:22–54.

Mashimbye, J. 2004. *Draft White Paper on Corrections in South Africa: Hearings*. Cape Town: Centre for Conflict Resolution, Correctional Services Portfolio Committee.

Matthews, B. 2006. *Intractable: Hell Has a Name: Katingal. Life Inside Australia's First Super-Max Prison*. Sydney: Pan Macmillan.

Mbeki, T. 1999. "Address by the Executive Deputy President, Thabo Mbeki, on the Site Tour of the New Kokstad Prison and Launch of the Skills Development Programme." April 17. http://www.unisa.ac.za/contents/colleges/docs/tm1999/ tm041709.pdf.

McCorkle, L. W. 1970. "Guard-Inmate Relationships." In *The Sociology of Punishment and Correction,* ed. N. Johnston, L. Savitz, and M. Wolfgang, 419–422. New York: John Wiley.

McIntosh, A. 1986. "Jail in PM's Riding 'Not Needed' Extra Cost for Taxpayers Is $41 Million, Dye Says." *Toronto Globe and Mail,* October 22.

Mears, D. P. 2005. "A Critical Look at Supermax Prisons." *Corrections Compendium* 30:6–7, 45–49.

———. 2006. *Evaluating the Effectiveness of Supermax*. Washington, DC: Urban Institute. http://www.urban.org/url.cfm?ID=411326.

———. 2008. "An Assessment of Supermax Prisons Using an Evaluation Research Framework." *The Prison Journal* 88 (1): 43–68.

Mears, D. P., and J. L. Castro. 2006. "Wardens' Views on the Wisdom of Supermax Prisons." *Crime & Delinquency* 52 (3): 398–431.

Mears, D. P., and J. Watson. 2006. "Towards a Fair and Balanced Assessment of Supermax Prisons." *Justice Quarterly* 23 (2): 232–270.

Meek, J. 1986. *Paremoremo: New Zealand's Maximum Security Prison*. Wellington: Department of Justice.

Miller, G. 2004. "Testimony to Senate Armed Service Committee, May 19, 2004." www.scvhistory.com/scvhistory/signal/iraq/sasc051904.htm.

Miller, J. 2009. "The Mexicanization of American Law Enforcement." *City Journal* 19 (4). http://www.city-journal.org/2009/19_4_corruption.html.

Miller, V. 2007. "Tough Men, Tough Prisons, Tough Times: The Globalization of Supermaximum Secure Prisons." In *Race, Gender and Punishment: From Colonialism to the War on Terror,* ed. M. Bosworth and J. Flavin, 200–215. New Brunswick, NJ: Rutgers University Press.

Minhoto, L. D. 2008. *Excesso e eficiência na penalidade contemporânea e expertise nacional*. Artigos DireitoGVDireitoGV. www.bibliotecadigital.fgv.br/dspace/handle/10438/2841.

Ministry of Justice. 1987. *Rapport van de werkgroep Opvang Vlucht-en Gemeengevaarlijke Gedetineerden*. The Hague: Ministry of Justice.

Ministry of Justice. 2000. *PSO 0900, Categorisation and Allocation*. London: HMSO.

———. 2005. *PSO 1810, Maintaining Order in Prisons*. London: HMSO.

———. 2009. *PSI 29/2009, Close Supervision Centre Referral Manual*. London: HMSO.

———. 2010a. *Noms Directory of Services and Provisional Timetable*. http://www.justice .gov.uk/about/docs/noms-detailed-directory-of-services.pdf.

———. 2010b. *PSI 03/2010, Category a and Restricted Status Prisoners*. London: HMSO.

———. 2011. *Prison Population and Accommodation Briefing for 25th Feb. 2011.* http://www.justice.gov.uk/downloads/statistics/hmps/10004C5F25022011_web_report.doc.

Minogue, C. 1994. "Isolation." *Eureka Street* 4 (8): 23.

————. 2005. "The Use of a Military Level of Force on Civilian Prisoners: Strip Searching, Urine Testing, Cell Extractions and DNA Sampling in Victoria." *Alternative Law Journal* 30 (4): 170–173.

Molenkamp, B. 2009. "De Extra Beveiligde Inrichting en de Terroristenafdeling." *Ontmoetingen: Voordrachtenreeks van het Lutje Psychiatrisch-Juridisch Gezelschap* 15 (1): 37–50.

Moll, H. 1992. "Je moet langgestraften fatsoenlijk behandelen." *NRC Handelsblad*, September 24, 7.

Mondragón, S. 2009. "La Corrupción y la Grandes Fugas." *Noticieros Televisa*, November 11.

Mooney, R. 1982. *Every Night! Every Night!* Montmorency, Australia: Yackandandah Play Scripts.

Moore, D., and K. Hannah-Moffat. 2005. "The Liberal Veil: Revisiting Canadian Penalty." In *The New Punitiveness: Trends, Theories, and Perspectives*, ed. J. Pratt, D. Brown, M. Brown, S. Hallsworth, and W. Morrison, 85–100. Cullompton: Willan.

Moore, J. 2004. *Bush's War for Reelection: Iraq, the White House, and the People.* New York: John Wiley.

Morgan, R. 2000. "Developing Prison Standards Compared." *Punishment & Society* 2 (3): 325–342.

Morris, M. 2006. "The UK Prison Service Close Supervision Centres." In *Humane Prisons*, ed. D. Jones, 87–99. Abingdon, UK: Radcliffe.

Morris, N. 2002. *Machonochie's Gentleman: The Story of Norfolk Island and the Roots of Modern Prison Reform.* New York: Oxford University Press.

Morris, T. 1968. "Review of Radzinowicz Report." *British Journal of Criminology* 8 (3): 312–314.

Morrison, W. 2006. "Rethinking Narratives of Penal Change in Global Context." In *The New Punitiveness: Trends, Theories, and Perspectives*, ed. J. Pratt, D. Brown, M. Brown, S. Hallsworth, and W. Morrison, 290–307. Cullompton: Willan.

Moura, Rafael Moraes. 2011. Presídios federais de segurança máxima já recebem até ladrão de bicicleta. *Estadão*, June 13. http://www.estadao.com.br/estadaodehoje/20110613/not_imp731562,0.php.

MSNBC. 2005. *Dateline.* September 28. www.msnbc.msn.com/id/9516628/.

Mubangizi, J. C. 2008. "Protecting Human Rights amidst Poverty and Inequality: The South African Post-Apartheid Experience on the Right of Access to Housing." *African Journal of Legal Studies* 2 (1): 130–146.

Muntingh, L. 2005. "Describing Prison Overcrowding." In *Pretoria: Conference on Strategies to Address Prison Overcrowding in South Africa.* Pretoria, South Africa: Institute for Security Studies.

Muzzatti, S. L. 2005. "The Police, the Public, and the Post-Liberal Politics of Fear: Paramilitary Policing Post-September 11th." In *Policing in the 21st Century*, ed. J. Hodgson and C. Orban, 107–127. Monsey, NY: Criminal Justice Press.

Naday, A., J. D. Freilich, and J. Mellow. 2008. "The Elusive Data on Supermax Confinement." *The Prison Journal* 88 (1): 69–93.

Nagle, J. 1978. *Report of the Royal Commission into NSW Prisons.* Sydney: NSW Government Printer.

National Institute of Corrections. 1997. *Supermax Housing: A Survey of Current Practice: Special Issues in Corrections.* Longmont, CO: US Department of Justice, National Institute of Corrections.

Neal, D., ed. 2002. *Supermax Prisons: Beyond the Rock.* Lanham, MD: American Correctional Association.

Newbold, G. 1989. *Punishment and Politics: The Maximum Security Prison in New Zealand.* Auckland: Oxford University Press.

———. 2003. "Rehabilitating Criminals: It Ain't That Easy." In *Convict Criminology,* ed. J. I. Ross and S. C. Richards, 150–169. Belmont, CA: Thomson/Wadsworth.

———. 2004. "The Control of Drugs in New Zealand." In *Hard Lessons: Reflections on Governance and Crime Control in Late Modernity,* ed. R. Hil and G. Tait, 53–72. Aldershot, UK: Ashgate.

———. 2007. *The Problem of Prisons: Corrections Reform in New Zealand since 1840.* Wellington: Dunmore.

———. 2009. *Crime in New Zealand.* Delhi: Indo-American Books.

Newbold, G., and C. Eskridge. 2003. "History and Development of Correctional Practices in New Zealand." In *Comparative Criminal Justice: Traditional and Non-Traditional Systems of Law and Control,* ed. C. B. Fields and R. H. Moore, 421–449. Prospect Heights, IL: Waveland.

Newburn, T. 2010. "Diffusion, Differentiation, and Resistance in Comparative Penalty." *Criminology & Criminal Justice* 10 (4): 341–352.

News 24. 2009. "Probe into Prisoner's Death." August 15. http://www.news24.com/SouthAfrica/News/Probe-into-prisoners-death-20090814.

NSW Council of Civil Liberties. 2008. "Shadow Report Prepared for the United Nations Human Rights Committee on the Occasion of Its Review of Australia's Fifth Periodic Report under the International Covenant on Civil and Political Rights and Second Optional Protocol to the ICCPR." http://www.nswccl.org.au/docs/pdf/ICCPR%20shadow%20report.pdf.

O'Brien, R. 1992. "Special Handling Units." *Forum on Corrections Research* 4 (3): 11–13. http://www.csc-scc.gc.ca/text/pblct/forum/e043/e043ind-eng.shtml.

Observer. 2003. "Iraq Nets Handsome Profit by Dumping Dollar for Euro." February 16. http://www.guardian.co.uk/business/2003/feb/16/iraq.theeuro.

O'Day, P. 2001. "The Mexican Army as Cartel." *Journal of Contemporary Criminal Justice* 17 (1): 278–295.

Office of Corrections Victoria. 1987–1988. *Annual Report.* Melbourne: Government Printer.

O'Malley, P. 1992. "Risk, Power and Crime Prevention." *Economy and Society* 21 (3): 252–275.

———. 1999. "Volatile and Contradictory Punishments." *Theoretical Criminology* 3 (2): 252–275.

Oppler, S. 1998. "Assessing the State of South African Prisons." *African Security Review* 7 (4): 41–56.

Ornelas, F. 2004. "Penal Islas Marías: Una Cárcel con Muros de Agua." *Envío,* November.

Othmani, A. 2008. *Beyond Prison: The Fight to Reform Prison Systems Around the World.* Trans. Marguerite Garling. Oxford: Berghahn Books.

People Against Gangsterism and Drugs. n.d. *South African History Online—Homepage.* http://www.sahistory.org.za/pages/governence-projects/organisations/pagad/pagad-briefhistory.htm.

Perkins, J. 2005. *Diary of an Economic Hit Man.* New York: Plume.

Perkinson, R. 1996. "Shackled Justice: Florence—The Cutting Edge of Social Control." In *Criminal Injustice: Confronting the Prison Crisis,* ed. E. Rosenblatt, 334–342. Boston: South End.

Physicians for Human Rights. 2005. *Break Them Down: Systematic Use of Torture by US Forces.* Washington, DC: Physicians for Human Rights.

Pike, J., and Federation of American Scientists. 2003. *People Against Gangsterism and Drugs.* http://www.fas.org/irp/world/para/pagad.htm.

Pizarro, J., and R. E. Narag. 2008. "Supermax Prisons: What We Know, What We Do Not Know, and Where We Are Going." *The Prison Journal* 88 (1): 23–41.

Pizarro, J., and V.M.K. Stenius. 2004. "Supermax Prisons: Their Rise, Current Practices, and Effects on Inmates." *The Prison Journal* 84 (2): 248–264.

Platt, T. 2004. "Challenging the Prison-Industrial Complex: A Symposium." *Social Justice* 31 (1–2): 7–8.

"PMG Report, Portfolio Committee on Correctional Services." 1998, March 25. http://www.pmg.org.za/minutes/19980324-new-prisons-briefing.

———. 2006, September 1. http://www.pmg.org.za/minutes/20060831-judicial-inspectorate-prisons-human-rights-and-privileges-inmates.

———. 2007a, November 7. http://www.pmg.org.za/minutes/20071106-sexual-offences-bill-deliberations-correction-services-ab-briefing.

———. 2007b, November 13. http://www.pmg.org.za/minutes/20071112-minister%E2%80%99s-progress-report-prison-escapes.

Porporino, F. J. 1986. "Managing Violent Individuals in Correctional Settings." *Journal of Interpersonal Violence* 1 (2): 213–237.Prados, J. 2004. *Hoodwinked: The Documents That Reveal How Bush Sold Us a War*. New York: New Press.

Pratt, J. 2002. *Punishment and Civilization: Penal Tolerance and Intolerance in Modern Society*. London: Sage.

Price, D. 2000. "The Origins and Durability of Security Categorisation: A Study in Penological Pragmatism or Spies, Dickie, and Prison Security." In *British Criminology Conference: Selected Proceedings*, vol. 3. http://www.britsoccrim.org/volume1/013.pdf.

Project for the New American Century. 2000. "Rebuilding America's Defenses: Strategy, Forces, and Resources for a New Century." Washington, DC: Project for the New American Century.

R v. Benbrika, VSC 80, 2008.

Raad v. DPP, VSC 330, 2007.

Ramesh, R. 2010. "More Black People Jailed in England and Wales Proportionally Than in U.S." *Guardian*, October 11. http://www.guardian.co.uk/society/2010/oct/11/black-prison-population-increase-england.

Ratner, M., and E. Ray. 2004. *Guantanamo: What the World Should Know*. White River Junction, VT: Chelsea Green.

Resodihardjo, S. 2009. *Crisis and Change in the British and Dutch Prison Services: Understanding Crisis-Reform Processes*. Burlington, VT: Ashgate.

Rhodes, L. A. 2004. *Total Confinement: Madness and Reason in the Maximum Security Prison*. Berkeley: University of California Press.

Richards, S. C. 2008. "USP Marion: The First Federal Supermax." *The Prison Journal* 88 (1): 6–22.

Risen, J., D. Johnson, and N. Lewis. 2004. "Harsh CIA Methods Cited in Qaeda Interrogations." *New York Times*, May 7. www.commondreams.org/headlines04/0513–03.htm.

Ritzer, G. 1997. *The McDonaldization Thesis*. Thousand Oaks, CA: Pine Forge Press.

———. 2004. *The Globalization of Nothing*. Thousand Oaks, CA: Pine Forge Press.

Riveland, C. 1999. *Supermax Prison: Overview and General Considerations*. Longmont, CO: National Institute of Corrections.

Roberts, D. 1993. "The Prison within a Prison Temporary Quarters: Neo-Nazi Is Being Housed in a Special Unit at Saskpen." *Toronto Globe and Mail*, March 16.

Roberts, J. V., and R. J. Gebotys. 2001. "Prisoners of Isolation: Research on the Effects of Administrative Segregation." *Canadian Journal of Criminology* 43 (1): 85–97.

Robinson, M. 2002. "McDonaldization of America's Police, Courts, and Corrections." In *McDonaldization: The Reader,* ed. George Ritzer, 77–90. Thousand Oaks, CA: Pine Forge Press.

Rodriguez, D. 2008 "A Reign of Penal Terror: United States Global Statecraft and the Technology of Punishment and Capture," In *The Violence of Incarceration,* ed. P. Scraton and J. McCulloch, 187–207. New York: Routledge.

Rogers, E. 1962/2003. *Diffusion of Innovations.* New York: Free Press.

Rogers, R. 1993. "Solitary Confinement." *International Journal of Offender Therapy and Comparative Criminology* 37 (4): 339–349.

Ross, J. I. 2006a. "Guantánamo y sus consecuencias." In *Tortura y Abuso de Podor,* ed. R. Bergalli and I. Rivera Beiras, 21–38. Barcelona: Anthropos-Editorial.

———. 2006b. "Is the End in Sight for Supermax?" *Forbes,* April 18. http://www.forbes.com/blankslate/2006/04/15/prison-supermax-ross_cx_jr_06slate_0418super.html.

———. 2007a. "Guantánamo Detainees." In *Battleground Criminal Justice,* ed. Gregg Barak, 320–329. Westport, CT: Greenwood.

———. 2007b. "Supermax Prisons." *Society* 44 (3): 60–64.

Ross, J. I., and S. C. Richards. 2002. *Behind Bars.* Indianapolis: Alpha Books.

Roth, M. 2005. *Prisons and Prison Systems: A Global Encyclopedia.* Westport, CT: Greenwood.

Rothe, D. L. 2006a. "Iraq and Halliburton," In *State-Corporate Crime: Wrongdoing at the Intersection of Business and Government,* ed. R. Michalowski and R. Kramer, 215–239. New Brunswick, NJ: Rutgers University Press.

———. 2006b. "The Masquerade of Abu Ghraib: State Crime, Torture, and International Law." PhD diss., Western Michigan University.

Rothe, D. L., and C. W. Mullins. 2006a. *The International Criminal Court: Symbolic Gestures and the Generation of Global Social Control.* Lanham, MD: Lexington.

Rothe, D. L., and C. W. Mullins. 2006b. "The International Criminal Court and United States Opposition." *Crime, Law, and Social Change* 45 (3): 201–226.

Rothe, D. L., and J. I. Ross. 2010. "Private Military Contractors, Crime, and the Terrain of Unaccountability." *Justice Quarterly* 27 (4): 593–617.

Rothman, D. 1980. *Conscience and Convenience: The Asylum and Its Alternatives in Progressive America.* Boston: Little, Brown.

———. 1998. "Perfecting the Prison: United States, 1789–1865." In *The Oxford History of the Prison: The Practice of Punishment in Western Society,* ed. N. Morris and D. Rothman, 100–116. New York: Oxford University Press.

Ruggiero, V., J. Sim, and M. Ryan. 1995. *Western European Penal Systems: A Critical Anatomy.* London: Sage.

Russell, C. 2006. *Incarceration Around the World (Incarceration Issues: Punishment, Reform, and Rehabilitation).* Broomall, PA: Mason Crest.

Russell, M. 1996. *Revolution: New Zealand from Fortress to Free Market.* Auckland: Hodder Moa Beckett.

Sá, A. A. 2007. "Os dilemas de prioridades e de paradigmas nas políticas de segurança dos cárceres e na formação dos agentes penitenciários." In *A criminologia do século XXI. IBCCRIM,* ed. W. B. Bittar, 1–5. Rio de Janeiro: Editora Lúmen Júris.

———. 2010. "Direitos humanos na execução penal." In *Direitos humanos e formação jurídica,* ed. J. Nalini and A. Carlini, 119–136. Rio de Janeiro: Editora Forense.

Saare, E., and V. Novak. 2005. *Inside the Wire.* New York: Penguin.

Salla, F. 2008. "Considerações sociológicas sobre o crime organizado no Brasil." *Revista Brasileira de Ciências Criminais* 71:364–391.

Sands, P. 2005. *Lawless World: America and the Making and Breaking of Global Rules.* London: Allen Lane.

Schlosser, E. 1998. "The Prison-Industrial Complex." *Atlantic Monthly,* December, 51–77.

Schmalleger, F., and J. O. Smykla. 2008. *Corrections in the 21st Century.* New York: McGraw-Hill.

Scholte, J. 2000. *Globalization: A Critical Introduction.* New York: Palgrave Macmillan.

Schönteich, M., and H. Boshoff. 2003. "Rise of Boeremag: A Case Study." In *"Volk," Faith and Fatherland: The Security Threat Posed by the White Right,* ed. M. Schönteich and H. Boshoff, Monograph 81, 55–78. Pretoria, South Africa: Institute for Security Studies.

Scraton, P., and J. McCulloch, eds. 2008. *The Violence of Incarceration.* New York: Routledge.

Security and Constitutional Affairs Select Committee. 2007. "PMG Report." November 7. http://www.pmg.org.za/minutes/20071106-sexual-offences-bill-deliberations-correction-services-ab-briefing.

Seddon, T. 2008. "Risk, Dangerousness, and the DSPD Units." *Prison Service Journal* 177 (May): 27–31.

Shalev, S. 2009. *Supermax: Controlling Risk through Solitary Confinement.* Cullompton: Willan.

Shane, S. 2006. "Seeking an Exit Strategy for Guantanamo." *New York Times,* June 18, sec. 4, 1, 4.

Sheldon, R. G. 2005. Prison Industrial Complex." In *Encyclopedia of Prisons and Correctional Facilities,* ed. M. Bosworth, 725–729. Thousand Oaks, CA: Sage.

Sheldon, R. G., and W. B. Brown. 2000. "The Crime Control Industry and the Management of the Surplus Population." *Critical Criminology* 9 (1): 39–62.

Shepherd, J. 2010. *Mr Asia: Last Man Standing.* Sydney: Pan Macmillan.

Sigcau, S. 2002. Speech presented at the opening of Kokstad Prison, Kokstad, South Africa, November 28.

Sinclair, Sir Keith. 1988. *A History of New Zealand.* Auckland: Penguin.

Sitole, K. 2010. "Media Statement by Mr. K Sitole, Commissioner of the Department of Correctional Services, on Transforming Dis-Used Mines into Super Maximum Security Prisons." Address presented at a Media Conference in Modderbee Prison, July 29. http://www.info.gov.za/speeches/1997/060311097.htm.

Sleiman v. Commissioner of Corrective Services & Anor, NSWSC, April 24, 2009.

Snacken, S. 2010. "Resisting Punitiveness in Europe?" *Theoretical Criminology* 14 (3): 273–292.

SourceMex. 2010b. "Violent Confrontations among Drug Cartels Extend to La Palma Federal Penitentiary: Three Murders Reported in 2004." January 12, 2005. http://ladb.umn.edu/sourcemex.

South Africa, Correctional Services Portfolio Committee, Correctional Services Department. 1998. *New Prisons: Briefing.* Cape Town: Correctional Services Portfolio Committee, Correctional Services Department.

South African Institute of Race Relations (SAIRR). 1997–1998. *Race Relations Survey 1997–1998.* Johannesburg: SAIRR.

Sparks, R. 2001. "Degrees of Estrangement: The Cultural Theory of Risk and Comparative Penology." *Theoretical Criminology* 5 (2): 159–176.

———. 2003. "State Punishment in Advanced Capitalist Countries." In *Punishment and Social Control,* ed. T. G. Bloomberg and S. Cohen, 19–44. New York: Aldine de Gruyter.

Spurr, M. 2005. "Her Majesty's Prison Service of England and Wales." In *Resource Material Series No. 67, 127th International Training Course*, 48–60. Tokyo: United Nations Asia and Far East Institute.

Star. 2010. "Awaiting-Trial Men Tell of Rights Abuses in Far-Away Prison." 2010. July 8. http://thestar.com.my.

State v. Makwanyane, CN.CCT/3/94, Constitutional Court of the Republic of South Africa, June 6, 1995.

Steinberg, J. 2004/2005. *Nongoloza's Children: Western Cape Prison Gangs during and After Apartheid*. http://www.scribd.com/doc/25431063/04–06-CSVR-Nongolozas-Children-W-Cape-Prison-Gangs-During-and-After-Apartheid-by-Johnny-Steinberg.

———. 2005. *The Number: One Man's Search for Identity in the Cape Underworld and Prison Gangs*. Johannesburg: Jonathan Ball.

Stern, V. 2002. "The International Impact of U.S. Policies." In *Invisible Punishment: The Collateral Consequences of Mass Imprisonment*, ed. M. Mauer and M. Chesney-Lind, 279–292. New York: New Press.

Stevenson, M. 2005. "Mexico Saves Infamous Island Prison." *Los Angeles Times*, March 13.

———. 2011. "Family Says Mexican Drug Lord Is Suffering in Jail." *Associated Press*, April 10.

Stewart, D. 2008. *The Problems and Needs of Newly Sentenced Prisoners: Results from a National Survey*. London: Ministry of Justice.

Strasser, S. 2004. *The Abu Ghraib Investigations*. New York: Public Affairs.

Strauss, S. 1982. "Isolation Studies for Inmates at Archambault, Official Says." *Toronto Globe and Mail*, August 19.

Sudbury, J. 2002. "Celling Black Bodies: Black Women in the Global Prison Industrial Complex." *Feminist Review* 70 (1): 57–74.

Suedfeld, P. 1974. "Solitary Confinement in the Correctional Setting: Goals, Problems, and Suggestions." *Corrective and Social Psychiatry* 141:10–20.

Suedfeld, P., C. Ramirez, J. Deaton, and G. Baker-Brown. 1982. "Reactions and Attributes of Prisoners in Solitary Confinement." *Criminal Justice and Behavior* 9 (3): 303–340.

Swackhamer, J. W., chair. 1972. *Report of the Commission of Inquiry into Certain Disturbances at Kingston Penitentiaries during April 1971*. Ottawa: Solicitor General of Canada.

Taguba Report. 2004. *Investigation of the 800th Military Police Brigade. Joint Interrogation and Debriefing Center*. US Military Occupation Facilities, Abu Ghraib Prison, Iraq. http://www.globalsecurity.org/intell/world/iraq/abu-ghurayb-prison-investigation.htm.

Tali, L., and L. Pongoma. 2009. "The Beast of C-Max Caged for Life." *Sowetan*, December 9.

Teixeira, A. 2009. *Prisões da Exceção: política penal e penitenciária no Brasil contemporâneo*. Juruá, Brazil: Curitiba.

Tenorio, R. 2005. "Trasladan a Matamoros a Rafael Caro Quintero." *Noticieros Televisa*, January 28.

Thompson, E. P. 1975. *Whigs and Hunters: The Origins of the Black Act*. London: Allen Lane.

———. 1987. *Writing by Candlelight*. London: Merlin Press.

Tinoco, A. 2009. "Las Islas Marías: Prisión con Muros de Agua." Noticieros Televisa, November 11.

Toch, H. 2001. "The Future of Supermax Confinement." *The Prison Journal* 81 (3): 376–388.

———. 2003. "The Contemporary Relevance of Early Experiments with Supermax Reforms." *The Prison Journal* 83 (2): 221–228.

Trouw. 1992. "Zware bewaking . . . en resocialisatie." September 23, 10–11.

Tyler, P. E. 2004. "Ex-Guantanamo Detainee Charges Beating." *New York Times,* March 12, A10.

Tyrer, P., C. Duggan, S. Cooper, M. Crawford, H. Seivewright, D. Rutter, T. Maden, S. Byford, and B. Barrett. 2010. "The Successes and Failures of the DSPD Experiment: The Assessment and Management of Severe Personality Disorder." *Medicine, Science, and the Law* 50 (1): 95–99.

Tuck, M. 1989. "Foreword." In *Special Security Units: Home Office Research Study No. 109,* by R. Walmsley, iii. London: HMSO.

UK Government. 2009. *Response of the United Kingdom Government to the Report of the European Committee for the Prevention of Torture and Inhumane or Degrading Treatment or Punishment CPT following Its Visit to the United Kingdom from 18 November to 1 December 2008.* London: UK Government.

United Nations Committee Against Torture (UNCAT). 2008. "Consideration of Reports Submitted by State Parties under Article 19 of the Convention: Concluding Observations of the Committee Against Torture Australia." May 16.

US Department of Defense. 2009. "Military Commissions." http://www.mc.mil/Portals/0/MCA20Pub20Law200920.pdf.

Useem, B., and P. Kimball. 1991. *States of Siege: US Prison Riots 1971–1986.* New York: Oxford University Press.

Vagg, J. 1994. *Prison Systems: A Comparative Study of Accountability in England, France, Germany, and the Netherlands.* Oxford: Clarendon.

Van Almelo, L. 1992. "Vluchtgevaarlijke bijna levend begraven. Commissie-Hoekstra vergist zich in effect strikte isolatie." *Nederlandse Staatscourant,* September 23.

Van Harmelen, W. 1992. "Extra beveiliging mag niet inhumaan zijn." *Trouw,* October 22.

van Zyl Smit, D., and F. Dünkel, eds. 2001. *Imprisonment Today and Tomorrow: International Perspectives on Prisoners' Rights and Prison Conditions.* Leiden: Martinus Nijhoff.

Verkaik, R. 2010. "Rising Number of Prisoners Is 'Out of Control.'" *The Independent* (London), April 24. http://www.independent.co.uk/news/uk/crime/rising-number-of-prisoners-is-out-of-control-1952976.html.

Vinson, T. 1982. *Willful Obstruction.* Sydney: Methuen.

Wacquant, L. 1999. "How Penal Sense Comes to Europeans: Notes on the Transatlantic Diffusion of the Neoliberal Doxa." *European Societies* (1): 319–352.

———. 2009. *Prisons of Poverty.* Exp. ed. Minneapolis: University of Minnesota Press.

Waddington, D. 1991. "Manchester Prison: The Woolf Report." *House of Lords Debates* 526 (February 25): cc791–cc802. http://hansard.millbanksystems.com/lords/1991/feb/25/manchester-prison-the-woolf-report.

Waldman, A. 2004. "Guantanamo and Jailers: Mixed Review by Jailers." *New York Times,* March 17, A6.

Walker, S. L. 2005. "Drug Lord Inmates, Corruption, Eroded Prison's Security." *Copely News Service,* January 20.

Walmsley, R. 1989. *Special Security Units: Home Office Research Study No. 109.* London: HMSO.

———. 2003. *Further Developments in the Prison Systems of Central and Eastern Europe.* Monsey, NY: Criminal Justice Press.

————. 2009. *World Prison Population List.* 8th ed. London: International Centre for Prison Studies.

Ward, D. A. 1994. "Alcatraz and Marion: Confinement in Super-Maximum Custody." In *Escaping Prison Myths,* ed. J. Roberts, 81–93. Washington, DC: American University Press.

————. 1995. "A Corrections Dilemma: How to Evaluate Supermax Regimes." *Corrections Today* 57 (4): 104–108.

Ward, D. A., and T. G. Werlich. 2003. "Alcatraz and Marion: Evaluating Supermaximum Custody." *Punishment & Society* 5 (1): 53–75.

Weinstein, C. 2000. "Even Dogs Confined to Cages for Long Periods of Time Go Berserk." In *Building Violence: How America's Rush to Incarcerate Creates More Violence,* ed. J. P. May and K. R. Pitts, 118–124. Thousand Oaks, CA: Sage.

Weisberg, R. 2004. "Loose Professionalism or Why Lawyers Take the Lead on Torture." In *Torture: A Collection,* ed. S. Levinson, 299–306. New York: Oxford University Press.

Weisburd, D., and C. Lum. 2005. "The Diffusion of Computerized Crime Mapping in Policing: Linking Research and Practice." *Police Practice and Research* 6 (5): 419–434.

Weiss, C. 2003. "O RDD e a lei." *Boletim IBCCRIM* (São Paulo) 10 (123): 9–10.

Weiss, R. P., and N. South, eds. 1998. *Comparing Prison Systems: Toward a Comparative and International Penology.* Amsterdam: Gordon and Breach.

Welch, M. 2004. *Corrections: A Critical Approach.* 2nd ed. New York: McGraw-Hill.

Whitman, J. Q. 2003. *Harsh Justice: Criminal Punishment and the Widening Divide between America and Europe.* New York: Oxford University Press.

Wicks, R., and H. H. Cooper. 1979. *International Corrections.* Lexington, MA: Lexington Books.

Wittes, B., and Z. Wyne. 2008. "The Current Detainee Population of Guantánamo: An Empirical Study." Washington, DC: Brookings Institution. http://www .brookings.edu/reports/2008/1216_detainees_wittes.aspx.

Wood, P. J. 2007. "Globalization and Prison Privatization: Why Are Most of the World's For-Profit Adult Prisons to Be Found in the American South?" *International Political Sociology* 1 (1): 222–239.

Woodward, B. 2004. *Plan of Attack.* New York: Simon & Schuster.

Worrall, A. 2000. "Globalization, the Millennium and the Prison." *Theoretical Criminology* 4 (3): 391–397.

Xinhua. 1997. "S. Africa to Build Most Secure Prison in World." September 28. HighBeam Research.

Yee, J., and E. Molloy. 2005. *For God and Country: Faith and Patriotism Under Fire.* New York: Public Affairs.

Zdenkowski, G., and D. Brown. 1982. *The Prison Struggle: Changing Australia's Penal System.* New York: Penguin.

Zinger, I., C. Wichmann, and D. A. Andrews. 2001. "The Psychological Effects of 60 Days in Administrative Segregation." *Canadian Journal of Criminology* 43 (1): 47–83.

Zinn, H. 1980/2003. *A People's History of the United States: 1492–Present.* New York: HarperCollins.

NOTES ON CONTRIBUTORS

DAVID BROWN is professor emeritus at the University of New South Wales, where he taught criminal law, criminal justice, criminology, and penology from 1974 to 2008. He has been active in criminal justice movements, issues, and debates for more than three decades and is a regular media commentator. He has published widely in the field, including over thirty book chapters. He has coauthored or coedited *The Prison Struggle* (1982), *The Judgments of Lionel Murphy* (1986), *Death in the Hands of the State* (1988), *Criminal Laws* in five editions (1990, 1996, 2001, 2006, and 2011), *Rethinking Law and Order* (1998), *Prisoners as Citizens* (2002), and *The New Punitiveness* (2005).

FRAN BUNTMAN is an assistant professor of sociology at George Washington University. She researches, writes, and teaches about prisons and other aspects of criminal justice, power, and resistance, focusing primarily on the United States and South Africa. In addition to her 2003 book *Robben Island and Prisoner Resistance to Apartheid* (Cambridge University Press), she has published numerous articles, chapters, reviews, and editorials, including the recent "Prison and Democracy: Lessons Learned, and Not Learned, from 1989 to 2009" (*International Journal of Politics, Culture, and Society*).

BREE CARLTON is a senior lecturer in criminology at Monash University. She researches and publishes in a wide range of areas relating to the history of punishment and prison studies nationally and internationally. Her recent articles have been published in journals such as *Punishment and Society, Australian and New Zealand Journal of Criminology,* and *Social Justice.* She was a recipient of the 2005 Australian Academy of Humanities Travelling Fellowship for her research on women and political imprisonment in Northern Ireland. In 2008, her book *Imprisoning Resistance: Life and Death in an Australian Supermax* (2007) was nominated in the True Crime category of the Eighth Davitt Awards. Her current research is focused on gender, imprisonment, and postrelease survival.

JOSÉ DE JESUS FILHO holds a bachelor's in criminal law from Universidade Estadual Paulista and a master's degree in criminal law from Universidade de

Brasília. He is a member of the Association for the Prevention of Torture Advisory Board and Brazilian Prison Pastoral Care Legal Adviser. As a member of the prison pastoral care, he has monitored prisons since 1995 and has worked on over one hundred torture cases as a lawyer. He is a member of the National Committee Against Torture, and in that capacity he has collaborated in drafting the current National Preventive Mechanism implementation bill. As a researcher, he has published a report about torture in prison based on the preventive perspective and articles about torture and other human rights violations inside prisons. In 2006, he created an online database to register cases of torture in Brazil, which is still available to volunteers.

LUKAS MUNTINGH is project coordinator of the Civil Society Prison Reform Initiative (CSPRI), a project of the Community Law Centre (University of the Western Cape, South Africa). He holds an MSoc (sociology) from Stellenbosch University. He has been involved in criminal justice reform since 1992 and has worked in Southern Africa and Central Asia on child justice, prisoners' rights, preventing corruption in the prison system, the prevention and combating of torture, and monitoring legislative compliance. His current focus is on the prevention and combating of torture and ill treatment of prisoners and detainees.

GREG NEWBOLD is a professor of sociology at the University of Canterbury, New Zealand. A former maximum-security prison inmate who served a 7.5-year sentence for drug dealing in the late 1970s and early 1980s, he has written seven books and more than seventy scholarly articles and book chapters on crime and criminal justice. His most recent book, *The Problem of Prisons* (2007), based on more than thirty years of research into and experience with the prison system in New Zealand, is a comprehensive history of correctional reform in this country.

THOMAS O'CONNOR is a comparative criminologist specializing in terrorism and homeland security. He holds a PhD from Indiana University of Pennsylvania, a master's degree from the University of Illinois and a bachelor's degree from Knox College. He is the author of the textbooks *Bringing Terrorists to Justice* and *Accounting Forensics* as well as articles in the *Journal of Contemporary Criminal Justice, Journal of Security Administration, Journal of the Institute of Justice and International Studies, Law Enforcement Executive Forum,* and the *Encyclopedia of Criminology*. He provides extensive information about a wide range of justice-related topics in the form of lecture notes at his well-known website called MegaLinks in Criminal Justice (www.drtomoconor .com). He is an associate professor in the undergraduate program in criminal justice/homeland security at Austin Peay State University, where he also directs the Institute for Global Security Studies.

PATRICK O'DAY is a comparative criminal justice specialist on the relationship between political mobilization and intergroup victimization, and also on the border dynamics in drug and people trafficking, policing, corrections, and political modernization in Mexico. He holds a PhD and an MA from the University of New Mexico as well as a bachelor's degree from Pan American College. He is the editor of the recently published book *In the Shadow of Lázaro Cárdenas* and has coauthored an article published in *Criminology*. He is also the author or coauthor of several articles published in the *Journal of Contemporary Criminal Justice*. He is retired from academia.

SANDRA L. RESODIHARDJO studied legal political science at Leiden University and received her PhD in 2006 from the Law Faculty of the Free University of Amsterdam. In 2007, she spent two months conducting research at the University of Manchester as a Hallsworth Visiting Professor. She currently works as an assistant professor at Radboud University Nijmegen, Institute for Management Research, the Netherlands. Her current research focuses on crises (the role of media in crises and blame games) and policy-making processes (agenda-setting processes and reform). She was an editor and contributor to *Reform in Europe* (Ashgate, 2006) and wrote *Crisis and Change in the British and Dutch Prison Services* (Ashgate, 2009). She has published in internationally reviewed journals such as *Acta Politica, Punishment & Society,* and the *International Journal of Production Economics.*

JEFFREY IAN ROSS is a professor in the School of Criminal Justice, College of Public Affairs, and a Fellow of the Center for International and Comparative Law at the University of Baltimore. He has researched, written, and lectured primarily on corrections, policing, political crime (especially terrorism and state crime), violence (especially criminal, political, and religious), and crime and justice in Indian Country for over two decades. His work has appeared in many academic journals and books, as well as popular outlets. He is the author, coauthor, editor, or coeditor of sixteen books, including *Beyond Bars: Rejoining Society after Prison, Behind Bars: Surviving Prison, Convict Criminology,* and *Special Problems in Corrections.* He has performed consulting services for Westat, CSR, the U.S. Department of Defense, the Office of Juvenile Justice and Delinquency Prevention, the National Institute of Justice, the U.S. Department of Homeland Security, and Intel Science Talent Search. From 1995 to 1998, he was a social science analyst with the National Institute of Justice, a Division of the U.S. Department of Justice. In 2003, he was awarded the University of Baltimore's Distinguished Chair in Research Award. In 2005–2006, he was a member of the Prisoner Advocate Liaison Group for the Institute of Medicine (part of the National Academy of Sciences). He worked close to four years in a correctional institution. His website is www.jeffreyianross.com.

DAWN L. ROTHE obtained her PhD from Western Michigan University and is currently an associate professor at Old Dominion University and the director of the International State Crime Research Consortium and ex-officio chair of the American Society of Criminology Division of Critical Criminology. She is the author of more than four dozen articles appearing in journals such as *Justice Quarterly*, the *International Criminal Law Review*, *Social Justice*, *Humanity and Society*, *Crime, Law, and Social Change*, and *Journal of Critical Criminology* and has authored dozens of book chapters. She is the sole author of *The Crime of All Crimes: An Introduction to State Criminality* (Lexington/Roman & Littlefield, 2009). She also coauthored (with Christopher W. Mullins) *Symbolic Gestures and the Generation of Global Social Control* (Lexington, 2006) and *Power, Bedlam, and Bloodshed: State Crimes in Post-Colonial Africa* (Peter Lang, 2008). She is the coeditor (with Christopher W. Mullins) of *State Crime, Current Perspectives* (Rutgers University Press, 2011).

LOÏC WACQUANT is professor of sociology at the University of California, Berkeley, and Researcher at the Centre européen de sociologie et de science politique, Paris. He is a MacArthur Foundation Fellow and recipient of the 2008 Lewis Coser Award of the American Sociological Association, and his research spans urban relegation, ethno-racial domination, the penal state, embodiment, and social theory and the politics of reason. His books are translated in twenty languages and include the trilogy *Urban Outcasts: A Comparative Sociology of Advanced Marginality* (2008), *Punishing the Poor: The Neoliberal Government of Social Insecurity* (2009), and *Deadly Symbiosis: Race and the Rise of the Penal State* (2013), as well as *The Two Faces of the Ghetto* (2012).

ANGELA WEST CREWS is professor of criminal justice and criminology at Marshall University in Huntington, West Virginia. She earned a BS in psychology from Tusculum College, an MA in criminal justice and criminology from East Tennessee State University, and a PhD in criminology from Indiana University of Pennsylvania. She is a past chair of the Corrections Section of the Academy of Criminal Justice Sciences and is the current president of the Southern Criminal Justice Association She has authored or coauthored several journal articles, book chapters, encyclopedia entries, and grant proposals and currently is developing a book on the international use of prison labor. Her most recent publications include a chapter, "Biological Theory," in *21st-Century Criminology: A Reference Handbook*, edited by J. Mitchell Miller (2009), and a chapter, "A House Divided: Corrections in Conflict," in *Cutting the Edge: Current Perspectives in Radical/Critical Criminology and Criminal Justice* (2nd ed.), edited by Jeffrey Ian Ross (2009).